So Much Reform,
So Little Change

So Much Reform, So Little Change

The Persistence of Failure in Urban Schools

Charles M. Payne

Harvard Education Press
Cambridge, Massachusetts

Fourth Printing, 2011

Library of Congress Control Number 2007941437

13-Digit Paperback ISBN 978-1-891792-88-5
13-Digit Library Edition ISBN 978-1-891792-89-2

Published by Harvard Education Press,
an imprint of the Harvard Education Publishing Group

Harvard Education Press
8 Story Street
Cambridge, MA 02138

Cover Design: Alyssa Morris

The typefaces used in this book are Adobe Garamond Pro and Optima.

*For my first teachers; my mother, Mrs. Beatrice Payne;
my aunts, Mrs. Mildred Payne Moore, Mrs. Grace Emma
Melvina Blackledge Plater, Mrs. Adele Key,
Mrs. Hattie Smith, and Mrs. Doris Stokes;
and the Honorable Harold Washington, for starting a conversation.*

Contents

Acknowledgments   ix

Introduction   1

CHAPTER 1
Dimensions of Demoralization   17

CHAPTER 2
"I Don't Want Your Nasty Pot of Gold":
From Social Demoralization to
Organizational Irrationality   49

CHAPTER 3
Weak Skills and Bad Attitudes:
Teaching in the Slums   67

CHAPTER 4
Sympathy, Knowledge, and Truth:
Teaching Black Children   93

CHAPTER 5
"You Can't Kill It and You Can't Teach It":
Bureaucracy and the Institutional Environment   121

CHAPTER 6
Missing the Inner Intent: The Predictable
Failures of Implementation   153

CHAPTER 7
A Curse on Both Their Houses: Liberal and
Conservative Theories of School Reform   191

Epilogue   207

Program Glossary   213

Notes   221

References   229

About the Author   249

Index   251

Acknowledgments

Students of the Civil Rights movement know that many of its younger members in the 1960s were profoundly skeptical of the "leader" model of social change. A corollary of that was skepticism about the notion that ideas are the product of a single person. One person may come to be identified with an idea, but important ideas are ordinarily the result of a social process. Anyone who writes books should be able to appreciate that sentiment. This book is what it is because I have lived for the past couple of decades in a remarkable network of scholars, educators, and organizers, a kind of Council of the Wise. They are smart, hard-headed—far be it from me to say "stubborn"—and passionate about the possibilities of poor children. That network includes Veronica Anderson, Joanna Brown, Teddy Bryan, Vickie Chou, Sandy Darity, Lisa Delpit, Fred Doolittle, Dick Elmore, Patricia Ford, Jack Gillette, Doug Gills, Louis Gomez, Paul Goren, Ann Hallett, Ed Joyner, Jim Kemple, Tim Knowles, Linda Lenz, Howard Machtinger, Bob Moses, Dick Murnane, Rochelle Nichols-Solomon, Theresa Perry, Janet Quint, Sharon Ransom, Steve Raudenbush, Ken Rolling, the late Cleetta Ryals, Warren Simmons, Priscilla Smith, Bruce Thomas, Charles Thompson, and Lauren Young.

The Consortium on Chicago School Research has given a new level of breadth and depth to our understanding of urban school change, and I have profited greatly from my relationship with Anthony Bryk, John Easton, Melissa Roderick, and Penny Sebring. This book draws significantly on my work with the Chicago implementation of James Comer's School Development Process. I am deeply indebted to the Comer principals and to the facilitators, especially Rodney Brown, Della Alford, Michelle Adler-Morrison, Sue Ann Lawrence, Shalewa Crowe, Chris Griffins, Thomas Barclay, Juan Alegria, Lisa Marth-Brock, and the inimitable Vivian Loseth. Among the very talented ethnographers who worked on the project, Dawn Corley, John Diamond, Ruanda Garth-McCullough, Karen Haskin, and Mariame Kaba played especially important roles. My experience with the Math Directors Network was also important to me, as is suggested in chapter 6. The best part of the experience was that it put me in contact with Jane David, Patrick Shields, and Brenda Turnbull. Comments from the anonymous reviewers for Harvard Education Press were particularly helpful in helping me revise the structure of the manuscript.

Various parts of this work have been supported by the John D. and Catherine T. MacArthur Foundation, the Chicago Community Trust, the Lewis-Sebring Family Fund, and an Alphonso Fletcher, Sr. Fellowship. The support of the Spencer Foundation, in the form of both a Senior Scholar Grant and a residential fellowship has been crucial. Few things mean more to a scholar than time to write, and I am indebted to the entire staff for making my time there productive, particularly to Paul Goren and Lauren Young for their advice and support. The fact that my time there overlapped with Bill Trent's and Mark Smylie's was the equivalent of finding a bird's nest on the ground, to borrow a phrase from Trent. I could hardly think of two more useful colleagues for the work I was doing.

For help with research and manuscript preparation in the final stages of this project, I am indebted to Connie Blackmore, Iman Washington, and Brenda Brock. My debt to Brenda is actually much deeper than that; suffice it to say I'm glad she returned to my life at just the right moment.

The one note of regret for me as I finished this project was the death of "Ackie" Arnold Feldman, my major adviser in graduate school. One of the great teachers of sociology, Ackie kept a shelf in his home of books by his students, and it is painful to think that this volume will never rest there. He modeled for many of us how one could hold the strongest personal beliefs—he called himself not a Marxist, but a Stalinist—without intellectual or moral compromise, in part by forcing oneself to be relentless about asking the same questions of the data, no matter what one felt about it. Chapter 2's discussion of the Corridor Principle is essentially his idea, although in the tradition of hard-headed graduate students I didn't acknowledge its importance at the time. The first essay I ever wrote for him was on the heuristic utility of Durkheim's theory of social solidarity. As shall be seen in the pages that follow, I'm still trying to get that assignment right.

Introduction

This book is about the persistence, the rootedness, of failure in urban schools and urban school systems. Its posture is guardedly optimistic. It strives never to lose sight of the overdetermined nature of failure but also to remember that urban systems are in fact showing signs of progress. In many respects, this work is an offspring of Chicago school reform. In the late 1980s, after an absence of more than a decade, I found myself back in Chicago, just as the city was embarking on an ambitious attempt to turn its schools around. True to the spirit of the City of Big Shoulders, expectations were high. The original legislation envisioned transformed schools within five years. In the early years of school reform, the dean of one of the local schools of education was saying there was no school in the city that couldn't be turned around in a year. When Dr. James Comer of Yale brought his program to the city, the foundations that were supporting it wanted him to start with eight schools, and then add eight more the second year. Dr. Comer, who by that time had been working with dysfunctional urban schools for about 25 years, suggested starting with two schools and waiting to see how they developed. Chicago foundations were an important part of that early energy in the school reform movement, and their stance was very much, "Give Us More Bang for the Buck!" They wanted programs that would grow aggressively.

I was an advocate of the bottom-up school reforms Chicago embarked upon, but I was also just about certain that optimistic projections weren't likely to pan out, although I could not then have said why I believed that. I had spent most of the previous five years as the director of a youth center in New Jersey, GOSPELL Academy. It was our mission to interest youngsters from Newark and the Oranges in math or science careers. I considered myself an experienced teacher and youth worker when I began the project. I very quickly learned how little I understood about what I had gotten myself into. Within a few weeks I was spending most of the afternoon yelling at the top of my lungs at children who were ignoring me. Everything was harder than it looked, everything took longer than it should have, often by an order of magnitude. Every time you managed to reach a new plateau, you saw, not the vistas of new possibilities you had anticipated, but new problems you couldn't see from the previous plateau. As so often happens, I was too busy doing the work to think analytically about the work, but I left with an inarticulate sense of an environment that just did not yield to good intentions and hard work (and with a permanent sense of gratitude to some of the staff at the Bank Street College of Education, who helped me reinvent myself as teacher).

That sensibility about an unyielding environment was sharpened as reform in Chicago unfolded. There was plenty to do and to learn for anyone interested in urban schools. I wrote a report for Chicagoans United for the Reform of Education that was ignored by some of the smartest people in town. I was the ethnographer for the Chicago implementation of James Comer's School Development Process and a member of the steering committee for the Consortium on Chicago School Research, the research advisory committee for the Chicago Annenberg Project, and the editorial board of *Catalyst*, a Chicago journal on school reform. I was an officer in the Citywide Coalition for School Reform, a member of the group that developed the Algebra Project in Chicago, and co-founder of a group—the Teacher Support Network—that tried to link external agencies rendering assistance to schools. At various times, I was a consultant to local foundations involved with school reform and to the Chicago Board of Education, the latter not always a comfortable position.

It would have taken a particular kind of obtuseness not to have learned something. I started, like many others, with the notion that there was some particular kind of programming or some particular form of pedagogy that was going to transform the system. It was just a matter of figuring out which one was best and then doing that all over the place. A few years into the process, it felt like I was back in New Jersey, not understanding anything. Programs that were hugely different from one another felt pretty much the same once they hit those schools, especially the more troubled schools. Very little was taking root, and almost everyone was caught off guard by how arduous and unpredictable the work was. That commonsense question, "What works?" came increasingly to feel underdeveloped. There was a prior question about the general pathology of schools that needed grappling with.

What was happening in Chicago was a particularly dramatic variation of the national experience. The late 1980s and the entire 1990s were a period of unprecedented experimentation with ways to improve schools serving low-income children. We saw the national commitment to state-wide accountability systems—led initially by states like North Carolina, Kentucky, and Texas—culminating in the 2002 No Child Left Behind legislation; the closely related standards-based reform movement and the restructuring movement that preceded it; the popularity of policies calling for the end of social promotion; the transfer of authority from traditional school boards to mayors; the complete or partial reconstitution of failing schools; state takeovers of failing districts; the $500 million investment of the Annenberg Foundation in improving schools; the National Science Foundation's attempt to reshape science and math education in the cities; the small schools movement, freshman academies, and other forms of personalization of the educational experience; calls for much more intensive forms of professional development and instructional support, including instructional coaching; the radical decentralization followed by the radical recentralization of the Chicago school system; an arguably even more ambitious effort to transform the New York system with its one-million-plus students; the attempt to duplicate the apparent success of New York's old District Two in San Diego and Boston; dozens of comprehensive school reform projects, including Success for All, Accelerated Schools, America's Choice, the School Development Program (more popularly the Comer Process), the Coalition for Essential Schools and the Talent Development Program. These interventions—and this, of course, has been only an illustrative list—took place against a certain social background: globalization, the outmigration of jobs from central cities, the resegregation of schools in much of the country, the increasing immiseration, criminalization, and isolation of the worst urban neighborhoods.

It is no easy thing to try to characterize the yield from all of this. A few years ago, two of our best-informed observers referred to the "sorry record of urban school reform for the past quarter-century" (Cuban and Usdan 2003: 159). That is not quite as apt now. The most recent report from the Council of Great City Schools shows 59 percent of fourth-grade students scoring at or above proficiency on their state's respective math test, compared with 44 percent in 2002, a 15 point improvement. For eighth-grade students, the improvement was from 35 percent at or above proficiency in 2002 to 46 percent in 2006. Reading scores are typically more difficult to move than math scores, but between 2002 and

2006 the percentage of at-or-above-proficiency fourth graders went from 43 percent to 55 percent, while the eighth-grade numbers went from 34 percent to 42 percent. A majority of urban districts made some progress in reducing achievement gaps based on income and ethnicity. The city of Philadelphia, which has seen a few challenges in recent years, has still managed five consecutive years of growth on the Pennsylvania state assessment, and in 2007 that included improved scores at every grade level with the exception of third-grade math (Snyder 2007b). Test scores are an unsatisfying measure (and state assessments highly variable in quality), but weak measure or not, we have seen some movement in the last few years where we saw little but stagnation for decades prior.

Some cities are showing progress on indicators more likely to mean that we really are making a difference in the lives of young people. Depending on how one computes graduation rates, New York City has seen at least a 14 percent improvement in the last three years (bringing the graduation rate up to a still disappointing 60 percent [New York City Department of Education 2007]).

Some systems, then, seem to be getting a slight grasp on some parts of the problem. Still, it's a slippery grasp at best, and, against the bright hopes and brave words with which the major reforms were launched, most interventions, local or national, have promised a good deal more than they delivered, to put it mildly. Let No Child Left Behind stand for the lot. As it limps into its sixth year, many observers on either side of the ideological divide seem to concede that it has helped some, but those who still believe it is going to be the major engine for reducing educational inequality are few—ignoring those paid to believe it (Dillon 2007; Davis 2006; Hoff and Manzo 2007). After a couple of decades of being energetically reformed, most schools, especially the bottom-tier schools, and most school systems seem to be pretty much the same kind of organizations they were at the beginning. "We've seen 'em come," teachers say of reforms, "and we've seen 'em go."

We have not learned from all this experimentation nearly as much as we might have. Much of this experience has just been wasted. From individual schools to school districts to the research community itself, the entities responsible for the management and analysis of urban schools are themselves constructed in such a way as to make it very difficult for them to learn from their own experiences. Still, we know more than we did even a decade ago. We have a compelling body of information about the roots of failure, we know a fair amount about what individual schools look like when they get better—not that there is any one pattern—and we now have the beginnings of a literature on successful urban school districts, which would have been a phrase without a referent in 1990.

The present volume is largely an analysis of failure and, particularly, the sociology of failure. No doubt some practitioners will look at that and think, "Surely, by now, we have had enough talk about and experience with failure? Let's focus on what works." I respect completely the impatience behind that question. Practitioners who don't have that sense of urgency about the work are not worth warm spit. Still, we can't get there from here. At the school level, the district level, and the national level, even where we see some progress, we continue to see attempts to implement reform in ways that are manifestly unlikely to work. Some of this is just political expediency or earnest incompetence, but some of it is that people in leadership positions do not have a systemic understanding of the causes of failure, in part because the same dysfunctional social arrangements that do so much to cause failure also do a great deal to obscure its origins. The process mystifies itself. This is a sphere in which the truth of the dictum about those failing to understand the past being condemned to repeat it has been amply demonstrated. The best ideas out there are not necessarily proof against systemic pathology unless they are implemented in ways that take those pathologies into account.

Put differently, most discussion of educational policy and practice is dangerously disconnected from the daily realities of urban schools, especially the bottom-tier schools; most discussion fails to appreciate the intertwined and overdetermined nature of the causes of failure. At the end of the 1990s, there was a sharp increase among foundations in concern for the role of leadership in changing schools, leading to a proliferation of training programs for administrators and teacher leaders. (We still don't have a handle on which of these programs actually *do* anything.) At the same time, there was growing appreciation, even among some relatively conservative leaders, for the power of small schools. Both points are valid enough. Better leadership at multiple levels of the system seems crucial to large-scale change, and smaller schools do have an impressive record of positive social and academic changes in students and teachers alike. Nonetheless, when even good ideas are understood out of context, when they are reduced to The Solution, they become part of the problem. Better leadership does not solve fundamental problems of maldistribution of resources; making schools smaller doesn't automatically mean that teachers will teach any differently. After all these years, we are still confusing the parts of the elephant with the elephant and trying to steer the beast from the nearest appendage.

The social dimensions of the problem are still almost certainly the least well appreciated. If the research of recent years has done nothing else, it has taught us how everything from efforts to get parents more involved to efforts to get teachers to take professional development seriously can be undermined by low levels of social capital, especially in our bottom-tier schools. Reform after reform fails because of nothing more complicated than the sheer inability of adults to cooperate with one another. Failing to appreciate the salience of social infrastructure and the irrationality of the organizational environment, both liberals and conservatives have spent a lot of time pursuing questions of limited utility. The questions that were arguably the defining questions of the 1980s and '90s had to do with the content of interventions. What's the right program for these schools? The right governance structure? The right way to teach? What's the information we need to get to teachers? In hindsight, we would have done better had we given more attention to trying to figure out how to implement anything under such inauspicious circumstances. Whether Success for All is a better program than Accelerated Schools, whether charters make more sense than small learning communities—these are not such important questions when there isn't much likelihood of being able to implement any of them well.

A few caveats about intellectual strategy: First, as much as the data will allow, I want to pay particular attention to the most intransigent schools, the schools at the very bottom. Once I would have thought that if we could understand these schools, we would automatically understand how to change less troubled schools. In retrospect, that may be a bit too linear. Nonetheless, the bottom-tier schools are particularly important objects of public policy, the places where the need is greatest and, sometimes, ironically, the places where there is the greatest hope.

Second, I share the general concern with an overreliance on test scores. There is considerable validity in the charges that tests don't reflect the whole child and don't tell us what we need to know; that the pressures on districts to cheat have increased dramatically; that some test-score improvement is just the result of narrow teaching. Nevertheless, tests are still the only widely available metric, and they hold a central place in policy debates, something that is not going to change in the foreseeable future. Right now, we cannot talk about change at scale without structuring much of that discussion around scores. The best we can do is be cautious in our interpretations and look at other measures where possible, particularly measures of graduation rates and postsecondary activities.[1]

Finally, I have tried to attend to the principle of methodological interocularity, to borrow a thought from the late Asa Hilliard (Perry, Steele, and Hilliard 2003: 143). That is, to the extent possible, I have tried to concentrate on the kinds of research findings that hit us right between the eyes, on robust, outlier findings. Social scientists need to wean their thinking from the tyranny of central tendency. Knowing what happens on the average in urban schools is often perfectly useless. We need to know more about what *can* happen, not what ordinarily *does* happen. One success, Robert Merton noted, tells us more than a thousand failures: one success tells us what is possible.

Much of what I am going to say will be understood to be critical of educators. That is not the way I intend it. I am trying to see educators as they really are, but understanding that not as representing *them* in any final sense so much as it represents their reaction to a profoundly alienating set of circumstances. I have already said that when I was failing in the classroom, I became the personification of the Ugly Ghetto Teacher, blaming students for my failure. The good news is that what we see on the average day from the average teacher in the average ghetto school is just a fraction of what that same teacher can do with support. I am trying to see teachers and principals the way good teachers see troublesome students, acknowledging the problems but not letting them obscure the potential.

In the late 1960s, when I first started thinking about these questions, it was nothing for a teacher, with a guest in the classroom, to spend a class period reading the paper or doing crosswords. There was no need to dissemble. The laissez-faire systems that dominated American cities for most of the second half of the century have gone the way of the hula hoop. From superintendents to classroom teachers, people are at least putting more effort into the work. (And we have conservatives to thank for this, to a significant degree, as the architects of accountability.) Leadership is more aggressive at every level of the system, and there is reason to believe the increased effort has translated into more attention to the poorest children (although not all agree with that, e.g., Neal and Schanzenbach 2007). Still, we cannot yet say with any confidence just how different these new systems really are. When we see a greater commitment to a more equitable distribution of resources, including human resources (often stymied by the self-same conservatives who gave us accountability), when urban educators take a less pessimistic stance about the capabilities of their children and a less cynical one about reform, when district leaders develop plausible visions of good teaching that go beyond generating test scores, when we see something akin to organizational rationality among these systems—then we might want to commence a conversation about fundamental change. What is happening now is as if the most determined activists and educators have seized parts of the system by the throat and are beating some sense into it. It's improvement, but it's not stable.

Still, practitioners are moving on the problem on a broader front and with greater energy; researchers are asking better questions and attacking them with more authoritative methodologies. Perhaps most important of all, there are embryonic signs of flexibility in a discussion that has been defined by rigidities, ideological and otherwise. Diana Ross and the Supremes had a hit song in which they sang:

> You used to be so proud,
> Now, your head's a little lower,
> And you walk slower,
> And you don't talk so loud.

That could be the anthem of urban school reformers. Reformers of every stripe got their butts kicked from one end of the 1990s to the other. When the funds from the Annenberg Foundation gift of $50 million to each of ten cities were used up, in many of those cities the liberal reformers who controlled those funds found themselves trying to explain that there really had been more progress than first appeared, if you look at things rightly, and $50 million isn't all that much, really, and real change takes time, you know. . . . Warren Simmons of the Annenberg Institute once teased a gathering of the progressive Cross City Campaign for Urban School Reform. When he first suggested the coalition study standards-based reforms, considered a stodgy conservative idea, he was booed down. Ten years later, Cross City was offering workshops on the subject. Some of the business-oriented reformers who came to ascendancy in the middle of the decade, promising that things would soon be set to rights with the application of good, hard-headed business practices, are now talking about how personalization isn't such a bad idea; relationships are important, after all, and real change takes time, ya know. . . . There is no doubt that ideological rigidity is among the main reasons it takes us so long to learn so little. Heads bloodied by reality, some reformers are now willing to reconsider the purity of their ideas, perhaps giving us a window of time during which a more complex conversation is possible.

"Make No Little Plans!": Background on School Reform in Chicago

This book tells a national story, but it is framed and illuminated by the experience of Chicago. Chicago is an important lens for understanding school reform in part because what happened there has had significant impact on the development of policy in other cities (e.g., the strong mayor model, ending social promotion), in part because the process of change has probably been documented more closely there than in any other major city. The Consortium on Chicago School Research is the closest thing we have to a Manhattan Project on urban schools, and from its inception it has maintained a commitment to combining quantitative and qualitative work, affording its work a complexity that cannot be achieved when the two are separated (and a complexity likely to be lost in the current fetishizing of random assignment research). Chicago's research community is "at the table" in a way that is rare. Researchers are in fairly constant conversation with educational power brokers, and sometimes what they have to say gets attended to; sometimes now they are present even as major new initiatives are being shaped. This represents a fairly recent change; ten years ago, the situation would have been far more conflictual, with researchers getting blasted whenever they said the pet policy of the moment wasn't producing. Attempts are afoot in other cities to create Consortium-like entities (Medina 2007).

Chicago also enjoys a probably unprecedented quality of educational journalism. The standard for educational journalism over the last decade has been set by the monthly journal *Catalyst: Voices of Chicago School Reform*. In the last year, there have been stories or special issues on new plans for merit pay for teachers, parent organizing, how well the system supports children with incarcerated parents, new policies for school autonomy, turnaround districts around the country, high-achieving Chicago schools serving low-income populations, the miseducation of special education children, and the question of equity in how technology is distributed across schools. To the everlasting chagrin of the powers-that-be, *Catalyst* gives school operations a transparency rare in big-city systems. (*Catalyst*, too, is spawning imitators in other cities.) Still, we may imagine that when Alexander Russo started his blog on Chicago schools (*www.district299.com*), school leaders began to look back fondly on the days when they had only *Catalyst* looking over their shoulders. The blog offers yet another level of scrutiny, often irreverent and proudly impolitic. Richard Wright once called Chicago "the known city"; in terms of education, that now has a certain aptness.

Chicago has a relatively high level of civic infrastructure; the corporate community is well organized and can sometimes speak with one voice—more or less—on educational issues. School reform in Chicago would probably not have been possible without business support (Russo 2004). More distinctively, Chicago boasts one of the country's most active traditions of neighborhood-based community organizations, a tradition that has long influenced community organizing in the rest of the country. Community groups and business groups naturally come out in different places on policy issues, but for a moment in the late 1980s and early 1990s, they were able to make common cause.

Chicago also provides an important window for thinking about school reform in the 1990s because the city gave both liberals and conservatives a fair shot. It is a story of at least two major reforms, one emphasizing bottom-up, democratic, decisionmaking; the other, top-down accountability. With over 400,000 students in the late 1980s and more than 30,000 teachers, Chicago was (and is) the nation's third largest school system, following New York and Los Angeles. In 1987 Secretary of Education William Bennett called it the worst district in all America, which wasn't giving Detroit, New Orleans, and Washington, D.C., their due, but which was probably only a slight exaggeration. During the 1980s, public frustration with the system was increased by a teachers' union that went on strike nine times in 18 years, culminating in 1987 in a 19-day strike that created a level of anger that helped stimulate a citywide reexamination of the school system. During the strike, it became clear that many citizens agreed with the *Chicago Tribune*—the schools "were hardly more than daytime warehouses for inferior students, taught by disillusioned and inadequate teachers, presided over by a bloated, leaderless, bureaucracy and constantly undercut by a selfish, single-minded teachers' union that has somehow captured and intimidated the political power structures of both city and state governments" (Staff of the *Tribune*, 1988). Discontent focused increasingly on the bureaucracy, and in 1988 the Illinois legislature sharply reduced the size and authority of the Chicago central office and gave individual schools expanded autonomy. The law created local school councils at each school and gave a majority of the votes to parents. The councils were given some real powers, including, most importantly, the power to hire principals, in addition to substantial authority over the discretionary budget, curriculum, and school-improvement plans. (By the late 1990s a typical elementary school had half a million dollars in discretionary funds, a typical high school twice that.) At the time, it was widely and reasonably considered the single most ambitious attempt to overhaul an urban district.

A 1993 report (Bryk et al.) from the Chicago Consortium on School Research suggested that about a third of the schools were taking advantage of their new freedom in ways that were likely to lead to better student outcomes. Still, there was enough dissatisfaction with the pace of improvement and with the system's continuing financial mess that the business community pushed to reform the reform, leading the legislature in 1995 to limit the ability of teachers to bargain over work rules, to further enhance the ability of principals to shape their teaching staffs, and, above all, to give control of the school board and the superintendency to the mayor, who appointed Paul Vallas, his budget manager, as chief executive officer of the system. A perfect exemplar of the city's can-do spirit, Vallas brought to the office a level of energy it had not seen in decades and the subtlety of a Sherman tank. With the mayor's clout behind him and with the enthusiastic cheerleading of the business community, he straightened out the system's longstanding financial mess in short order; expanded afterschool programs, preschool programs, and tutoring; ended social promotion; put 109 schools on probation; reconstituted several high schools; removed the principals of low-performing schools; put 150,000 children into mandatory summer school; found a way to buy eyeglasses for tens of thousands of kids; and initiated an ambitious program for the physical renovation of the system. During his six years, Vallas extended the school day for many students, built 76 schools and rehabilitated 500 more, and solved a $1 billion deficit, leaving behind a $355 million surplus. Less tangibly but arguably more importantly, Vallas put an end to the excuse-making of school leadership. If a principal started talking about how hard it was to work with children from deprived backgrounds, Vallas was likely to point to a school with similar demographics that was doing better. If some schools could do it, then why not *all* schools? In a thousand ways, he sent the message that there are no excuses, that we are not going to stand pat around here, and that we can move this damn thing. Against the decades of stagnation, it was the message the city needed to hear.

Under Vallas, the Chicago system was simultaneously decentralized and recentralized. On the one hand, most schools retained (despite Vallas's best efforts, it seemed to some) much of the authority they had gained in the first reform; on the other, they had to contend with an unusually powerful and active chief executive. It was a situation with multiple tensions built in, but for the first four years or so, it seemed to work. Test scores were rising. Pre-Vallas reformers argued that Vallas was reaping the harvest of the work that had been done before he entered office, but most of the public seemed to give credit to Vallas. The press was largely laudatory. Black and Latino parents found his energy and push refreshing (and he spared no effort to make himself accessible to them). Vallas was getting so much positive press that there were murmurings that the mayor who appointed him was getting tired of hearing his name. Whatever the reason, after two years of fairly flat test scores, the mayor allowed Vallas to resign in 2001. (After losing a close bid for the governor's office, Vallas became superintendent of the Philadelphia system, where he again presided over a period of rising test scores. More recently, he has moved on to New Orleans, escaping a looming budget mess in Philadelphia.)

When he left office in 2001, his frequent adversaries at *Catalyst* tipped their hat in respect:

> Most cities would die for the consistency of purpose and track record of accomplishment that CEO Paul Vallas and School Board President Gery Chico provided. To repeat the litany: financial stability, labor peace, new and rehabbed schools, higher expectations for students and staff, a sense of accountability and a new public confidence in the public schools. (*Catalyst* 2001)

The *Catalyst* editors added, though, that he had been both "enormously receptive to good ideas and a hot-tempered overseer who brooked no criticism" and that he had made fear the primary motivational tool inside the system, squelched debate of complex issues, and failed to understand the importance of building a stronger teaching staff.

To almost everyone's surprise, the mayor appointed 36-year-old Arne Duncan to run the system, which seemed like throwing a choirboy into the whorehouse. Still, many reformers and community activists were pleased, thinking that Duncan was likely to bring a less combative and punitive style to the job and more concern with instruction and with developing human capital in the system (Kelleher 2001; Anderson and Lenz 2001). It seemed like the perfect third act. First, the city has a period of bottom-up democracy, under which some schools flourished in ways they could not have under the old, controlling bureaucracy. Then a period of tough-guy leadership, a good kick in the pants for schools that hadn't been able to take advantage of freedom. Finally, in Act 3, the synthesis—leadership that comes in talking the language of human-capital development and instruction and organizational transparency.

Through it all the system has managed to lurch forward, at least at the elementary school level. In 1991, 23 percent of the city's grade school children read at or above grade level; by 2005, it was 47 percent. In math, the rise was from 26 percent to 46 percent. Particularly interesting is that by 2005, the number of Chicago children reading in the nation's bottom quartile was reduced to 24 percent, down from 48 percent in 1991, suggesting that over time the kids traditionally least well served by the system were getting a different kind of teacher attention (CPS website; http://research.cps.k12.il.us/cps/accountweb). Overall attendance in the system was up slightly from 89 percent in the early 1990s to 92 percent in 2002.

As is true across the country, high schools generally remain stagnant. By the 2003–04 school year 12 percent of all high school students dropped out, but even that was better than nearly 16 percent in the 1993–94 school year. There has been a significant rise in the number of Black and Latino students taking Advanced Placement tests and a modest increase in the numbers of students passing the algebra/geometry sequence. Such changes as did occur happened while the student body was becoming poorer. Students from low-income families went from 68 percent of all students in

13

1993 to 85 percent by 2002, while the percentage of students with limited English skills went from 9 percent to 14 percent over a 14-year period (*Catalyst* website; CPS website; Kelleher 2004).

One interesting change that is typically underanalyzed concerns the mobility rate (the percentage of students who move in or out of schools in a year), which went from hovering around 35 percent in the early 1990s to about 25 percent in 2004 (*Catalyst* website). It is not clear to what extent this fall facilitated or resulted from the improvements in schools, but some observers are convinced that as they become more satisfied with the local school, poor parents find ways to move less often. Conceivably, economic conditions could have improved in the worst neighborhoods so that people didn't need to move, but there is no obvious evidence to suggest that. In any case, we should probably think of declines in mobility rates as desirable in and of themselves. Schools are just better off when students aren't constantly shipping in and out.[2]

This is still very much a failing system. The National Assessment of Educational Progress (NAEP) is a more intellectually substantial test than those Chicago uses, and Chicago performance on it has been mediocre, a fact local newspapers gave little play, according to Linda Lenz, editor of *Catalyst*. If one compares Chicago to Boston, a city with similar demographics, 61 percent of Chicago's Black fourth graders scored in the lowest achievement category, compared with 45 percent for Boston (Lenz 2004). Of those CPS graduates who start college right after high school, only a third have college degrees six years later, about half the national average, suggesting that even the system's better prepared students are not well prepared (Roderick, Nagaoka, and Allensworth 2006: 64). Between 1994 and 2003, the number of elementary school students who were suspended more than doubled, with African American students accounting for a disproportionate share of them, suggesting a less than hospitable school atmosphere.

Thus, as with several other cities, we can point to some improvements yet come up well short of suggesting fundamental change. It is a long way still from the kind of revolution Chicago reformers thought they were authoring in 1988, but there has been motion, enough that we can learn something from it.

I noted at the outset that this book is another product of Chicago school reform. I should have noted what a special moment that was—a moment when people who thought they knew what poor people could

or would do repeatedly found out otherwise; when poor people working with corporate leaders were finding that there were real people inside some of those suits. It was one of those moments when the horizon
seemed right there to be touched. That was the moment, and "this book
is of it, with something of the fever and the fret. Nor does the writer
regret it. . . . Written under different circumstances it would have been a
different but not necessarily a better book" (James 1963: xi).

Chapter 1

Dimensions of Demoralization

What is wrong with the schools in urban America? Why do their problems appear so intractable? How is it that, after years of effort and expenditures of billions of dollars, we have so little to show for our efforts?

—Paul Hill

It isn't that they can't see the solution. It is that they can't see the problem.

—G. K. Chesterton

"I Appreciate Your Enthusiasm, But . . ."

For social scientists, the newest members of a social setting often make the best informants; they "see" things that older inhabitants have come to take for granted. With her master's degree from Columbia University's Teachers College, Joyce Kingon came to the public schools of New York City with stronger-than-average credentials, which hardly meant much for her school in the South Bronx, one of the city's worst:

> "Twilight Zone" begins the minute I enter my new school . . . and see that every clock has hands pointing to different times. In a place where at least half the children cannot tell time, no one seems concerned about the clocks.
>   "You get used to it," says one veteran teacher. "Wear a watch. Work around it." (Kingon 2001: 30)

Actually, there were signs even before she got to the school. As part of the certification process, she had to take a workshop on child abuse, during which she learned that should she suspect a case of abuse, she should report it to not one, but two, supervisors. Someone asked why that was necessary.

"To cover yourself," said the instructor, introducing a phrase I would hear with incredible frequency from teachers over the next year.

A discussion followed. Some principals might not want to do anything about a problem because there are so many already that one more would put the school over the top and make the principals look like poor managers.

"But if this is a serious concern, can't you go around the principal to a higher authority?" someone asked. There was laughter and the rolling of eyes. (30)

Kingon thought she had fallen in with a group of disgruntled teachers. In fact, she was entering a world where distrust of higher authority was the norm as well as a world where procedure would regularly triumph over common sense. When she was hired at the city's recruitment hall on Court Street, she was told to go over to 110 Livingston Street—a mythic address, for many years the home of New York's Board of Education, the place where old bureaucrats went to die—to get her papers signed. After waiting there for an hour, an official told her to return to Court Street to get her papers "processed correctly." After waiting two hours there, she was called in by the same man she had spoken to on Livingston Street, who glanced at her papers and signed them, prompting her to ask why he couldn't have done that three hours ago. "The procedure is handled here in this office," she was told.

That was benign, compared to some of what she saw when she got to the school. Some kids showed up all dressed up for the first day of school, only to find that their names were not on anybody's list. Their parents were told to take them home and try again the next day. Even on the second day, the school couldn't find all of them in its records.

The school was using Success for All (see Program Glossary) as its reading program. Kingon received no training beyond a manual to read. On the first floor, she came across a textbook graveyard, with books that had been ordered to support the previous year's reading program, no longer of any use. The experienced teachers tell her this is the norm. Programs come, programs go. In this case, the training was especially poor "because the supervisor, also new to the program, is only one page ahead of the teachers, who are one page ahead of the students." If past practice holds, the veterans add, after two or three years, just when teachers are becoming comfortable with the new program, it will be changed because of disappointing results. By the time they reach eighth grade, some kids may have been exposed to three or four different programs.

As frequently happens in high-stakes environments, the school's curriculum had been narrowed. The principal didn't allow field trips. Geography, history, music, and art were low priorities, with social studies and science taught on alternating weeks. Teachers were not altogether happy with the Success for All program—Stress for All, as one called it—finding it rigid and complicated. They were getting contradictory feedback from the SFA consultants and the office at the Board of Education that oversaw SFA. Scores were going up, but one teacher pointed out that all new programs get a bounce in the beginning. It will flatten out, she said.

The powers-that-be seemed unable to address these real problems, but they had a laserlike focus on bulletin boards. "Although the children rarely look at the bulletin boards, visitors from the district, city and state put great stock in them and spend a long time looking at them" (33). Every teacher did a board every month. The principal was not above ripping down the ones she didn't like, without consulting the teachers who made them—who, of course, had to do them over. At the same time, there was little indication that the principal was concerned with creating anything approximating a professional culture among her staff. When Kingon suggested that some staff-development time could be devoted to having more experienced staff share expertise with younger staff, the response was, We are not here to teach you Education 101.

In the lunchroom a teacher announces that a particular student is on medication and is like a zombie. Cheers go up. Kingon asks a senior teacher nearing retirement how he keeps order. "I scream in their ear," he says. A second-grade teacher refines that: "I scream in their face." When she starts to use the children's drinking fountain, a colleague warns her against it: one can't be sure what these kids have put into it.

Some of the harshness toward the children may have reflected teacher frustration with the discipline process, which the school handled with a six-step procedure only a bureaucrat could love. A disruptive student was to be written up repeatedly, followed by a meeting with the parents, which must also be documented, followed by a 7- to 10-day cooling-off period. At step 4, reports were given to the guidance counselor. Nothing reached the principal's desk until step 6. All of this took enormous amounts of teacher time and energy, so teachers were unlikely to do it for more than one or two students. Teachers didn't believe the process was likely to do much good in any case. It did keep the principal isolated from the day-to-day problems in the classroom. When that broke down, of course, the principal could always just shoot the messenger. If a teacher wrote up too many students, the principal could just proclaim that the real problem was the teacher, who didn't have control of her students. If something went really wrong while the process was still unfolding, the principal could always say, "Why wasn't I told of this before?"

Kingon indeed manages to get on the principal's bad side, apparently for writing up too many students, which she stops after a veteran teacher reminds her that too many negative reports makes the administration look bad. Even when she opens a closet door to find a second-grade boy simulating sex with a frightened girl, she doesn't submit a report: "I comfort her and write up something to cover myself. If there is trouble, I'll be asked if I documented the incident, not if I did anything about the incident" (37).

Kingon finally goes to the custodian to ask about those darned clocks. He explains to her that every time he asks for something to be fixed, he fills out a blue request form and puts a copy on his wall. When the request is taken care of, he takes the blue form down. He asks her how many different colors of paper she sees on the wall. Three, she says; blue, pink, and white. "Wrong," he says. "They're all blue. First the blue fades to pink and then the pink fades to white. That white one is about the clocks" (33).

Getting a few clocks to work isn't an insurmountable problem. Surely, with a bit of persistence, someone among the 40 or 50 adults typically associated with an elementary school can figure out a way to fix the clocks. That it doesn't happen, that such a simple problem becomes insuperable, is an indication of how beaten down these adults are, a process that begins as soon as teachers enter the profession. First-year teachers in urban schools may come expecting trouble with the material or with the children, but they are frequently caught off guard by the difficulty of working with their more experienced colleagues.

The history of Teach for America, for example, which recruits graduates of America's best universities to teach in high-need schools, could be written in terms of its struggle to get these talented and idealistic young people accepted. A Teach for America teacher in New Orleans realized that his students had a dangerous walk home—to the notorious Desire

Street projects—so he started walking them home. He was surprised that some veteran teachers were annoyed with him and some were outright angry. In Utah, Brian Wilcox threw himself wholeheartedly into his first teaching job but found that everything he did brought criticism from his colleagues:

> I ate with my students at lunch ("Wilcox shouldn't do that—"); I played with my students at recess ("That's unheard of—"); I read with my students in the library ("He's wasting his time—"); I even stayed after school with some boys who got in trouble with the principal ("He's undermining the school's entire discipline program—"). (Kane 1992: 118)

He worked, the older teachers carped, and his students flourished—enough so that eventually a few parents of other sixth graders asked to have their children transferred to his room. This was just too much for his colleagues; they went to the principal and complained (and it would be interesting to know exactly how they framed it).

> The principal called me into his office. "I appreciate your enthusiasm. But do you have to be quite so . . ." he fished for the right word, "so energetic?"
>
> "I'm sorry. I don't mean to be a problem. What am I doing wrong?"
>
> He pawed awkwardly through his mental thesaurus. "You're not doing anything wrong. But can't you just tone it down and keep the peace?"
>
> His advice rankled all evening long. Tone it down? Tone it down? Do I have to do less than my best job to keep peace with colleagues in today's educational system? (Kane 1992: 119–20)

In demoralized schools, the answer is "yes." Hostility from older teachers is sufficiently common and sufficiently unsettling to new teachers that Teach for America has had to change its mode of implementation. They began to prefer clustering, sending several people into the same school, partly so that they might be able to give one another some of the support they cannot count on from veteran teachers.

Once a certain style of work becomes normalized among a workgroup, those who violate it are deviants and can expect to be sanctioned like deviants in any social setting. The fact that here the style of work that has become normalized is associated with the failure of children and that the style of work that gets treated as deviant is associated with success makes little difference. Sociologically, the gung-ho teacher is the equivalent of the rate-buster in factories, the worker who sets such a pace as to make things difficult for other workers (Whyte 1955). If one teacher starts walking students home, parents may start asking why other teachers don't. If one teacher starts staying after school with students, the principal may think that others should, too. The rate-buster threatens settled social arrangements.

Teachers who get too much training may find that such training can make their colleagues uncomfortable. The hope of many principals is that they will get a few teachers who have been certified by the National Board for Professional Teaching Standards and that there will be ripple effects, that those few will somehow affect their colleagues. Any sociologist could tell them that rate-busters are seldom honored:

> When Kathleen Reeves began the long, intensive effort to gain national certification as an outstanding English teacher, it was big news in suburban Detroit. . . . [An] article and . . . photo went up on the bulletin board in the teachers' lounge at Seaholm High School in Birmingham, Mich. It didn't take long for Ms. Reeves' colleagues to let her know what they thought about the publicity. Within days, someone had drawn a red mustache across her upper lip. "That was pretty much the attitude," Ms. Reeves, who went on to become certified, said recently. "One teacher said, 'Well, there's the master teacher.' She was very sarcastic." (Bradley 1995)

Her union, of which she was a vice president, was also less than enthusiastic. "They don't want to acknowledge me for fear of offending those who were not certified," she said. One of the first teachers to become certified in a Virginia district started finding garbage in his mailbox and heard a few of his co-workers regularly making snide remarks. A Utah teacher of the year had his colleagues circulate an insulting note about him, suggesting that he thought he was a hotshot who knew more than they. He thought the teachers who were most upset were the worn-out teachers who had grown comfortable just collecting a paycheck, suggesting something of the ideological character of these rejections.[1]

We have many examples of these patterns in relatively privileged schools, but they are likely to be even more pronounced in urban schools. People who meet the highest standards of their profession are

22

held up for ridicule, a perfect example of what Jean Anyon (1997) means by the "degraded professional culture" of inner-city schools. One of the most popular models for staff development, sometimes called a Train the Trainer model, involves sending a few teachers out to be trained so that they can come back and train others. It looks cost-effective; in practice, the stronger the norms of collegial leveling and isolation, the less likely it is that anything will come of these ventures. Part of what is involved in the current discussion about Black kids accusing their more academically successful peers of "acting white" is the idea that successful students have to somehow negotiate their success, perhaps by being a good athlete or by becoming the class clown (Fordham 1996). Being the relatively successful teacher in an unsuccessful school can require similar negotiation. One learns to not talk with other teachers about what is going well in one's classroom, or one learns simply to minimize contact with other teachers (Kozol 1967; Rosenfeld 1971). Presumably, the insecure find reassurance in keeping everyone at their level.

If we take organizational morale to be "the enthusiasm and persistence with which a member of a group engages in the prescribed activities of that group" (Manning 1991), the fact that an institution needs to squelch and marginalize its most energetic, most enthusiastic, or best-prepared members tells us these are demoralized institutions. Observers of urban schools have given us three decades of variations on the basic story of institutional contradiction and impotence in bottom-tier schools (Kohl 1967; Kozol 1967; Leacock 1969; Rogers 1969; Rosenfeld 1971; Gouldner 1978; Payne 1984; Fine 1991; Anyon 1997; Devine 1996; Staff of the *Tribune* 1988; Lipman 1998; Noguera 2003). They tend to be places governed by an overarching sense of futility and pessimism; where colleagues may distrust their supervisors and perhaps one another; where there can be a certain harshness in the way children and parents are dealt with; where many children seem to be disengaged much of the time, but not necessarily more so than the teachers; where the levels of human capital are at their lowest; where instruction is uncoordinated and uninspiring; where there are too few resources, and those few are often badly used; where the curriculum is narrow, boring, and frequently changing; where teachers have profound skepticism about "programs"; where there is a general feeling of instability—personnel come and go, students come and go, programs come and go—all of it presided over by a dysfunctional bureaucracy.

All this stands behind clocks that don't get fixed and broken windows that don't get repaired. Failed institutions make the simplest things difficult. The problems manifest themselves in so many ways that they may obscure the fact that many of the discrete problems are either generated by or reinforced by the sheer lack of connectedness among people. Giving up on the institutional mission goes hand in glove with giving up on one's colleagues. The denizens of demoralized social spaces do what they have to do but without much heart or hope.

Leading with the Negative

Whenever we talk about the social climate in inner-city schools, we need to make a special effort to remember that what we are seeing has structural roots. It is all too easy to see grown people acting like fools and assume that's all they are. Take a decently functioning suburban school, take away 40 percent of its funding, most of its better teachers, and the top-performing 50 percent of its students, and see how much fun faculty meetings would be after that. If we give people an enormously challenging task and only a fraction of the resources they need to accomplish it, sooner or later they start to turn on one another, making the job more difficult still. If we are not mindful of the inadequacy of the resource base, it always seems as if the problem is just those nutty people teaching in urban schools, as opposed to the conditions under which we expect them to teach.

In her study of Marcy School in Newark, Jean Anyon records an event that captures much of the tragedy of social relationships in bottom-tier schools. An assistant superintendent has arranged for two retired white executives from the National Executive Service Corps to advise parents at the school on how to collaborate. At the first meeting they attend, five members of the Parent Corps are sitting at one table in the library, the two executives at another, "wearing expensive-looking suits . . . and holding pencils above long yellow pads" (1997: 21). Most of the parents are seated with their backs to the executives, and at no time during the conversation do they look at them. One of the executives says, "We each had our own company. We've had a good deal of experience. What problems do you have that we—with our background—could help with?" The leader of the parent group responds that the only problems are maintenance and a lack of gym equipment, after which one of the executives says again "But [*pause*] if there is anything we can do for you, we'd like your suggestions." The parent leader ignores that and takes conversation in a different direction, but the executive tries again, asking about plans to get more parents involved. The parent leader lets him know they already have a lot of parents—not true, they only have eight—and they have learned over time how to get parents, after which she turns back to speak to the parents about something else. The executives stop asking questions. "They sit quietly at the back of the room during the rest of the meeting, and Mrs. Williams does not acknowledge them again."

We can probably assume good intentions on the part of all concerned, but they never learned to *hear* one another. One of the great paradoxes of the inner-city school is that when resources are made available, social and political barriers often inhibit their being brought to bear. Replace our square businessmen with (hip?) university professors who come to offer help with the teaching of reading; or with the National Science Foundation who comes to offer more engaging materials to teach science—materials they've spared no expense to develop; or with the Gates Foundation come to support more personalized forms of education. In bottom-tier schools, it is unlikely to matter. Outsiders coming to "help" are going to be rejected, just for being Outsiders, so it seems.

Figure 1.1 summarizes some of the ways in which weak social webbing manifests itself. One of the factors cutting across the particular expressions of pessimism and disconnection in figure 1.1 is what we can call the Principle of Negative Interpretation. Whatever other people do is interpreted in the most negative way possible. If parents don't show up at school, what does it mean? That they don't care. If a colleague fails to make hall duty, what does it mean? That she's blowing off her responsibility. If a principal fails to observe classes? She doesn't care about the kids. But if parents do show up? They're just coming to stick their noses in our business. If the colleague shows up for hall duty? Sucking up to the principal. If the principal does start doing observations? She's just trying to impress the people downtown—and why is she just starting now? If a teacher is really nice to students, they may take that as proof she thinks they're dumb and won't hold them to any standards. If she's mean? Racist bitch. Ambiguous evidence is consistently interpreted in the most negative way possible; no one gets the benefit of the doubt.

Figure 1.1. Social Barriers to School Change

- Lack of social comfort among parents, teachers, and administrators
- Low mutual expectations
- Predisposition to suspicion of "outsiders"
- Generalized belief in program failure; "I've seen programs come, I've seen programs go."
- Distrust of colleagues; the Principle of Negative Interpretation
- Tensions pertaining to race, ethnicity, age cohort; predisposition to factions
- Generalized anger; consequent withdrawal as major coping strategy
- "Happy Talk" culture; tendency to put the best face on everything
- Poor internal communications
- Institutional inability to learn from experience, intensified by a tendency to particularize, to treat one's school as if it were unique, making the experience of all other schools irrelevant
- Ego fragility, touchiness, emotional fatigue
- Disproportionate leverage for the most negative teachers
- Inability of teachers to share professional information

This is similar to the principle of Ingroup Virtue–Outgroup Vice (Allport 2001). The same behaviors are evaluated in opposite ways, depending on whether the actors are members of the ingroup or the outgroup. If Abe Lincoln studies late into the night, that's a sign of character and determination. If Asian American students do it, they're nerds. The difference is that in demoralized schools, the outgroup is generalized to become, at the extreme, everyone who is not in one's faction.

James Comer's School Development Program is among the reform models most sensitive to relationship issues, but even the staff doing the Chicago implementation of Comer initially underestimated the depth and tenacity of those problems. They were aware, for example, of the tensions between teachers and parents and of the very strong sense among Chicago teachers that most inner-city parents don't care about education. Thus, in their first schools, they put a great deal of energy into increasing the visible participation of parents in schools, thinking that would reduce some of those tensions. In fact, in almost every case, increased parental involvement led to increased parent-teacher tension, at least temporarily. (Teachers: "They're only coming to spy on us.") Merely interacting more didn't change the deeply ingrained tendency of one group to interpret the behavior of the other group in the most negative way possible.

A negative climate is fertile ground for the development of factions—older teachers versus younger ones; primary-grade teachers versus upper grade; third-floor teachers against first-floor teachers; constructivist, inquiry-oriented teachers versus traditional ones; teachers in the annex against teachers in the main building; Spanish-speaking teachers against English-speaking ones; U.S.-born Spanish-speaking teachers against Spanish-speaking teachers born elsewhere. Race and ethnicity are powerfully implicated in these divisions—as well as in most aspects of school interpersonal dynamics—but rarely acknowledged, the 800-pound gorilla that everyone pretends not to see. Lipman says of one of the schools she studies in a southern city, "All of the students identified by teachers as 'problems' were African American. However, the teachers assiduously avoided discussions of race and racial identification" (Lipman 1998: 112).

If you go into schools and ask about racial relations, you can get an almost offended response: "Well, of course, it's not an issue. We are color-blind. We don't see race. We don't see ethnicity. We only see children, and all children are the same to us." Then you look at how the teachers sit at lunch, at how teachers shape their own cliques, and how information flows. All that is likely to be racialized. Teachers are likely to be sitting in racially identifiable groups as they tell you there is no race in their world.

There is currently a good deal of discussion among social scientists about the posture of color blindness and the increasingly prominent role it has come to play in American racial discourse (Bonilla-Silva 2004; Lewis 2003; Pollock 2004; Wellman 1977). One theme in that discussion is that color blindness as an ideology can function as the new, acceptable face of racism. Arguing "I am color-blind" may in fact reinforce the racial status quo. You cannot change racial inequality if you pretend that race isn't there. Color blindness gives the person claiming it the advantage of not having to think about how negative outcomes are distributed. If, in fact, we all tell ourselves that in each individual encounter we interact without reference to color, then the fact that there are no Black boys in the honors track cannot be put into the conversation, because it has nothing to do with their blackness but only with their characteristics and capabilities as individuals. We treat everybody the same, after all. Color blindness precludes a discussion of the distribution of privilege by race.

New programs coming into a school may be racially coded almost immediately. The people who did the introductory workshops for the Comer process in Chicago, for example, were Black. They impressed teachers, particularly some of the African American teachers. The race of the presenters and the fact that Dr. Comer himself is African American led many Black teachers to think of the process as a "Black" program, and they supported it on that basis. They then felt betrayed when a white facilitator was assigned to their school.

External partners in Chicago are agencies—some university-based, some community-based, some for-profit—that help in schools in some way. A part of the untold story of external partners is the way that the most successful of them help schools learn to work through race. Ordinarily, if expertise comes into a demoralized school in the wrong racial packaging, the school may not be able to make use of it. Expertise just gets rejected. A learning process may be necessary to get schools to the point where they can accept expertise irrespective of how it is packaged.

In the Comer case, there were two young women facilitators whose experience typified for me some of the dilemmas faced by white facilitators in nonwhite schools. In terms of the quality of their work as professionals, their commitment to children and parents, I couldn't say there was a dime's worth of difference between them. But their presentational styles were different in ways that played into the school's racial imagery. One woman was flat-out shy, not outgoing, not effusive, did not necessarily take the lead in creating certain kinds of interactions. If you created them, she'd respond very effectively as a professional. She would spare no effort to get the job done. In this context, though, shyness is likely to be read as racial hostility. If you're one of the few white folks in a building and you seem to hold back, your holding back can be read as a statement about your racial identity. And that's how it was read in this case.

The other facilitator, working in one of the South Side schools, caught the devil from everyone. The parents led the charge. Usually teachers lead this charge, but it was the parents in this school. You would see them standing in the halls, all indignant, fists on hips, talking about "the White Girl this" and "the White Girl that." If she was nearby they would whisper about "the White Girl" just loudly enough for her to hear it.

They would walk down the hall and look her right in the face and not say anything, or walk away if she walked up to them. In the face of all this, she did not wither. She called a meeting of parents at which she said something like, "I understand some of you are upset because I'm white." The parents fell all over themselves denying it. "You're white? We didn't even notice." None of us want our smaller selves called out in public, and the parents knew that according to their own best values their behavior was small and petty. They were making judgments without giving the person a chance, and poor people know, better than most of us, how destructive that is.

Still, had they not been confronted, they would have probably kept on until they made it impossible for "the White Girl" to do her job. In this case, the facilitator said something like, "There's not much I can do about being white. I'm not here to be white, I'm here to work with your children. I want six months. I want people to just let me do my job and if, at the end of six months, you are not satisfied with what I have done on behalf of your children, I will leave. You will not have to run me out of here." A year later, she was arguably the single most socially central person in the building. She had the deepest relationships across the constituency groups, and when she had to leave because of funding, her departure was a crisis. It was traumatic for almost everybody in the building, but especially so for the parents, who had come to think of her as their special advocate, the source of their empowerment. We can be sure that there are other people with just as much talent, just as much dedication, who don't have the confidence of the second facilitator. They allow racial definitions to be imposed on them rather than imposing themselves on the definitions. It takes enormous emotional resources and/or an effective support system to weather being marginalized in this way, all the more so since most outside change agents are going to be caught unawares. Almost without exception in my experience, outside agencies rendering assistance to schools were unable to prepare their staff for the emotional beatings they were going to suffer.

A common experience among school reformers is going into a new school, quickly establishing a beachhead, but then finding themselves unable to move off the beach. That is, they find right away a small group of teachers open to trying whatever the innovation is, but two or three years later, they are still working with that same little group. Other teachers don't come on board as anticipated. A common reason for this is that the favorably predisposed teachers are socially defined by other teachers as a faction, so the mere fact that they have endorsed any program guarantees that other factions will shy away. In Chicago during the 1990s, the eager adopters were often young, primary-grade teachers, fresh out of college where they had been immersed in the language and theory of reform. School reformers from the outside, typically rejected by most staff because they are outsiders, are glad to find a receptive group talking their language. Becoming involved with that group, typically a low-status social clique, immediately embroils the reform in preexisting cleavages of race, cohort, and teaching philosophy, often before the reformers are aware that such cleavages exist.

A longstanding racial issue in Chicago schools has to do with differing standards and styles of discipline. African American teachers often see white colleagues as too lax about discipline—because they are afraid of the children or because they don't care about the children or because they don't understand African American culture—while white teachers may see some of their Black colleagues as rigid and punitive. When white staff members propose or endorse reforms, the reactions of Black staff may be conditioned by the perception that the white teachers who are so quick to talk about new programs have been unwilling to shoulder their share of the load when it comes to maintaining discipline.[2]

Color blindness might be regarded as one example of a larger phenomenon. One of the ironies of weak social infrastructures is that they can contribute to the development of "Happy Talk" public culture. In public discussions everyone accentuates the positive, even if it has to be made up. In schools where only 5 or 6 percent of students are reading at grade level, teachers sit around talking about how well they're all doing, all things considered, and how professional they all are. Even in the poorest-performing Chicago schools, the great majority of teachers traditionally received either a superior or an excellent rating every year (*Chicago Tribune* Staff 1988). If a school is already doing well, of course, there is no need to talk about how to do better, no need to talk about who is not doing their job—stressful conversations in any environment, but especially so where there is little underlying trust and respect. When every suggestion for improvement is highly likely to be construed as a personal attack, it's best to keep conversation light.[3]

It bears repeating that climates of pervasive distrust mean that schools cannot make use of financial and technical resources even when they become available. Inner-city schools are criminally under-resourced; still, in demoralized schools, making resources available hardly means they will ever be brought to bear. Expensive teaching materials sit on a shelf because teachers don't believe they will make any difference, or they wind up in the room of a teacher who has political pull but no notion of how to use them. Those conservatives who say urban school systems waste substantial resources are exactly right, however little they understand the context.

One year an experienced, deeply concerned teacher coordinates several programs and participates on a number of committees. The next year, she does none of that. Asked why, she explains that she had her "feelings hurt" by a principal who "is constantly telling people what they are not doing." She told the principal to find someone else to coordinate programs. An observer coming into contact with her the second year would write her off as another disengaged teacher. The emotional culture of schools is such that it is extremely unlikely that the offended party will ever explain her wounded feelings outside of her clique, which means nothing can be done about them, even if someone were so inclined. What was most likely an oversight by an overworked principal alienates a valuable staff member. The weak social webbing of bottom-tier schools makes it difficult for the schools to use resources from the outside, but it also degrades the human resources already there. In the toughest schools, change agents would be well advised to proceed as if operating in a place suffering from collective depression.

Social demoralization also means that communicating the simplest information accurately is difficult even when no one is deliberately sabotaging the flow of information. People read things into messages that were never intended. This is a contributing factor to one of the most frustrating characteristics of these institutions: their inability to learn from experience. What does it mean when a school has implemented 10 or 15 different programs within the space of a few years, which is not unusual numbers at all—none of which has gone particularly well— and continues to implement more programs in ways that reflect little or no learning from the previous attempts? Why doesn't experience count for more? In part, the inability to learn from experience has to do with the lack of time for shared reflection and pooling of information, but even if there were more time, distrustful people have difficulty learning from one another. It is hard to analyze anything when people are so prone to interpret everything negatively. The Inadequate Personnel Paradigm ("It didn't go well because the people I put in charge blew it") becomes an omnibus explanation, pushing out more instructive explanations. Some teachers in bottom-tier schools consistently produce better student outcomes than their peers. In more rational social environments, people would be able to learn from that and build on it.

Inadequate social infrastructure may also mean that inner-city schools are distinctively personality-driven institutions. In socially chaotic environments, strong personalities may find a kind of leverage not available in more structured environments. Suburban schools have plenty of staff personality problems of their own, but it is a reasonable hypothesis that the lack of structure in urban schools leaves them particularly vulnerable to strong, aggressive personalities. That is, given a weak professional culture, inadequate evaluation of personnel, protectionist unions, and dauntingly complex procedures for disciplining uncooperative teachers, there are fewer institutional constraints on individual behavior than one might find elsewhere (*Chicago Tribune* Staff 1988: 61–85; Vander Weele 1994: 61–74). Thus, the constellation of personalities associated with a particular reform effort may be a critical predictor of how implementation will fare.

Understandably, many reform initiatives of the 1990s agreed on the need for more collegiality and collaboration among teachers. It was an important part of the rationale for peer coaching, school governance teams, career academies, small schools, communities of practice, small learning communities, and many others. The idea lends itself to multiple mechanisms and means. In many versions, it may also make untenable assumptions about the social environment. To say "team" is to presuppose a great deal. There may be personality conflicts. Teachers may not see how collaboration is going to resolve the problems with which they are most concerned. Norms of isolation and competitiveness may be very strong. In their study of 200 Louisiana teachers, Leonard and Leonard (2003: 4) found that "Teacher work continues to be characterized by competition and individualism and lacks the type of trusting, caring environment that is more conducive to collaborative practice" (see also DiPardo 1997; Kruse and Seashore 1997). Like other researchers, they also found that teachers frequently feel they don't have time for all the collaboration they are being asked to do; it feels like an add-on, no matter what its proponents say. Then, of course, there is always the problem of inept implementation. In New York, "Many of the official programs (for teacher collaboration), young teachers complain, are empty shells, reserved as plum positions for teachers who can no longer stomach being in the classroom all day" (Hartocollis 2000). The most we can expect from such programs is "contrived collegiality" (Hargreaves 1991).

Kim Marshall tells an instructive story about his fifteen-year attempt to improve Boston's Mather School. He came to the principalship at Mather with some propitious background experience. He had directed the development of Boston's citywide curriculum as well as a system-wide strategic planning process. Prior to that, he had studied with Ron Edmonds, perhaps the leading figure in the effective schools movement. When he came to Mather in 1987, Marshall was not wanting for ideas. Early on, he tried to address the isolation and lack of teamwork among teachers. He tried to focus staff meetings on instruction, published a school newsletter that was largely about teaching, and revised the schedule so that teachers teaching the same grade had the same preparation time and, later, a weekly 90-minute team meeting. "But morale never seemed to get out of the basement. Staff meetings gravitated to student discipline problems." In team meetings, "there was a strong tendency for the agendas to be dominated by field trips, war stories about troubled students, and other management issues, with all too little attention to using student work and data to fine-tune teaching" (Marshall 2003: 107).

Part of the difficulty in getting teachers to talk substantively about teaching was due to what Marshall calls "curriculum anarchy." Having been involved in the creation of Boston's citywide standards, Marshall was "stunned" to find teachers simply ignored them.

> While teachers in one grade emphasized multiculturalism, teachers in the next grade judged students on their knowledge of traditional history facts. While one team focused on grammar and spelling, another cared deeply about style and voice. While one encouraged students to use calculators, the next wanted students to be proficient at long multiplication and division. (107)

While many teachers were unhappy about the uneven preparation of their incoming students, they were unwilling to talk with their colleagues about it for fear that it would lead to confrontation. The absence of professional dialogue was the price of maintaining morale. The situation was hardly helped by the fact that the official curriculum was in fact badly aligned with the local assessment tests, which themselves were not much respected by teachers.

Almost inevitably, teacher pessimism was a significant barrier: "Discouraged by the visible results of poverty and having never seen an urban school that produced very high student achievement, many teachers found it hard to believe that it could be done. They regarded themselves as hardworking martyrs in a helpless cause." The most negative individuals virtually declared war on the principal. While he was preaching that "all children can learn," they circulated a parody of one of his memos: "For Sale: Rose-Colored Glasses—Buy Now—Cheap—Get that glowing feeling while all falls apart around you."

> I was aghast at the vehemence with which these teachers attacked me. Monthly confrontations with the faculty senate invariably got my stomach churning, and I took to quoting Yeats: "The best lack all conviction, while the worst / Are full of passionate intensity. . . ." On several occasions, I failed to set limits on outrageous and insubordinate behavior, didn't assert my prerogatives as principal, and lost face with the rest of the staff, who secretly wanted me to change the negative culture that had dragged down the school for years. (109)

Marshall brought in a program to address the low expectations, brought in curriculum consultants, searched for better assessment tools, increased the quantity and quality of professional development, and considered a range of whole-school reform options—Effective Schools, Success for All, Efficacy, Accelerated Schools, the Comer plan, Whole Language, Multiple Intelligences, and others—all of which failed to get the necessary level of teacher buy-in, so the school continued to map its own way.

Much of what Marshall tried to implement was sensible and appropriate. These were good ideas being pushed by a serious and well-informed principal, yet most of them went nowhere for a long time. Time and again, he found that the kinds of structural changes he could make did not affect the core dynamics of his school. Repeatedly, the most difficult barriers proved to be the warped character of social relationships. The moral of the story is that good ideas will not save us. Just bringing good ideas into schools with severely damaged social infrastructure is tantamount to bringing a lighted candle into a wind tunnel.

Mather is emblematic of the national experience in another way: it got better. Mather's test scores went from among the worst in the city to about two-thirds of the way up the list. In 1999—twelve hard years after Marshall came there—the school made larger gains on the Massachusetts Comprehensive Assessment System than any large elementary school in the state. Leading change in a demoralized environment is among the most daunting jobs imaginable, but it is not impossible.

Counting Dysfunction

I noted earlier that the basic picture of life in inner-city schools has not changed much in several decades. What has changed in the last ten years is our ability to supplement that picture with a still-emerging body of quantitative research, including the work of the Consortium on Chicago School Research. In some of their early field studies, it became evident that the quality of relationships among adults determined much of what did or did not happen in schools. This led to a series of studies. In one of them, the Consortium surveyed staff at 210 schools in an attempt to identify those characteristics shared by schools that were getting better. When the 30 most highly rated schools were compared with the 30 poorest, a battery of questions about the quality of relationships proved to be one of the best predictors. While teachers almost unanimously agreed that relationships with their colleagues were cordial, that did not always mean they respected or trusted one another. Forty percent of teachers disagreed with the statement, "Teachers in this school trust each other." The degree to which teachers in a given school trusted one another correlated well with whether the school was improving or stagnating:

> Social trust is a highly significant factor. In fact, it may well be that social trust is the key factor associated with improving schools. Teachers in the top 30 schools generally sense a great deal of respect from other teachers, indicating that they respect other teachers who take the lead in school improvement efforts and feel comfortable expressing their worries and concerns with colleagues. In contrast, in the bottom 30 schools, teachers explicitly state that they do not trust each other. They believe that only half of the teachers in the school really care about each other and they perceive limited respect from their colleagues.

There were similar patterns in terms of teacher-parent trust: "In the bottom 30 schools . . . teachers perceive much less respect from parents and report that only about half of their colleagues really care about the local community and feel supported by parents" (Sebring, Bryk, and Easton 1995: 61). As suggestive as these findings are, they are only correlational. One could reasonably argue that the absence of trust is as much a reaction to school failure as a cause of it. Subsequently, Anthony Bryk and Barbara Schneider (2002) published a more complex analysis of what they call *relational trust*. Their scale for teacher-teacher trust included the following items:

- How many teachers in this school really care about each other?
- Teachers in this school trust each other.
- It's okay in this school to discuss feelings, worries, and frustrations with other teachers.
- Teachers respect other teachers who take the lead in school improvement efforts.
- Teachers at this school respect those colleagues who are expert at their craft.
- To what extent do you feel respected by other teachers?

The scale for teacher-principal trust included:

- It's okay in this school to discuss feelings, worries, and frustrations with the principal.
- The principal looks out for the personal welfare of the faculty members.
- I trust the principal at his or her word.
- The principal at this school is an effective manager who makes the school run smoothly.
- The principal places the needs of children ahead of her personal and political interests.
- The principal has confidence in the expertise of teachers.
- The principal takes a personal interest in the professional development of teachers.
- I really respect my principal as an educator.
- To what extent do you feel respected by your principal?

Thus, relational trust is a multidimensional concept, involving issues of respect, integrity, personal regard, and confidence. It is more a way to think about the quality of social relationships generally than a way of thinking about trust narrowly. The sheer concentration of distrust in some schools, then, is all the more disturbing. In 1997, in the bottom-quartile schools, over 60 percent of teachers reported having no or minimal trust in their colleagues, compared to about 25 percent in the top-quartile schools (which, on the face of it, might be regarded as a pretty high figure in its own right). Bottom-quartile teachers actually trusted their principals a little more than they trusted their colleagues: "only" 51 percent of teachers were in the two lowest trust categories vis-à-vis the principal. By contrast, in top-quartile schools, a whopping 88 percent of teachers expressed strong or very strong trust in their principal.

The most interesting results come from looking at improving and non-improving schools over time using a composite trust measure. In 1991 the schools that would eventually be identified as improving showed a quality of school relations only slightly better than schools that would not improve. By 1994, they had much higher levels of trust, and after that they began to take off academically. By 1997, schools that had had weak trust reports in 1994 had less than a 15 percent chance of being among the system's improving schools. Schools that had had strong trust reports in 1994 did almost three times as well. By 1997, they had a 50 percent chance of being in the improving group in both reading and mathematics. In addition, "schools with weak trust reports in both 1994 and 1997 had virtually no chance of showing improvement in either reading or mathematics" (Bryk and Schneider 2002: 111). High-quality human relationships are strongly predictive of whether or not a school can gather itself together to get better. When one controls statistically for the usual suspects—racial and class composition of the student body, stability of student body, school size, teacher credentials and experience, and concentration of poverty in the neighborhood—the relationship between trust and school improvement remains strong.

Clearly, then, we need to know something about the proportion of urban schools that might be thought to have severe deficits in social capital. Fortunately, the Chicago research allows us to at least begin getting a handle on that. The best available data come from the 211 schools of the Chicago Annenberg Challenge (see Program Glossary), a sample in which high schools are somewhat underrepresented but in which the elementary schools have demographic and achievement levels that almost exactly match the city as a whole. Those data tell us that, according to a 1997 survey of teachers, about a quarter of the schools reported minimal principal support for change, about the same proportion as reported that their principal worked to create a sense of community and that they had limited cooperation among teachers. One-third of schools reported a weak focus on student learning, and a little more than a third reported weaknesses of joint problem-solving (and we should suspect the direction of bias on these questions to be in the direction of underestimating the problem). When we consider trust, the number of problematic schools goes up dramatically. Forty-two percent of schools report minimal trust between teachers and parents, but a full 52 percent report no or minimal trust among teachers (Sconzert, Smylie, and Wenzel 2004: 15–16). Trust levels that low are likely to undermine most change initiatives all by themselves, even if a school had no other problems to contend with. Considering that some schools had already improved their climate by 1997 (Sebring et al. 2006) and that having a proportionate number of high schools would almost certainly have made the numbers more negative, it is probably conservative to say that in the early 1990s half of all Chicago schools had such deeply dysfunctional social arrangements as to have been considered fundamentally demoralized. They were socially defeated institutions, whipped before they even took the field.

It goes without saying that the schools with the weakest social webbing are likely to be concentrated in the neighborhoods with the weakest social capital. The stronger a neighborhood's sense of collective efficacy (e.g., residents trust one another, feel the community is closely knit, think they can call on one another for help), the higher its level of religious participation (e.g., belonging to a religious institution, attending such an institution, talking to religious leaders) and the lower the level of crime in that neighborhood. Also, the more friends people say they have outside the neighborhood, the healthier the schools in that neighborhood are likely to be (Sebring et al. 2006). In neighborhoods where religious participation is high, for example, 39 percent of schools were judged to have high capacity for improvement; where it is low, only 5 percent. We get about the same split between neighborhoods where collective efficacy is strong and those where it is weak (38 percent against 6 percent). In neighborhoods where residents have strong connections to people outside their neighborhood, 33 percent of schools had high capacity, against 8 percent in more socially isolated neighborhoods. That is, neighborhoods with strong social capital are four or five times as likely to have high-functioning schools as neighborhoods where the residents feel disconnected from one another. At the neighborhood level and at the school level, our most vulnerable students are vulnerable precisely because they are surrounded by adults who cannot cooperate with one another. Schools in the ghetto become schools *of* the ghetto.

There is nothing surprising to social scientists about the notion that social capital is an important determinant of educational outcomes (e.g., Coleman 1988; Schneider 2001), but we can be more precise now about how it operates. Weak social infrastructure means that conservatives are right when they say that financial resources are likely to mean little in such environments. It means that expertise inside the building is likely to be underutilized, and expertise coming from outside is likely to be rejected on its face. It means that well-thought-out programs can be undermined by the factionalized character of teacher life or by strong norms that militate against teacher collaboration. It means that schools are unlikely to learn from experience; it is difficult to learn from people whom one does not respect. It means that we have to think differently about the timeline for change. Many programs may have to spend the first year or two of implementation doing nothing but trying to cut through the social underbrush, trying to establish working networks. That does not necessarily mean these are bad programs.

The Politics of Demoralization

By treating teachers in ways that empower them, such as involving them in decisions about policies and practices and acknowledging their expertise, administrators can help sustain a healthy school environment.

—Reg Weaver,
President, National Education Association

In schools, no good idea ever goes anywhere; it gets buried in endless discussion and power plays that make you sorry you ever got involved in the first place.

—Anonymous teacher
(quoted by Sarason)

If demoralized environments problematize social trust, they also problematize the use of power and authority. Figure 1.2 lists some of the ways those problems express themselves. If trust is one way to facilitate collective action, power and authority constitute another, and they may be especially important in situations of low trust. Enough top-down pressure may get people to move in the same direction no matter what they think of one another. Similarly, in a context where the leadership has high levels of legitimacy, where followers feel leaders have a moral right to lead, what followers think of one another may matter less. The ghetto school, though, presents its own challenges to the establishment of legitimacy. What does it mean to be the leader of an enterprise that is constantly failing? Other factors constant, we would have to think that failure automatically undermines the legitimacy of the leadership. If the job isn't getting done, and if you're the person responsible and you can't fix it, why should you get to boss me around? Why should I defer? Why should I obey? The question hangs there in the air even if no one ever gives it (public) voice. We should look at inner-city schools, then, as places where the legitimacy of leadership is ordinarily problematic, ordinarily being negotiated. One could imagine a situation in which principals might be able to buttress their claims to legitimacy by emphasizing their strengths as instructional leaders, by stressing their command of the core business at hand. One would have to imagine it. Instructional leadership is not common among inner-city principals—nor principals, period, for that matter (Elmore 1999).

Figure 1.2. Micropolitical Barriers to School Change

- Perception of principal patronage, favoritism
- Tendency to protect existing power arrangements, formal or informal
- Pattern of contested or stalemated power among principal, teachers, union, others
- Tendency to give new programs to "safe" people
- Pattern of autocratic power or vacillation between autocratic and collaborative styles
- Staff not willing to take part in decisionmaking
- Principal not open to criticism; inability of principal to understand how he or she is perceived by staff
- Reluctance to talk about certain issues for fear of offending the principal, other powerful actors
- More generally, the tension between the need for positive PR and the need for realistic assessment

A theme of the next two chapters is that demoralized environments lead to people being invested in the failure of those around them. My failure gives me reason to hope for yours. The more plausibly parents can point the finger at teachers, the less they need to worry about how good a job they are doing as parents. The more teachers can point to the inadequacies of principals, the less reason for scrutinizing their own behavior. At the same time, principals have to answer to the people downtown, and, as chapter 5 will argue, that has meant answering to people who are collectively incompetent and technically irresponsible. There has not been much connection between the things that animate them and the lives of children and parents and teachers. Yet if principals want to keep their jobs, they have to keep these people happy. This, then, is the terrain against which inner-city principals must lead, with the legitimacy of their position up for questioning from the very beginning, with the people around them predisposed to being critical and carping and the people above them capable of doing little more than posing new problems. Small wonder that the micropolitics of many failing schools becomes particularly contentious or that many principals can't find a better way to negotiate their situation than by becoming petty autocrats.

In wealthier schools, political considerations are likely to be offset to some degree by a higher level of professional consensus, by a greater availability of resources (and thus less need to squabble over who gets what), and by more stable power arrangements. Where restraints are less evident, any reform has potential for destabilizing distributions of power, prestige, and privilege. Someone gets more resources, someone gets fewer. Whether the reform takes root depends in part on whether someone negotiates those politics. Principals, for example, can hardly be faulted if they want to put people they can depend upon in charge of a new initiative, but in conflicted buildings, any program run by one of the principal's pets will be given a wide berth by other teachers.

Providing teachers with an instructional coach became a fairly popular intervention in the late 1990s. It is still a promising intervention, but it is not easy to implement. If a principal brings in a coach for English teachers, what does that say about the chair of the English department? Even more important, what does it do to principals? How do they supervise someone who knows more than they do about the core business of the enterprise? When the coach enters a classroom, what does she represent? Is she there to uphold a particular vision of teaching or to help the teacher?

Or is she there as the principal's representative, sent to evaluate the teacher? A great many coaches find they cannot be effective with veteran teachers because they are seen as "spies." This is becoming a major strain in the development of an emergent professional role. In practice, coaches often wind up working mostly with new teachers because they cannot negotiate the politics of getting into other classrooms.

Any program facilitator can destabilize existing power relations. The facilitator who fights the good fight, who works her way through the initial rejection to become a valued member of the school community, may find that the principal—even if it is the principal who brought the facilitator in—is not entirely comfortable with the emergence of another influential one, who typically cannot be controlled in the way principals control others. Assistant principals are even more vulnerable. The facilitator's role is typically a kind of ill-defined assistant principalship, and real assistant principals can't be blamed if they are nervous about what the new role means for them. The situation is structured so as to make assistant principals the enemies of change, and their roles are so structured as to allow them to do a great deal of mischief to programs they don't like.

During the implementation of the Comer School Development Process in Chicago, it became clear that a public confrontation between the program facilitator and the principal was almost a normal part of the program's evolution. Principals would typically adopt the program's rhetoric right away—collaborative decisionmaking, no fault-finding, a renewed focus on the interest of the children—but it took longer for their behavior to catch up (see the next chapter). This would put the facilitators in an awkward position. If the staff saw them silently watching principals do things that contradicted the spirit of the program, things that clearly were not in the interest of the children, it proved that this was just another jive program, just as the staff had thought. To retain credibility and the moral high ground, the facilitators had to speak out eventually, invariably after numerous private conversations with the principal had come to naught. Typically, the Shootout at the OK Corral boosted facilitators' status among teachers. They became a kind of buffer, able to say things to principals that would have been difficult for teachers to say, giving voice to the previously voiceless. (That is to say, facilitators reduced vulnerability, which can be an important component in building trust [Bryk and Schneider 2002].) Initially, the Chicago facilitators, mostly consensus-oriented, conflict-aversive social workers, absolutely dreaded the idea of these confrontations. As they became more experienced, it came to seem more like just another part of the job. (And the principals who learned to let the process work itself through typically became more powerful than they had been previously.)

Nationally, from the mid-1980s through the mid-1990s, many of the most popular reform models involved some form of decentralization of decisionmaking, including Chicago school reform in its initial phase. The rationales were certainly compelling. If people have some say in what goes on, they are likely to have higher morale, likely to be more invested in the business at hand. The more that people who actually do the work can impact decisionmaking, the more decisionmaking is likely to reflect information that supervisors by themselves would not consider. In industrial settings, the research base for the advantages of devolving authority downward is considerable. Nevertheless, in retrospect, it is clear that researchers and policymakers, once again, oversold a model they only half understood. In practice, schools often found they still had little control over some of the things that mattered most to them—union contracts, fiscal policy, and curriculum (Hill, Pierce, and Guthrie 1997). Even when that is not true, there are real difficulties at the building level. Teachers don't necessarily want democratic involvement in the way that reformers shape it. They may find that sharing in decisionmaking requires too much time, too many meetings with ill-defined outcomes. Teachers clearly want to have a sense that they are listened to on the issues they care about, but they don't necessarily equate that with formal involvement in a shared decisionmaking process designed by outsiders (Malen, Ogawa, and Kranz 1990; Wohlstetter and Mohrman 1994).

On the other hand, principals in demoralized schools know perfectly well that some of the people being invited to share power are going to use it in vindictive and disruptive ways, at least at first. Small wonder that many principals go through a stage of democratic pretense during which they mouth the rhetoric of sharing power while, in fact, finding a variety of ways to control what actually happens, reinforcing staff skepticism about reform rhetoric.

We have seen enough cases where schools have had real success in sharing power to know that if schools can work through the difficulties, sharing decisionmaking really can help move schools to a higher level of functioning. Many reform efforts, though, greatly underestimate the difficulty that bottom-tier schools are likely to have working through the problems. This is a specific case of the more general problem of reformers trying to put something into a school without thinking about the structure of power in schools. The saddest cases by far are not those where a school is doing a poor job of implementing some trendy model of school governance, but those where no one has much power to get anything done, where the various factions and interest groups exist in a state of permanent checkmate.

One of the first casualties of autocracy is free speech. One of the reasons conflicted schools have such trouble getting better is that honest self-assessment may be all but impossible. It is all right to talk about what is going well, but talking about what is going badly is just too tricky, too likely to offend someone—and probably the people in leadership positions. For schools trying to initiate some kind of reform initiative, of course, this makes sensible mid-course corrections unlikely. It also exacts a toll that we don't understand on teachers who experience their own failure to speak up as moral compromise, a betrayal of their children and of their own better principles. Some of the generalized anger of teachers in these situations may be anger at themselves for not having the fortitude to tell the emperor his breath is funky.

> An organized group is characterized as having high morale when it performs consistently at a high level of efficiency, when the tasks assigned to it are carried out promptly and effectively. In such units each member is likely to contribute his share willingly doing what he believes to be worthwhile and assuming that his associates will do their part. When necessary, the men help one another without even being asked. Mutual encouragement is commonplace, and those whose zeal is exemplary are singled out for praise. The few who do not share the prevailing orientation feel pressures to comply: those who fail repeatedly to live up to expectations are scorned as "slackers" and efforts may be made to expel them from the group. The successful completion of each transaction occasions no surprise; it is the expected thing. Members of such groups usually place a high evaluation on themselves. They often develop a strong sense of identification with each other; they develop pride in their unit, become conscious of its reputation, and take pleasure in displaying emblems of belonging to it.

That is Shibutani's (1978) description of a high-morale military unit, and it sounds like a perfect inversion of what we know about the social functioning of bottom-tier urban schools, where we find instead a pervasive sense that one's colleagues and leaders cannot be depended on ("Cover your own butt!"), disdain for those who bring enthusiasm to the task ("They'll learn . . ."), a lack of support for new members of the group, a tendency for people to define their jobs in the narrowest terms possible ("Is it in the contract?"), and unbounded surprise when anything goes right.

I suspect that one of the reasons we have such persistent difficulty appreciating how damnably hard it is to change urban schools is the lack of respect we have for the people who work in them, which then predisposes us to simplistic answers. It is useful to be reminded that it is not, fundamentally, a problem that can be reduced to just the people in schools. The people in inner-city schools are reacting to sustained failure much as people in other failed institutions do. Institutional failure can create a social environment that encourages yet more failure, one downward spiral generating another. At the same time, positive synergies can be slow to come, if they come at all; one positive development does not necessarily lead to others in an unsupportive environment.

Yet if we could so arrange the world that urban principals only had to deal with social issues to improve their schools, they would be better off. At the same time they confront social demoralization, they also confront an irrational organizational context, a bureaucracy that, without exaggeration, can be called pathological when it isn't just out-and-out corrupt, and a situation in which the cultural, social, and material supports for teaching and student development all tend to be minimal. All this is taking place in an atmosphere of ideological rigidity and smug contempt for educators. Yes, weak social infrastructure, all by itself, can undermine the best-intended reforms, yet school leaders do not experience it by itself but in conjunction with a series of other problems, any one of which, all by itself, can also undermine initiatives. The patient has multiple diseases, and any of them can be fatal.

The fundamentally ahistorical, nonsociological, and decontextualized thinking that dominates this discourse makes it hard to appreciate the overdetermined nature of failure in the inner city. If we did appreciate it, we wouldn't have so many proposals that assume that if we *just* had more accountability, if we *just* had better teachers, if the teachers *just* cared more about children, if we *just* paid them more, if we could *just* operate schools under free-market principles, if we could *just* operate them more democratically, if we *just* put a computer on every desk, if we could *just* get schools to make decisions based on data, if we could *just* make lifelong learners of teachers, if we *just* put teachers in professional learning communities, if we *just* guaranteed every child a college education, everything would be all right. There is a mammoth disconnect between what we know about the complex, self-reinforcing character of failure in bottom-tier schools and the ultimately simplistic thinking behind many of the most popular reform proposals. What this seems to imply is not an argument for this or that program, but rather, for a style of work, a more intensive and robust way of intervening.

The Consortium on Chicago School Research has given us one way to think about this. The framework for much of their work is what is now called the Five Fundamentals for school improvement:

1. Instructional Leadership, which includes principal instructional leadership and teacher-principal trust

2. Professional Capacity, which includes the quality of professional development available in a school, the capacity of teachers to talk about their teaching with one another, and the degree to which the adults in a building take collective responsibility for what happens there

3. Learning Climate, including the degree to which students perceive high expectations, feel that teachers are personally attentive to them, and feel safe

4. Family and Community Involvement, including how teachers and parents communicate and the level of human and social resources in the community

5. Quality of Instruction, including the level of intellectual challenge in instruction and the degree to which students are academically engaged

There are other reasonable ways this kind of framework might be arranged, but the Consortium has amassed a great deal of data supporting the predictive power of this way of thinking about it. "We found that schools strong in most of the essential supports were at least ten times more likely than schools weak in most of the supports to show substantial gains in both reading and mathematics" (Sebring et al. 2006: 2). The supports work differently, though, in different kinds of communities. In communities with higher levels of social capital and lower numbers of the neediest children, schools can get better if the fundamental supports are just at average levels. Not so for the toughest schools. For schools in communities with the lowest levels of social capital and large numbers of the neediest children, "the essential supports needed to be exceptionally robust to result in improvement" (3–4), and that means robust in more than a single area. "The importance of strength in multiple essential supports suggests that narrow interventions will have limited success in improving student learning" (4), which could stand as the epitaph for most of what we have been calling reform for the last two decades.

If we take seriously the idea that failure in the inner city is overdetermined, it follows that there is no one lever we can move that will give us the purchase we need. We do not need to catalog and address every factor that contributes to failure—in fact, we cannot. We do need to be thinking about how we move in a deep way on more than one front at a time. Talent Development, developed at Johns Hopkins, is one of the more successful models of high school reform (Quint 2006). Their motto is Comprehensive, Sustained, and Intense. That captures it. Rhetoric notwithstanding, most of what we call school reform has not had the depth nor the intensity to cut into the deeper tangle of problems. Thus, we throw enormous resources at the problem, but those blue slips of paper keep right on turning into white slips of paper.

Chapter 2

"I Don't Want Your Nasty Pot of Gold": From Social Demoralization to Organizational Irrationality

Seems a stranger strolled into an urban school one day and asked if he could address the teachers. When they were gathered, he held up a big, shiny pot of gold and announced that it belonged to the school; he had brought it as a gift. The teachers, especially the veteran teachers, immediately started firing hostile questions at him. How come he was being so nice to them? And who was going to divide the gold up? Did the union approve of bringing gold into schools? Besides, some of them had heard he had already given a pot of gold to the school down the street. Was this pot of gold as large as the pot of gold he gave the school down the street? Because if not, they didn't want it. They didn't need any second-rate pot of gold, thank you very much. One stern matron rose to her feet, shaking a finger at the befuddled stranger, to testify that she had been teaching for thirty-five years, and if you needed gold to teach she sure would have figured it out before now, and anyhow, she knew the students and parents in this neighborhood, which was more than she could say for the stranger, and they just weren't the kind of parents and kids who could appreciate gold. Maybe gold made a difference in other neighborhoods, but it wasn't going to do a bit of good here.[1]

It is one thing to describe the social demoralization of schools, another to appreciate that after a certain level of density, demoralization becomes something other than a series of problems in interpersonal relations. Demoralized schools become different kinds of organizations, nearly incapable of certain kinds of collective decisionmaking. The most thoroughly demoralized organizations are best thought of as technically irrational; there is no predictable relationship between what they do and the ends they have in sight. More specifically, the members of the organization cannot act in their own self-interest, even when they agree on what that is.

One of the things this means is that certain kinds of reform, predicated on motivating people by sanctions (be they positive or negative), will repeatedly have more trouble getting purchase than would be the case in rational organizations. We can consider the story about the blue slips of paper turning white, a kind of First Heuristic, a reminder of the centrality and power of noncooperation in our worst schools. The Pot of Gold Story can be the Second Heuristic, a symbol of how irrational organizations can become less than their constituent elements, incapable of doing the simplest things, even of accepting good things that are plopped into their laps.

Woodbine School serves an overwhelmingly low-income, Black, and Hispanic population on Chicago's West Side.[2] In the early 1990s, it had fewer than 20 percent of its students reading at grade level, which actually is on the high side for bottom-tier schools. Its assets included an engaged, energetic principal, who was capable of accepting some criticism—an important issue for principals—and a hardworking staff. While many Chicago schools are virtually empty of staff soon after the afternoon bell, Woodbine has several teachers who regularly come early and stay late, suggesting a staff that has higher expectations for their students than is normal in inner-city Chicago. At least two well-known street gangs operate in the area, but this was not a school serving one of Chicago's housing projects—with all the additional social problems that entails.

Even with its relative advantages, Woodbine was a school where the staff had significant problems trusting one another, some of which started with problems on the leadership team but emanated out to complicate relationships throughout the building. Mrs. Clinton, the principal, was very concerned with test scores but, like most Chicago principals, would be considered more of a manager than an instructional leader. Her classroom observations—which were infrequent—seemed geared toward identifying the weaker teachers so that she could weed them out, not toward working with them on their weaknesses. She had hired some assistant principals, though, who were more respected by staff for their knowledge of instruction, something not all principals are secure enough to do. The principal's operating style, though, made it difficult for her to get the best out of her staff. She was described as impetuous, much quicker to reprimand—often in public—than to praise. The principal was not very patient with the frequent criticisms of insensitivity to staff; her position was that she hired people because she hoped they would be professional enough to do their jobs without being stroked every few minutes. Despite the fact that the school was officially committed to shared decisionmaking, Clinton had difficulty making her staff, even the senior staff, feel like they had a real voice. She vacillated between asking for collaboration and consensus one day and expecting staff to respect her decisionmaking prerogatives as principal the next. Her vacillation kept senior staff constantly off balance. Is this a day when it is okay to disagree with the boss or not?

Guess wrong, and you could wind up in big trouble. At one point, the principal decided that she wanted to reshuffle job assignments of the members of the leadership team (the assistant principals, the counselor, the social worker, the curriculum resource specialist) in ways that, from her viewpoint, would allow for more effective curriculum supervision and more support for teachers on disciplinary matters. From the viewpoint of almost everybody else, it looked like the reassignments failed to take advantage of the particular strengths and weaknesses of team members. Clinton originally presented the decision as a done deal, but when she saw how clearly shocked team members were at not being consulted sooner, she claimed she was only making suggestions, after all. Still, she had presented the realignment so forcefully that no one really believed that it was open for discussion. Few objections were voiced until she stepped out of the room and the Comer facilitator pressed people for their reactions, which turned out to be almost entirely negative. Clinton was clearly annoyed to walk back in the room and find the issue still under discussion. According to the field notes, she "sighed and in a combative tone asked the group, 'What is the problem? Is there someone here who is unable to do what I have asked them to do?'" When Mrs. Johnson, one of the assistant principals, expressed her doubts about the new plan, Clinton repeatedly asked her if she was saying she could not accomplish what she had asked her to do, and the AP repeatedly responded that she was "perfectly willing" to do her "very best," but she still had concerns. After going back and forth for a while,

Clinton pushed her chair back from the table and said, angrily, "This is an administrative decision and I am the administrator. This is no longer up for discussion. As far as I am concerned, this meeting is adjourned." With that, she stormed out.

The observable fallout from this little brouhaha continued for months. In the short term, Mrs. Johnson was frightened, almost to tears at one point, that, for voicing an honest professional opinion, she was going to get written up. Mrs. Clinton was certainly in a mood to do that for a while. She felt betrayed—that was her word—by her assistant. This was not the first time that Clinton thought that Johnson had betrayed her by speaking out of turn, but it marked a turning point in their relationship. Clinton several times expressed skepticism about Johnson's intentions, and Johnson, who prided herself on being a hard worker, seemed to withdraw for a while. She did her job, but she was not always invested in it the way she had been. Perhaps it's not surprising that the assistant principal's relationship with teachers sometimes replicated her relationship with the principal. Johnson made several decisions that directly affected teachers without consulting them and then seemed surprised when teachers were upset or felt devalued.

It may seem that Mrs. Clinton overreacted to a minor disagreement, but consider the context within which she works. Like all Chicago principals, she lived on a four-year contract, renewable at the pleasure of her local school council. For much of the period under discussion here, relationships between the principal and the council were markedly tense. The principal seemed to be right in her judgment that some members were out to get her. At least two members seemed to automatically take the opposite side from her on any issue. There were periods, negotiated by the Comer facilitator, when the hostile council members tried to be less oppositional, but even during those truce periods the principal had a hard time believing they were sincere. She continued to interpret their current behavior in the light of their previous behavior, perceiving attacks where it was pretty clear that nothing of the sort was intended.

The principal was thus always on the defensive, confronted with a central administration that was becoming increasingly aggressive about test-score improvement and a council that seemed to be waiting for her to slip up. The last thing she needed was senior staff openly disagreeing with policy. From the principal's point of view, that kind of betrayal was not merely personal; it also jeopardized her ability to continue to run and improve her school. A principal may firmly believe in collaborative, egalitarian ideals—after all, Clinton brought the Comer program, which stresses those principles, to Woodbine—and yet bracket them off as not being applicable to particular situations. You can't have everybody expressing their feelings on every single point when you are in the middle of a battle. The principal felt, with some justice, that there were plenty of issues on which she had gone out of her way to solicit and respond to staff input. She couldn't do it on every issue.

Her leadership staff would almost certainly have agreed with her on that. Still, they wanted to know, more clearly than the principal had communicated, which issues were to be the principal's prerogative and which would be open for input. Realistically, though, principals were negotiating the reform context for the first time; the political context was shifting all the time. They could not always know in advance which issues could comfortably be thrown open for discussion.

However understandable, what is perceived as inconsistent behavior from principals can wreak havoc with their staffs. Soon after the blow-up, Mr. Ford, another assistant principal and perhaps the member of the leadership team least likely to disagree with the principal, seemed to become the fair-haired boy. He seemed to have Clinton's confidence in a way the others did not and seemed to have access to information sooner than anybody else. Other members of the team resented what they saw as favoritism, and in subsequent meetings when people disagreed with Ford, it wasn't always clear whether they were disagreeing substantively or just because he was the principal's new boy. At least one other member seemed to be always trying to protect Ford from any criticism. For several months, the atmosphere on the team was defensive and mutually suspicious, enough so that there were open discussions about distrust on the team, and the simplest administrative tasks—supervising the lunchroom, devising a detention policy—became exercises in Byzantine intrigue, with each faction trying to discredit the other and always questioning the motives of the other.

In between squabbles over lunchroom duty, this group was supposed to be leading Woodbine School through a thoroughgoing revision of its K–8 curriculum. This was a project the school had embarked upon a year and a half earlier, intended to spur more professional collaboration among teachers and to align the material taught in one grade with that taught in contiguous grades while encouraging the use of more innovative teaching methods. It seemed to be largely an idea that the administration was pushing, but there was some degree of enthusiasm among staff at the beginning, which rather quickly got frittered away. The external consultant who was brought in got off to a rocky start; teachers initially thought he was talking down to them. From the very start, many—perhaps most—teachers were visibly uncomfortable with the idea of sharing what they were doing in the classroom. The reexamination of curriculum required dozens of meetings, after school and on weekends, and even the initially hopeful became resentful about all the extra time. Some teachers made earnest efforts to coordinate with teachers in other grades but many others didn't, and some of the latter involved cases of preexisting friction among teachers. Other disagreements started off as curricular—including one between a proponent of whole language in the early grades and a proponent of phonics—but came to take on a personal cast as well, preventing any rational search for compromise. It seems that when the administration failed to react forcefully to these problems, they sent a message to teachers about just how serious they were. In any case, most teachers seemed to find the whole process pretty abusive (but even so, it was clear that they learned a great deal about what their colleagues were doing; for all the problems, it was a new level of professional dialogue). The fruit of their mighty labor was a sizeable new curriculum handbook, completed just about when the long-festering leadership tensions were coming to a boil. The administrators acted as if the handbook were a great victory; teachers generally shrugged.

With or without a handbook, school leadership was far too fractured to actually implement anything in the classroom. Mrs. Johnson, the assistant principal, was probably the staff member with the most pertinent expertise, but the project was assigned to one of the assistants with whom Johnson was frequently at odds. Johnson clearly knew about some of the problems while they were developing but, given her tenuous relationship with the principal and some of her colleagues, did not feel comfortable about raising issues too forcefully. Nevertheless, raise them she did, and, as she expected, her questions were interpreted as personal attacks, and the other assistant countered with a series of optimistic reports that glossed over reality. Eventually, Johnson was given more direct responsibility for the project, but teachers' attitudes were pretty well hardened by that time. They didn't want to hear the phrase "curriculum revision." The very idea of visiting someone else's classrooms was still commonly referred to as "spying." Eight or nine months after the handbook was produced, it appeared that not many teachers could have found a copy of it, much less were they teaching it. With reasonable leadership, the process might have had a chance; other schools got a good deal more out of the effort. At Woodbine, the fragile social situation made it impossible, over the near term, for the school to use expertise it actually had on staff. It is almost certain that the whole episode deepened teacher cynicism about large-scale change. Pity the next person who tries to sell this group on a new academic program, no matter how valuable.

Curricular revision is one of the most complicated tasks any school can undertake. Naturally, it requires building-level leadership. It is perhaps even more instructive that when Woodbine School attempted more modest initiatives, they too frequently foundered on the social infrastructure. Consider a teacher-initiated attempt to address discipline problems. Teachers had long complained that the central office didn't do enough to help them with misbehaving students. Largely at the urging of Mr. Steele, a white fifth-grade teacher, the middle-grade teachers initiated their own discipline policy. Each transgression earned students a certain number of points, and as points added up, so did sanctions— calls to parents, detention, loss of in-class privileges, and so on. Maybe it wasn't the most creative response, but it worked. There was apparently unanimous agreement that so long as all teachers were doing it, and kids faced the same rules and punishments in every classroom, it made a real difference. Classrooms and corridors were noticeably more quiet, referrals to the office were reduced. Most of the changes occurred pretty rapidly, but even the most chronic offenders seemed to improve after a couple of marking periods. So, teachers had collectively identified a problem of vital importance to them, collaborated, and had come up with a way to substantially alleviate the problem.

Naturally, it didn't last. It is hard to say exactly when things started falling apart, but it was clear that by the end of the first year, there was less consistency of effort. Mr. Steele, the person most visibly associated with the project, lost some leverage after getting involved in a conflict with the administration that took on a personal tone—such as Steele referring to the main office as "the lunatics." At least one teacher pretty much decided to stop doing the point system. By the beginning of the next year, there were two nonconformists, one of whom went so far as to badmouth to kids the teachers who were enforcing the rules. Her colleagues thought she was trying to win a popularity contest with the kids. Some thought was given to asking the administration to intercede and get everybody back on the same page, but the teachers decided that there was no purpose in that. Their thinking may have been affected by the fact that one of the nonconformists was widely perceived to be among the principal's pets. The program just kind of withered away, as teachers gradually tired of beating their heads against the wall. Midway through the second year, only a few classrooms were even trying.

We can't be entirely certain what was happening at the level of individual motivation, but outwardly we seem to have an inability to sustain minimally cooperative relationships—even when all involved seemed to have been profiting from them—along with an apparent absence of professional respect and confidence in the ability of the administration to behave impartially. In that context, teachers could craft small victories, but holding on to them took more than they had.

It would be an error to think of these problems as merely incidental. If only this particular teacher didn't get into a spitting match with this particular principal, maybe things would have worked out. In fact, the likelihood is that if that hadn't happened, something else would have. In the inner city, it is misleading to think of hostility as merely interpersonal. Put underprepared people in a highly stressful, under-resourced, stigmatized environment where no one typically has the authority to invoke effective sanctions, where class and racial tensions are ever-present, and you create an environment where dysfunctional relationships become structural, as much a part of the social landscape as outmoded textbooks.

Remember that Woodbine School was emphatically not among the worst of the bottom-tier schools in Chicago. In the worst schools, you wouldn't have a principal giving conflicting messages; you might have an out-and-out autocrat running the school with some little in-group, whose members would be distinguished only by their skill at political intrigue or ardor at butt-kissing or who just happen to be of the same racial group as the principals. Teachers elsewhere can be so intimidated that it is difficult to get them to talk inside the building. For all the problems Mrs. Clinton had, her staff almost universally acknowledged her desire to see children learn and her willingness to select staff on the basis of professional competence. While she might fly off the handle, she would listen to criticism—from some sources—when she came down. Maybe Woodbine could not implement the new curriculum policy, but in other schools it would have been impossible to get teachers working cooperatively long enough to rewrite it. The tragedy of Woodbine is that with a staff that had decidedly not given up, they still couldn't sustain a level of internal cooperation that would allow them to predictably keep even simple positive innovations in place, even when the staff had some ownership over the innovations.

The problems of elementary schools are exacerbated in high schools. This is at least partly because of their greater size, partly because the departmental structure of high schools adds an additional barrier to interaction among teachers, partly because it is so much easier for students to just fall between the cracks, and partly because student behavior becomes so much more problematic. I first started thinking about institutional ability to get the simplest things done, to hold on to small victories, when I studied Chicago's Westside High School, which had been for a very long time among the city's most disorganized and dangerous schools.[3] At various times, certain parts of the building were virtually ceded to some of the street gangs that infested the schools (and teachers in bad odor with the principal might find themselves regularly assigned to hall duty in those parts of the building). The school had some of the city's lowest test scores. Relationships between the faculty and administration were so dysfunctional that kids could often do pretty much what they wanted. On most days, one could get a sense of an institution out of control just walking up to the building, where there were normally clusters of students hanging about who should have been in class. Entering the hallways didn't change much. There, too, students would be hanging out, much as if they on a street corner, talking and joking, playing radios, playing cards, or grabbing a quick smoke. Late in the day or during an assembly or approaching a holiday, the situation could get much more chaotic. The cop who said, shortly before one Christmas vacation, that he'd like to take a nap at his post but was afraid he'd be robbed, was only half-joking.

There were individual teachers, teachers who had a "rep," who could clear the halls almost anytime they wanted. Many of these were Black teachers and some were coaches, both groups thought to be less afraid of students. The normal institutional arrangements for controlling the halls were formidable, but only on paper. The school had a detachment of police officers in the building at all times; several paraprofessionals, all males, were assigned primarily to hall duty; students carried ID cards with their class schedules on them; and teachers were assigned to monitor virtually every section of hallway and every stairwell throughout the school day. Part of the problem, of course, was that the adults didn't really do what they were supposed to do. Teachers regularly just didn't show up for hall duty, and the administration seldom made an issue of it. Some further aggravated the problems by letting students leave class early or, even more commonly, by not challenging students who chose to come late. There were a few teachers who locked the classroom door when the late bell rang, which at least encouraged students to get to class on time, but, more immediately, it left a few more students with nothing to do but join the general melee in the halls. Teachers assigned to do study halls frequently failed to show up, which students took to mean they didn't have to stay there.

Teachers commonly talked about the hall problem as if it were beyond solution, because either the kids were just too wild or the administration too incompetent, or both. Nevertheless, the school actually found several ways to ameliorate the problem. The real problem was that as soon as something worked, it was discarded. For a while they tried the so-called snatch-and-grab program. When the late bell rang, teachers were to go into the halls and pull any nearby students into their classrooms. It seemed to work fine for a while, but then it faded away. Then, there were the hall sweeps. Groups of teachers, beginning on the upper floors, would walk the halls, pushing students before them in a dragnet toward the first-floor auditorium, where they would be given either a warning or a suspension. This straightened out the hall problem for a while, but the program gradually just died away. Some months later, hall sweeps were reinstated, but this time only during certain unannounced periods of the day. After a bit, though, the program once again just faded away.

Eventually, a much more aggressive assistant principal was given responsibility for the halls. He used police officers more actively, put stronger teachers on hall duty when possible, and put a great deal more pressure on all teachers to do hall duty. Once again, while the program lasted, it worked. This, obviously, is not a pattern of unrelieved failure. Rather, it is one where the school repeatedly finds a measure of success and then somehow backs away from it. We can call this backing away from small successes the Corridor Principle. The adults in the building couldn't sustain collective action long enough to maintain policies, which, it would seem, benefited almost everyone. Part of the underlying problem seemed to be that both teachers and students expected any innovation to fail. When a new program was announced, the dominant opinion was that it couldn't work. When it seemed to be working, people said it wasn't going to last. In that climate, any problems that cropped up were seen as proof of impending failure. Let a teacher or two fail to show at the appointed time, and other teachers saw that as a sign that things were falling apart, which then justified taking their own responsibility less seriously. If it's not going to work anyway, why knock yourself out? Gradually enough people would pull back so that the program really couldn't function well anymore, at which point there would be a chorus of people saying, "Told you so!", often in tones that were relieved, even triumphant, as if they had been once again rescued from the nasty prospect of succeeding at something.

It sounded very much like what Shibutani saw in his dysfunctional army company:

> Consistently shoddy performance develops in a cumulative process. . . . But if the others notice that these [slipshod performers] are getting away with their dereliction, they will join them. As it becomes clear that such transgressions are difficult to punish, increasing numbers join them. Men then begin to cooperate in avoiding duties; they prearrange absences from their posts and cover for each other. (1978: 417–18)

At Westside, the most gung-ho teachers and police officers might continue trying long after others had given up, but eventually many of them would decide it was pointless to keep beating their heads against a wall. Even the strongest eventually succumbed to the self-fulfilling prophecy, one that happened to work in their narrow interests in the sense of getting them out of an unpleasant obligation.

In his classic essay on self-fulfilling prophecies, Robert Merton (1948) noted that they could operate only in the absence of institutional controls. Clearly, teachers were not very worried about administrative response. The expectation was that the administration might huff and puff for a while but sooner or later would turn its attention to something else before doing anything serious. In a crisis-ridden environment—where administrators felt they had few sanctions to bring against uncooperative teachers, where the lack of cooperation was massive, where it had the sanction of tradition, where there was good reason to fear that anything that looked like heavy-handed administration might lead to a fight with a very strong and protective teachers' union—teachers were making a safe bet.

My first encounter with blue slips of paper turning white involved teacher attendance books at Westside, which probably said more about the social character of the school than did the battle for the corridors. Teacher attendance books bore no particular relationship to any known reality. One year, outside auditors determined that only 2 of 140 books had been done correctly. The errors were anything but subtle. Different teachers' books differed as to the total number of school days, largely because different teachers stopped taking attendance at different times. Over half the teachers in the English department had students marked absent on holidays, during a teachers' strike, or at other times when school was not in session. Apparently, teachers were not taking attendance daily. Rather, they were filling in the books long after the fact, presumably giving students whatever number of absences felt about right. That teachers felt no need to even try to make the books look plausible is almost certainly a function of how little they respected the administration. Let us concede that teaching in the ghetto is difficult, that establishing order in ghetto schools can be difficult. There is nothing difficult about taking attendance. If it doesn't happen, it doesn't happen because the responsible adults feel free to make only the most minimal efforts.

Disorder is a double-edged sword. In one sense, it obviously works to everyone's disadvantage. In another, though, disorder means a measure of freedom people in more regulated environments don't have. Teachers in better-organized schools are not thrilled about hall duty and recordkeeping either, but they are much less likely to have a choice about it. Once people come to accept the idea that the overall mission of the school is futile, it makes sense for them to cut the best deal they can for themselves, which means taking advantage of such freedoms as the situation offers. One can do minimal preparation for class, skip committee meetings, make a practice of not coming in on Fridays—generally blow off the least pleasant aspects of the job. It may not be much but it's something, something that gives teachers another kind of investment in failure.

The fact that they exploit the situation doesn't mean that teachers are any more craven or irresponsible than the rest of us. They understand their own misbehavior as a reaction to the larger failure, not a cause of it. If they could really be convinced there was a chance of making Westside a place that worked for children, no doubt they would prefer to be a part of that. Veteran Westside teachers saw the old days, when the school had a more assertive administration, as a golden period, but that didn't keep them from taking what small compensations they could from disorder, even as they decried it. A teacher may say that under the last strict principal she enjoyed coming to school much more, even though more demands were placed on her. Even as she says that, she looks at a memo on her desk from the current principal and says she may or may not get around to responding to it. If one talks to students who have been in more orderly environments—which, on the West Side, often meant Catholic schools—they say the same thing. They preferred the other environments, worked harder there, but once back at Westside, they found it hard not to yield to the temptations of being free.

For Max Weber, organizational rationality exists when an organization can match its ends to appropriate means. In the Weberian sense as well as the colloquial sense, it would make sense to think of the worst urban schools as being irrational institutions. People have institutionalized ways of perceiving the world that make the whole less than the sum of its parts; individual capacity does not add up to organizational capacity. We have to think about demoralized schools as if they were clinically depressed individuals, people whose emotional state makes every task, even the smallest, seem overwhelmingly difficult, makes it difficult for them to do that which they would otherwise be capable of, makes it likely they will fail to recognize good fortune even when it is beating them about the ears. Much of our policy discussion, though, proceeds as if schools were sane places. Thus, reformers of both the left and the right continue to act as if making this or that change in school structure will, by itself, lead to real change, when actual experience has been very much the opposite. As a report from the Wisconsin Center for Educational Research puts it:

> Our research suggests that human resources—such as openness to improvement, trust and respect, teachers having knowledge and skills, supportive leadership and socialization—are more critical to the development of professional community than structural conditions.
>
> Structural conditions—including time to meet and talk, physical proximity, interdependent teaching roles, communication structures,

and teacher empowerment—are important to be sure. But if a school lacks the social and human resources to make use of those structural conditions, it's unlikely that a strong professional community can develop.

This finding adds weight to the argument that the structural elements of restructuring have received too much emphasis in many reform proposals, while the need to improve the culture, climate, and interpersonal relationships in schools have received too little attention. (Kruse, Seashore-Louis, and Bryk 1995: 8)

For more than a decade, some conservatives have touted charter schools and voucher plans as paths to large-scale change. Such a notion turns out to be a bit more complicated than expected. One respected choice advocate recently noted, "It is time to acknowledge that getting dramatic results from school choice will be harder than expected" (Hill 2007). Part of the rationale for choice models, perhaps the primary rationale, has been that if public schools were faced with competition, they would find a way to do better work. The argument greatly overestimates the capacity of such schools. It assumes they are more or less rational entities that can respond appropriately to a changed political environment. That's not a reasonable expectation for our most troubled schools and systems. Unless the internal problems of such schools are addressed, neither threats by themselves nor the provision of additional resources by themselves are likely to produce much more than temporary bursts of frenzied activity. The idea of performance pay for teachers, which seems to be coming back in vogue, as it does periodically, might be thought of in the same way, as presuming more rationality than the system supports.

If the right expects too much from sanctions, the left retains a touching faith in reasoning, in one form or another. To make a point to be repeated in the next chapter, the fact that the inmates have an investment in seeing that the asylum isn't too well run changes the game considerably, adding an important additional level of irrationality. Demoralized teachers are not just people who don't trust; they are people invested in not trusting, invested in believing that better practice isn't possible or wouldn't make a difference. When people are in that position, it may not be possible to change their thinking with "evidence." Actually experiencing some success, as we have argued, may not suffice, calling into question an idea much beloved of liberals: that good practices will spread once people see the success of those practices. Ideology yields neither to evidence nor to experience.

The discourse around Best Practices is problematic for just this reason. The basic idea is that we should identify those practices that seem to make the most difference for children and replicate them as widely as possible. As usually practiced, it can be a pretty decontextualized way to think about change. If you are in a school with a culture of faculty cooperation, inquiry-based learning, let us say, can look like a really good thing. Try to export that to a building where faculty don't help one another solve problems, and you may not recognize the result. On a grander scale, we have the history of East Harlem's Central Park East. For a long time, it held an almost iconic position in the national discussion as the place where inner-city education was working, and this at a time when there were very few such places at which to point. In the 1980s and 1990s, educators would go on pilgrimages there and then return home to replicate what they saw, usually taking replication to mean imitating the instructional practice, or the programming, or the faculty organization, usually not thinking that they were trying to transfer ideas from a situation where the initial faculty was highly skilled—sharing a common educational vision and a personal and professional commitment to its success—to situations where none of that was likely to be true.

That is, the Best Practices discourse lends itself to decontextualized thinking, reducing the problem of urban schooling to a cognitive one: if only our teachers and principals knew how they do it the Big City. In fact, taking the idea of organizational irrationality seriously means that we have to be careful about all reforms that are essentially cognitive, that is, all reforms which take the form of saying that we just need to get some particular information into the heads of people in schools, and that will make a fundamental difference. It is an ahistorical, apolitical way of understanding the world. There is some of this in the current fashion of calls for data-based decisionmaking in schools. Presumably, the world already knows that decisions are likely to be better if they are based on a little information. If people don't do that, presumably they have their reasons, and perhaps we should spend some time thinking with school people about what those reasons might be rather than just issuing more exhortations from on high.

In fact, taking seriously the idea of organizational irrationality might help us reevaluate some of the clichéd language now substituting for thought in too many high-level discussions, particularly language which assumes that new and different is inherently good. We are reaching a point where it is hard to go to a meeting without hearing calls for "innovation." Or the even more vulgar references to "out-of-the-box" thinking! "Newness" becomes a goal in itself. The presumptions embedded in that deification of the new are largely insulting to educators. If we begin with the assumption that there are many smart, talented, hardworking people in these schools, we are less likely to accept the notion that there is some bright new idea that's going to fix everything. If that's all it took, the good people in our schools would have figured it out already. We are not smarter than they. Our energies would be better devoted to trying to understand the organizational and environmental characteristics leading people to do so much less than they can.

Thus, a word of caution about the Pot of Gold story. That story works because on first telling, almost all of us hear it ahistorically. That is, we hear it as a commentary on teachers, one that gives us the right to look down on them. We are unlikely to stop and ask, What has led teachers to think this way? What is the history through which they are seeing the Benevolent Stranger? How many times have they seen other reformers coming through, coming down from the University, or Central Office, or the Big Foundation? How many times have they come, probably people who have never spent a day in front of 35 screaming kids, never been cursed by a kid or threatened by a parent, with their overdressed, overpaid, patronizing selves, knowing nothing about the leadership problems in that school, knowing nothing about the history of failed reforms in that school, reforms that took up teachers' time and then were never mentioned again? How often have they come, knowing nothing and promising everything, full of missionary zeal and intensity, bringing the Next Bright Idea, coming to *tell* teachers, not to listen to them, brushing aside teachers' real-world objections, conveying, in ways subtle and not so subtle, their very real contempt for teachers?

From the viewpoint of official institutional goals, the most demoralized schools have a kind of structured irrationality. In terms of the lived history of the people in schools, their reactions are perfectly rational. The greater irrationality, the deeper contradiction, is that we think we can treat teachers the way we do, approach them the way we do, and then expect them to make decisions in the best interest of children.

Chapter 3

Weak Skills and Bad Attitudes: Teaching in the Slums

He just sat in his chair, didn't do nothing, just wrote how many questions [we were supposed to do], like one to six or what page and he'll say do it Friday and he don't explain. . . . When somebody ask him something, he act like he don't hear them, he'll just be sitting up there and keep on writing.

They don't listen to him. He explains nothing. He be talking about something that nobody be interested in, that don't have nothing to do with that class. And he be talking and the students be talking over him.

—Chicago high school students, quoted in
Getting What We Ask For (Payne, 1984)

And of course, the defeatism comes from witnessing injustice after injustice. And this does not refer solely to the students who tell me about their parents who have beaten them or kicked them out, or the violence they witness, or even the plain old poverty that dictates much of their lives. It also refers to the teachers in my school who scream, antagonize, insult and demean the "bad" kids— who somehow manage to survive getting yelled at by eight adults between 8 [a.m.] and 3 p.m.

—Second-year teacher,
New York City, 2004

Helen Gouldner's *Teachers' Pets, Troublemakers and Nobodies* (1978) offers one of the most instructive portraits we have of the initial encounter between inner-city children and inner-city schools. These are all-Black schools, and the classrooms Gouldner looked at had Black teachers. What stands out most in her analysis is how quickly teachers began sorting students into the Chosen and the Lost. In some kindergarten classrooms, it happened as early as the first week of classes. Teachers began dividing students by presumed ability. "Presumed" because at that point, teachers had no data on which to base decisions. Teachers claimed that they could tell right away which kids "got" school and which would have a hard time catching on. In fact, that initial sorting was strongly correlated with a set of social cues—whether children were light-skinned or dark-skinned, whether they had body odor, whether their hair was straight or kinky, how well dressed they were, how well their language conformed to standard usage, how comfortable they were interacting with the teacher. Once students had been divided into groups, teachers proceeded to teach them differently. They interacted more favorably and frequently with those doing well. They covered more material with them, were more animated in conversation, more affectionate in interaction.[1]

The low kids, meanwhile, began acting like low kids. They began to withdraw, participating less and less in the life of the classroom, spending more time just looking out the window or interacting among themselves. They stopped answering questions even when they knew the answers, and the irony is they knew more answers than the teachers imagined. Just by overhearing the lessons taught to the high kids, the low kids picked up some things, but because the teachers tended to ask low kids only low-kid questions, they never got a chance to show that they learned more than they were taught.

> Good natured or sullen, passive or hostile, compliant or troublesome, [the low child] did worse and worse in his schoolwork and as the year progressed, he failed more and more often to live up to the academic standards of his grade level. . . . But for most, self-doubt and low self-esteem combined to create a fear of putting forth the increasingly difficult effort to catch up. At this point the teachers interpreted a child's poor performance as a confirmation of their initial evaluation of his poor potential. (62)

Paradoxically, one of the ways low-group children, especially boys, reacted was by turning both to one another and turning on one another. On the one hand, the boys developed stronger peer associations, looking to each other for support and companionship. On the other hand, there was a certain fragility to their relationships, especially in classrooms where either the teacher or the high-group students looked down on them. Low-group students seemed to internalize those attitudes, calling each other "stupid," "dummy," and the like. This is consistent with an older body of research on classroom climate, which finds that the more harshly the teacher interacts with her class, the more harshly students interact with one another (Johnson 1970).

At the end of the first year, the high kids have both learned more and developed better attitudes about being school citizens. They move on to first grade where they will be sorted again, but this time the teacher has objective data that says where they belong; subjective judgments have been transformed into hard truths. Of course, there may well be some correlation between these social cues and readiness to learn as teachers understand it, but even if so, we don't want teachers using aggregate patterns to make decisions about individual children. Gouldner only follows her kids through the third grade—and for educational ethnography, unfortunately, that is a long time—but one can imagine a process in which each additional year of poor teaching makes the objective differences between students more real, where each year further encourages the low students to build an identity on something other than school. By the time the child is in the upper grades, whatever academic and social deficits, whatever attitudinal issues the child brought to school have been magnified and ossified. Kids have been labeled and those labels built into their sense of self and patterns of performance, but by a process so fragmented and so mystified behind ideologies of "merit" that no one involved is likely to understand how it happened, least of all the child. Nobody has done anything to anybody. Kids have just been sorted, according to talent, for their own good. It is the perfect engine for the reproduction of inequality. In the sense that Marxists speak of capitalism as alienating the worker from the fruits of his or her own labor, we can think of schools as playing a role in alienating children from their own intelligence.

Nilda Flores-Gonzalez (2002) has looked at the process of how kids construct school identities from the other end, interviewing Latino high school students and dropouts in Chicago about how their understandings of their relationship to school evolved. She finds that the ones who stayed in school tend to remember their early school years rather warmly. They talk about grade school as a place where they found social support and respect, but "it was really their relationships with teachers that they mostly remembered" (33). Those early experiences helped them develop identities as "school kids," while kids not getting that kind of reinforcement were more likely to develop as "street kids." Early on, some students began to find in street culture a supportive network that is the source of prestige, reward, and positive evaluations not found at school. They soon realized that, while not being good in school matters, they excel in street ways. "Being good at being bad" furthers their exploration of street culture at the expense of schooling (39).

Gonzalez points to the eighth-grade year and summer before high school as an especially important moment of passage, a point when many kids are going to make some pretty definitive choices about how they are going to relate to street culture. In gang-infested neighborhoods, the transition to high school means figuring out how one is going to ensure one's physical safety. It's a very different moment, of course, for different kinds of kids. Street kids, who are likely to have learned over the years to not think of adults at school as resources, have to think about how to negotiate this new and dangerous terrain relatively alone. School kids have a wider range of options to draw on and thus, we would think, feel at least a little less pressure to join a gang for protection. What Gonzalez does is help us see the social history out of which the bad-ass eighth grader grows. Ordinarily, the institutional roots of that process are completely obscured.

Gouldner and Gonzalez give us important opportunities to think about how the early encounter with schools can shape intelligence and identity. Certainly, there are questions be to raised about how far we can generalize from their work and about the relative importance of school-based processes as opposed to family- and street-based factors. What we know definitively is that one part of the pattern they identify—giving inferior teaching resources to the students who most need them—has been implicit national policy, at least until very recently. We should understand, first, that poor children start off as a more-difficult-to-teach population. Perhaps the best compilation of the data is found in Lee and Burkam's work (2002). Children from the highest SES group start school with achievement 60 percent higher on average than children from the lowest SES group. They start out behind, and then we systematically undermine them with poor schools. Poor children start their school careers in much lower-quality schools where they will be in larger classes, with less well-prepared teachers who have a weaker sense of collective responsibility and professional community than the teachers of more advantaged children (Lee and Burkam 70–74). That pattern continues throughout a child's school career, as we shall see. Children in our bottom-tier schools are going to be disproportionately served by teachers with weak skills and bad attitudes—and who won't be staying around long, in any case.

One of the more encouraging aspects of the national conversation around school improvement is the growing attention to teacher quality and its maldistribution. What we know isn't pretty. In 2002 nearly half of the 7,400 new teachers hired in New York City were uncertified, meaning they had failed the state exams, lacked required coursework, or both (Goodnough 2002). In 2004 half the seventh- and eighth-grade teachers in the Philadelphia school system failed certification exams in English, math, social studies, and science (Woodall 2004). In North Carolina, where 10 percent of the state's teachers have earned National Board certification, half of them serve in the 20 percent of schools with the smallest percentage of disadvantaged students (*www.teachingquality.org/pdfs/ncnbctrecs. pdf*). Nationally, children in the highest-poverty schools are assigned novice teachers almost twice as frequently as children in low-poverty schools. Nearly half the math classes in high-poverty or high-minority high schools are taught by teachers without a major or a minor in something related to math. The figures are even worse in high-poverty, high-minority middle schools, where 7 of 10 classes are taught by someone who doesn't even have a minor in a related field (Peske and Haycock 2006: 2–3). In 1999, 48 percent of Chicago principals said lack of knowledge and skills among teachers was at least "somewhat of a roadblock" to school improvement (Martinez 2001). In recent years, some large cities—New York, Chicago, and Philadelphia—have made progress improving the quality of their teaching force, but in Philadelphia, at least, there hasn't been commensurate progress getting better-certified teachers equitably distributed across schools (Useem, Offenberg, and Farley 2007).

We know that teacher quality "matters, and matters most to the most disadvantaged schools" (Presley, White, and Gong 2005: 1). Illinois has constructed a relatively sophisticated Teacher Quality Index. At the elementary and middle school levels, as TQI increases, so does the percentage of students meeting state standards, even with student background characteristics held constant. Getting anything to improve in high schools is difficult, of course, but the Illinois data suggest that teacher quality has its largest impact at that level. Among schools with at least 50 percent poverty, the percent of students meeting or exceeding state standards increases from nearly 14 percent to nearly 33 percent as the TQI moves from the lowest quartile to the second highest (Presley, White, and Gong 2005: 11).

While the Illinois index is certainly better than most, it is still fairly crude, based on such easily quantifiable information as teacher test scores, certification, experience, and quality of undergraduate institution. As we look more closely at the quality of actual teaching rather than of teachers, we can find even stronger results. One of the most discussed such studies is William Sanders's study of teacher effectiveness in Tennessee, which concludes that students who get three highly effective teachers in a row score 50 percentile points higher than students who start with the same test scores but get three highly ineffective teachers in a row (Sanders and Rivers 1996). "Differences of this magnitude . . . are stunning. For an individual child it means the difference between a 'remedial' label and placement in the accelerated . . . track" (Peske and Haycock 2006: 11). Moreover, sustained good teaching seems to inoculate children. If children have had three good teachers in a row, they do not fall back if they then get a poor teacher.

Bottom-tier schools are, of course, less likely to get highly effective teachers in the first place, but then they can't hold on to the teachers they get, especially the good ones (Guarino, Santibañez, and Daley 2006). In New York City, 44 percent of new teachers are gone by their fourth year, while a nearby small city like Scarsdale still has 82 percent of its teachers after 5 years (Winerip 2005). Asked about a particularly large exodus of teachers in 2004, "the city schools' human resources director says her office doesn't do exit interviews and doesn't know the reasons" (Winerip 2005). If the human resources director doesn't know that, what, pray tell, would she know? In Chicago, about 40 percent of new teachers are gone within 5 years. Nationally, exiting teachers cite money—the largest problem—discipline problems, lack of administrative support, and too little freedom to do their jobs as the main reasons for leaving. Of course, turnover is concentrated in certain schools, which means that the unluckiest classrooms will have 3 or 4 teachers in a year, occasionally more.[2]

Bad Attitudes: Failure as Ideology

If teachers were coming into schools with weak skills but those schools could meet teachers where they were and help them improve, this would be a different conversation. In fact, bottom-tier schools are about as good at helping teachers develop as they are at helping students develop, largely because of what Anyon (1997) calls the "degraded professional culture" of demoralized schools, a culture defined in part by isolation. Whatever deficits teachers have are unlikely to be fixed by professional interaction with colleagues. In a 1997 survey, 68 percent of Chicago teachers said they get meaningful feedback from a colleague less than once a month; 25 percent reported they had never visited a colleague's classroom (Duffrin 1998).

Principals, urban or otherwise, have not been known for their skills at instructional supervision. The reform movements of recent years have meant that principals who haven't been comfortable supervising traditional instruction are being asked to lead the implementation of all kinds of new, often more complicated, instructional initiatives. Principals claim with much justice that the other things they are required to do leave them with little time for classroom supervision, but other factors seem to play a role—fear of confrontation with individual teachers or with the union, a sense that classroom observations don't really do any good, a lack of confidence among some principals in their own instructional skills. Richard Elmore notes that research on administrators shows that "direct involvement in instruction is among the least-frequent activities performed by administrators of any kind at any level, and those who do engage in instructional leadership activities on a consistent basis are a relatively small proportion of the total administrative force" (Elmore 1999: 11).

If principals show little sense of agency when it comes to instruction, the same is true of many teachers. In our toughest schools, the modal teacher belief is that by the time students start school, the great majority of them have already been so damaged that only a handful can be saved; thus, it doesn't matter much what teachers do (e.g., Anyon 1997; Staff of the *Chicago Tribune* 1988; Lipman 1998; Gouldner 1978). With luck and hard work, teachers say, some of them can learn some basic skills, but the kind of conceptual, abstract learning that many reformers advocate is altogether out of the question. This is an ideology in the sense that teachers are clearly invested in the idea of the ineducability of most children and the apathy of their parents, so much so that when teachers encounter evidence to the contrary there is a predisposition to reject it (Kohl 1967; Rosenfeld 1971). Within the context of school reform, teachers may try new methods, but they do so with the same old attitudes. Poor instructional skills and bad attitudes certainly reinforce each other. People who don't understand good practice are likely to be predisposed to believing that it doesn't matter anyway, or that they are already doing it.

Pygmalion in the Classroom, the classic study of the effect of teacher expectations on student learning, found that if teachers could be given higher expectations of student performance, somehow the students began performing better. The effects were stronger for younger students and for more minority-looking students (i.e., darker-skinned Mexican Americans). The authors end by noting the practical implications of their project:

> If further research shows it is possible to select teachers whose untrained interactional style does for most of her pupils what our teachers did for the special children, it may be possible to combine sophisticated teacher selection and placement with teacher training to optimize the learning of all pupils. (Rosenthal and Jacobson 1968: 181)

Further proof that psychologists don't need to be making policy recommendations. If we thought of expectations as just characteristic of the individual, this would make some sense. In fact, in bottom-tier schools, low expectations are part of the culture of the institution. Sending in one or two teachers with higher expectations is hardly likely to change very much. Indeed, the most likely thing is that they will bring their beliefs into alignment with those of the host culture.

One of the studies that best captures this sense of a deeply engrained culture of failure is *Shut Those Thick Lips,* by the anthropologist Gerry Rosenfeld (1971), which is based on his time teaching at a Harlem elementary school. The interview he has to go through to "qualify" is a joke—they are not interested in what he knows about children or teaching or subject matter—and his interview with the principal of his building is more of the same. It is very clear that the principal will be satisfied with any warm body. The principal tells him that he can start off with a slow learners' class, and Rosenfeld understands that all he has to do to be considered successful is keep the lid on.

Before he ever sets foot in a classroom, Rosenfeld has been told multiple times that little is expected of him or his charges. When he finds he has no books, he is told that there weren't enough to go around, so books were given to the "better" kids first since his weren't going to learn anything anyway. As a new teacher, he is surprised to find that his principal doesn't supervise him at all. He is just thrown into a classroom and left to fend for himself. When he protests a midyear transfer to another class, he is told the same—his kids won't be hurt by it. When he goes into the teachers' lounge, he finds that conversation frequently takes the form of Competitive Admission of Failure (Payne 1984), in which teachers compete with one another telling stories about how dumb their students are. When he manages to greatly increase the class's performance on standardized tests, everyone assumes he cheated and they insist on retesting them. *Those* kids can't get scores like that! Rosenfeld encounters low expectations as beliefs held by more powerful and experienced persons than he, but also as more than beliefs: that is, as a set of institutionalized practices that reflect and reinforce low expectations.

In an action research project, some perceptive Philadelphia high school students have captured the structural roots of teacher expectations nicely (Enoch and Zuviri 2006). They found that at their high school, most teachers feel they have a good relationship with their students, but most also feel the students aren't going very far in life. That struck the student researchers as a contradiction, but they saw teacher expectations as largely a reaction to the context. They saw teachers as reacting partly to the scarcity of instructional resources, to the mismatch between the resources they do have and the instructional needs of students, to poor leadership in the building, to poor communications. By failing to provide what the school needed to function, higher-ups were sending a signal. It didn't make sense for teachers to have high expectations in a context where they knew the environment didn't have the resources it would take to do the job. "The teachers realized the whole administrations' (district, region and school) decisions created low expectations for students" (10). It is too easy to take a reductionist view of teacher expectation, so that it is just a matter of a teacher's judgment of a youngster's potential. In fact, teacher expectations are composed of several elements, some rational, some less so. To some degree, the Philadelphia teachers are offering a pessimistic assessment not of their students but of the obstacle course their students have to navigate.

There is a famous study of the nature of socially invested belief by Leon Festinger and his colleagues. What happens when a group belief is unequivocally disconfirmed, as, for example, when a religious group believes that the world is ending on a certain date but the date comes and nothing happens? If the investment in the belief is great enough—and in this case, people sold their homes, quit their jobs, and so forth—disconfirmation can lead to an intensification of belief.

> Man's resourcefulness goes beyond simply protecting a belief. Suppose an individual believes something with his whole heart; suppose further that he has a commitment to this belief, that he has taken irrevocable actions because of it; finally suppose that he is presented with evidence, unequivocal and undeniable evidence, that his belief is wrong: What will happen? The individual will frequently emerge, not only unshaken but even more convinced of the truth of his beliefs than ever before. Indeed, he may even show a new fervor about convincing and converting other people to his view. (Festinger, Riecken, and Schachter 1956: 3)[3]

Thus, when Rosenfeld comes along with test scores suggesting that some of the lowest-achieving students in the school can make two or even three years' progress in a year, he is hardly the bearer of hope. He is positioning himself as the heretic, disrespecting the sacred beliefs of the tribe, or, in Festinger's terms, he is the source of cognitive dissonance. People placed in a failing situation are likely to want to do something to distance themselves from failure. By adopting as pillars of the collective belief system the ideas that the kids are unteachable, their parents unreachable, and the administration hopelessly political and inept, teachers absolve themselves of any responsibility for the failure around them.

This is not merely a matter of what it takes for teachers to feel good about themselves despite being in a failing situation. Rosenfeld's colleagues resented the fact that he took his kids on trips on Saturdays, that he spent considerable time with their parents. Why should they care about that, he wondered, any more than they cared about what television shows he watched at night? This is another expression of the "rate-buster" phenomenon. The person who outworks everyone else is widely disliked precisely because he or she threatens the settled conditions of work for everyone else. Workers can have both a psychological and a material investment in failure. It is not that teachers want to fail but that they don't see much likelihood of succeeding, and in such a context, it is natural that people try to get what they can from a bad situation. Someone once said that the inner-city school is the ultimate free school; everyone is free to do any damned thing they please. As we have seen, when everyone has low expectations of everyone else, it may be okay if one doesn't do hall duty, or lets the paperwork slide, or doesn't assign anything that will be difficult to grade. If trying isn't going to make a difference, we can just relax a little. The low standards that work to the detriment of the collectivity over time can get mighty comfortable for the individual in the short term.

One of the fondest hopes of liberal-progressive education reformers is that change can come without forcing anybody to do anything; change can be—some would say *must* be—noncoercive. If we can demonstrate better classroom practice, teachers will see better results and will sign on voluntarily. We will consider the idea of voluntary change in more detail later, but for now suffice it to say that as a way to think about large-scale change, it is simply nonsense. It presumes a rational organizational context, a context in which information and training by themselves can make a large difference. That is hardly what bottom-tier schools offer. Again, once people have given up hope, once they have developed emotional and material investments in failure, those investments skew both their perceptions and their interpretations of what goes on around them. A taste of success—as reformers understand success—may not be nearly enough to cut through that. Students, for their part, are doing exactly the same thing, developing various kinds of investments in failure and the freedom it allows them. Each side is reacting to a depressing, alienating context in ways that reinforce the hopelessness and confusion of the other side, without realizing it. Once schools have been remoralized, if you will, given a renewed sense of possibility, maybe we can talk about voluntary change again.

Race helps shape a sense of limited possibilities, partly because it becomes a signifier of intelligence. In his review of the literature on what we know about the relationships among race, expectations, and performance, Ron Ferguson (2003) finds that, after decades of research, this is not a particularly strong body of research, but the evidence at hand suggests that race, ethnicity, and class all affect teacher perception and teacher behavior. One of the more convincing lines of research on how that happens deals with teacher persistence. When a child is trying to figure something out, how long will the teacher wait? When a child doesn't figure something out, how many alternative explanations will a teacher offer? All this seems to be significantly affected by these social cues, clearly reminiscent of Gouldner. Literally and figuratively, majority-group children are going to get more chances.

For a number of years, I was a member of a group of researchers who tried to stay in touch with several cities around the country that were trying to implement some form of progressive, inquiry-based mathematics.

It's interesting that, across the country, there's no clear pattern to the way that form of instruction gets racially coded. There are some places where this would look like the elite, upper-class program. This is the way those kids do math; everybody else gets workbooks. There are other places, depending on the politics of the system and how the program is introduced and by whom, where this becomes the Black and Latino math program. This is math for *those* kids. In one of the latter cities, one where implementation has been strong, they have had several years of rising test scores among Black and Latino students. The strongest improvement, not surprisingly, has been among Black and Latino boys—the previous low achievers. Scores went up on the state test—which was not particularly friendly to progressive math—as well as the SAT, with rising numbers of students taking the SAT. Chemistry and physics teachers were happy because they were getting more kids who could apply the math they had learned. As the old folks say, it was too much like right. When *those* kids start demanding entry into higher-level math courses, the courses that are almost always the preserve of a white or white and Asian elite, the system reacts. Principals balked at creating additional upper-level courses; they couldn't believe that so many students were qualified. Parents of the kinds of kids who had done well in traditional math courses began questioning the whole progressive math program. The new courses must have been watered down if all these kids got through. The mere fact that Black and Latino students are doing well at something is taken to imply a lack of rigor in the something that they are doing. Their success damns the program. The fact that the principals and parents felt comfortable publicly voicing their doubts about the ability of the kids says something about how deeply entrenched is this notion that some kids are supposed to fail. (In another version of the same phenomenon, college students, including African American college students, assume in advance of any experience that courses in African American Studies will be less rigorous than others.)

When I first started studying urban schools, I was caught off guard by the way teachers would make disparaging comments about a child in front of a child and even more surprised that some nonwhite teachers would do it. In fact, it shouldn't have been surprising. Being nonwhite hardly makes one impervious to dominant narratives about race. I suspect that some nonwhite teachers, reacting to the frustration of their position and perhaps reacting to some level of embarrassment over being identified with disreputable kids and parents, can be even harsher than others in their statements about the kids and their potential or lack of it. To the person doing it, rejecting the kids and parents may feel like a way of defending the race. They may be saying, in effect, "Don't think all of us are like that." If they sometimes seem even harsher, even sharper than their white colleagues, that may be because they do not have to be concerned about the accusation of racism. Their color gives them a license to be negative without fear of being misinterpreted. At the opposite end of the spectrum would be a group of teachers of color who feel a deep sense of common fate with their children and who stay in tough schools precisely for that reason.

If my experience is any guide, the way teachers talk about student potential among poor rural whites in North Carolina is not much different from the way teachers talk on the West Side of Chicago. It would be naïve to think these judgments are not racially inflected, but they are not racism in any simple sense of the term; they are not saying the race to which these kids belong cannot learn. Teachers tend to frame their beliefs more narrowly, to particularize. Negative judgments are framed by place, not race. These particular kids, with these particular parents, living in this particular neighborhood, going to this particular crazy school, can't be expected to amount to much, but the fault is in their circumstances, not their genes. The Philadelphia teachers were giving us one version of this. The more particularized the belief system, the more useful it was for fending off intrusions from the outside. Such-and-such a program may have worked somewhere else, but not here, not with these kids. I know these kids. If this kind of thinking isn't exactly racist, perhaps we should call it racialist thinking to retain a sense of the continuity between what appears to be the dominant construction of students in urban schools and the traditional racist hierarchies.

Low expectations are part of the fuel for what we usually call teacher "resistance," although that is probably not the best term for what we are talking about. "Resistance" is an accusation, not a description. It normalizes the reformers' point of view and withdraws validity from the teachers'. The implication is that we have all these good ideas and programs, but teachers just resist doing them. Teacher *skepticism* is less judgmental and probably comes closer to expressing how teachers feel about what they are doing. Given that teachers have a clear understanding of the limited capacity of the district, given that they have lived through any number of programs that were going to fix everything, given what they know about the very real limitations of reformers, it is perfectly sensible for teachers to be skeptical of this year's snake oil. Given the historically weak performance of most reforms, teachers would have to be fools to get all excited over every idea that comes down the pike. Indeed, by not cooperating with change, teachers may feel that they are protecting their students from additional disruption of their learning.

Noncooperative teacher behavior is patterned in certain predictable ways. It is frequently the case that veteran teachers are more likely to be uncooperative with change than younger teachers. This may especially be the case where the reforms involve any form of progressive pedagogy. Progressive pedagogy is so much the fashion in schools of education that younger teachers are likely to have had it presented to them as the right way—often, the only right way—to teach and to have a certain comfort level with it. Primary-grade teachers generally seem more optimistic, more willing to accept change than those who teach the higher grades, seventh and eighth grade in particular. Early resistance seems especially likely to come from the weakest teachers, those most likely to be embarrassed if teaching is more closely scrutinized. (At least at the elementary school level, there is normally considerable consensus in a building as to who are the best and the worst teachers.) It is also common for early resistance to come from some of the relatively successful teachers, people who feel they are already doing well and don't need outsiders coming in to tell them how to teach.[4]

Earlier, I noted that one of the distinguishing features of urban schools is the way a few negative people can exercise power all out of proportion to their numbers. As one principal put it, "It's been observed that inner-city schools attract and nurture strong personalities and can develop a negative culture. When a leader starts to mess around with the unspoken expectations and mores of such a culture, he or she is playing with fire" (Marshall 2003: 109). The social distribution of the predisposition to noncooperation may have something to do with this. If it were only the weaker teachers attacking reform, it might be relatively easy to isolate and neutralize them. The misgivings of the stronger teachers, though, give legitimacy to the doubters. A fairly common situation seems to be a group of successful teachers who are split about reform, a group of younger teachers who are pro-reform but whose opinions weigh less than others because of their youth and inexperience, and a group of older, higher-status, less successful teachers who are adamant in their opposition. The anti-reform group thus has the advantage of greater social status in the school and, for some, a deeper emotional investment in their position. Even when their numbers are small, this may be enough to give them disproportionate leverage in shaping the discussion in their schools. Theirs is a more desperate kind of struggle.

Teaching and Learning in the Big City

If we were to just list the factors interfering with a higher level of instruction in urban schools, we would want to include at least the following:

Figure 3.1. School-Level Impediments to Instructional Capacity

- Weak pre-professional training; lack of certified teachers
- Teacher skepticism about students' learning capacity
- Weak sense of teacher agency
- Inadequate instructional supervision of teachers; absence of accountability for instructional program
- Teacher isolation: "What goes on in my classroom is my business"
- Rigidity of teacher attitude about how students learn
- Fragmented staff development; "drive-by" staff development
- Reluctance of teachers to accept leadership from colleagues: "She must think she knows more than we do"
- Poor content knowledge of staff; poor classroom management skills
- Disconnect between curriculum and assessment procedures; being made to teach one thing while being tested on another
- Ineffective discipline; atmosphere not conducive to teaching
- Generalized belief in program failure: "We've seen programs come, we've seen 'em go"; generalized disbelief in professional development
- Inadequate informal staff knowledge about students' backgrounds and interests
- Resource needs: personnel, material, and space
- Instability of good instructional staff; the best people move on
- Fragmented, poorly-paced curriculum
- General lack of programmatic coherence; the parts of the school don't interact with one another

---

Just a partial listing of the component parts of the problem should help us appreciate what leaders on the ground have to confront, but the Consortium on Chicago School Research has given us a more precise way to think about the epidemiology of bad instruction. Over a period of

15 years, they have sponsored a series of studies that, taken collectively, offer a revealing and instructive portrait of what goes on in the city's classrooms, almost certainly the most detailed such portrait available for any big city. These studies paint the usual disheartening picture, but the details are instructive.

We can start with their work on time and how it is used. When one is in an urban school, one is constantly reminded of how little time there is to do the most important things. (I recall one teacher-leader in Washington, D.C., who was always asking, "How come there's never enough time to do it right but there's always enough time to do it over?") Oddly, the issue of the sheer amount of time available for instruction has received relatively little attention in the national discussion about reforming urban schools. In Chicago, the situation is particularly poor. The city allocates less time for instruction than do most districts, but the amount of time actually available for instruction is a good deal less than what is allocated. According to BetsAnn Smith's exacting study (1998), Chicago's elementary schools officially operate on a 330-minute day, expecting to be able to use 300 minutes of that for instruction. A more common arrangement nationally would be for a system to operate 360–400 minutes a day in order to provide 330–360 minutes of instruction.[5] Chicago, ever the city of the optimistic, appears to believe that teachers can take care of all noninstructional tasks—lunch, transitions from one activity to another, from one place to another, attendance-taking, bathroom breaks, packing up at the end of the day, emergencies—in half an hour. In the real world, according to Smith, even those teachers who are most aggressive about protecting time cannot cram all noninstructional activity into half an hour. The most effective half of Chicago teachers still need 14 percent of the available 330 minutes, or 46 minutes a day, for noninstructional activity. The half of Chicago teachers who are the least effective time managers need almost 28 percent of the day, an hour and a half.

The problem is compounded by the fact that some days are devoted largely to special events—holiday celebrations, assemblies, standardized testing, report card pick-up days. Some teachers decide that Fridays are special days: "They forgo substantive instruction in favor of shortened lessons, playing quasi-educational games, watching videos, taking a 'mental health break,' or other less than academic pursuits." Smith conservatively estimates that 35 days, nearly a fifth of the year, are typically compromised in some way. Certainly, some of the special events have, potentially, real educational value, but it is safe to assume that the more demoralized the school, the more teachers will see these opportunities as break time.

All this assumes that teachers are showing up every day. In fact, prior to reform, Chicago's Substitute Center typically fielded 1,200–1,400 requests for subs every day, which would affect 6 percent of the city's classrooms.[6] Teachers were most likely to be out on Mondays and Fridays; May has traditionally been the worst month for teacher absences. Not all requests for subs could be honored. In 1987 the *Chicago Tribune* revealed that on an average day, 5,700 students were without a teacher at all, but even when subs are available, it was widely agreed that they are not very effective instructionally (Staff of the *Chicago Tribune* 1988: 93, 97).

In practice, teachers can count on two fairly sustained periods devoid of major interruptions—the seven weeks from early October to the Thanksgiving break and the six weeks from mid-January till early March. Much of September is wasted because of personnel issues. School staffs have to be adjusted in light of enrollment changes, which means that some schools will lose teachers and some will gain. Some teachers who thought they were going to be teaching one grade find out they will be teaching another. This is going on while schools and classrooms are trying to establish their routines. Some classes may not have all their instructional material at the very beginning of the year. In a 1997 survey, 42 percent of teachers reported that it took them three weeks or more to get their classes fully operational (Smith 22). During the year, schools have to contend with the holiday slowdowns, the tendency for teaching to drop off for several days before Christmas, Halloween, spring break, and the end of the year. The pre-Christmas swoon seems to be especially bad, with student and teacher attendance both falling off while disruptive student behavior seems to increase. March brings the testing season, and the school year in some schools is pretty much over after that. Spring sees a lot of field trips, science fairs, and assemblies, so that some schools never regain their focus during the last 12 to 15 weeks of school. In the 1997 survey of teachers, half reported that in April, May, and June they spend less than 50 percent of all class time on the introduction and study of new material.

Schools can certainly do more to protect instructional time. Some issues can only be handled well at the district level—defining the length of the school day, building professional-development time into the contract—but schools can reduce the number of special events or make very sure that those which occur are clearly related to instructional priorities. Teachers can, as BetsAnn Smith recommends (1998), be taught time-management skills as a part of their professional development. Principals can see that the slowdown in teaching which typically precedes major holidays—which takes weeks out of the school year in some schools—just doesn't happen. Not a few teachers would be grateful if their principals could just refrain from using the public address system at times when it cuts into instruction. Conservatively, it looks like many bottom-tier schools could add two weeks of instruction to their academic year without spending a dime, and some are clearly frittering away a full four to six weeks of instructional time. Quite apart from the direct impact on teaching, schools and teachers who fight to protect instructional time send a strong and important message about institutional priorities and norms. It would be a step in the direction of the remoralization of schools.

In theory, Chicago elementary school children should receive about 900 hours of instruction each year. In practice, they may be getting 40 to 60 percent of that. Smith estimates that under optimal conditions, students get only about 540 hours, going down to a meager 454 hours in poorly managed classrooms in poorly managed schools. Nearly half of Chicago students are receiving half the officially allocated hours of instruction.

"Life in Chicago classrooms," Smith concludes, "is nothing like the steady flow of academic lessons we all like to imagine. More accurately, it is a series of stop-and-go learning opportunities that compete with one another for scarce time" (17).

We have no thorough studies of time usage in Chicago high schools, but we do know that so-called study halls were traditionally egregiously misused. Students could take as many as three unsupervised study halls a day, many of them scheduled at the beginning or end of the day, encouraging students to come to school late or leave early, which is just as well since virtually no work could get done in study hall, chaotic as some of them were. For the system, the promiscuous use of study halls created substantial savings in teacher salary costs (Staff of the *Tribune* 1988: 93).

One could make the case that what we know about the quality of instruction in Chicago schools is even more troubling than what we know about the quantity of instruction. To borrow Booker T. Washington's quip about tainted money, the most important thing to say about quality instruction is t'ain't enough of it. One series of Consortium studies looked directly at the level of intellectual challenge embedded in the assignments typically given in Chicago classrooms (Newmann, Lopez, and Bryk 1998; Newmann, Bryk, and Nagaoka 2001; Bryk, Nagaoka, and Newmann 2000). They were trying to get a sense of what proportion of assignments had something one might think of as intellectual challenge. By intellectually authentic (or "intellectually ambitious," in some of the later work), they meant work that called for original application of knowledge and skills, as opposed to just routine use of facts and procedures; work that involved disciplined inquiry into a problem and that led to a product that has meaning beyond school. Over three years, the study sampled over 2,000 writing and math assignments from over 400 classrooms in 19 elementary schools and developed rubrics that teams of teachers used to judge the complexity of each assignment. This is apparently the largest such body of data we have ever had on what actually gets taught in disadvantaged urban classrooms.

At the sixth-grade level, a high-scoring writing assignment might ask students to pick any topic they feel strongly about, write an essay that will persuade the reader to the writer's point of view, and convince the reader to take some action. There is an element of knowledge construction in that students are required to select and organize information; an element of disciplined inquiry since they must use evidence to support their arguments; and a connection to students' interests outside of school since it allows students to select a topic they care about. By contrast, a low-scoring assignment might give students some sentences and just ask them to identify the parts of speech. In sixth-grade math, an intellectually ambitious assignment might ask a student to follow a stock for several weeks and write a paper analyzing its performance. A worksheet assignment asking students to solve problems with no context would be an example of a low-scoring assignment (Newmann, Bryk, and Nagaoka 2001: 24).

The essential finding is that there wasn't much chance in the late 1990s of the average Chicago child encountering anything remotely challenging. At the third-grade level, 43 percent of assignments fell into the *no challenge* category, typically fill-in-the-blank or short-answer assignments. In third-grade math, the same 43 percent of all assignments analyzed were judged to have no challenge, largely assignments that required only routine application of facts or procedures. Across all grade levels, a majority of both writing and math assignments fell into the two lowest categories, *no challenge* or *minimal challenge*. In eighth-grade math, that figure rose to a staggering 86 percent of all lessons (Newmann, Lopez, and Bryk 1998:

17–18). On the whole, the situation was somewhat better in writing; at each grade level at least 17 percent of all writing assignments were judged to have *extensive challenge.*

When Chicago students do encounter intellectual challenge, it matters a great deal. No one would think the Iowa Test of Basic Skills or the Illinois Goal Assessment Program is designed to measure higher-order skills, yet students who have been exposed to higher-order teaching do better on them—much better. "Even after controlling for race, socio-economic class, gender, and prior achievement differences among classrooms, the benefits of exposure to assignments that demand authentic intellectual work in writing and mathematics are quite substantial" (Newmann, Bryk, and Nagaoka 2001: 18–19). "Substantial" means that classrooms where students were most exposed to high-quality assignments recorded learning gains 20 percent greater than the national average; classrooms with low-quality assignments—the great majority of classrooms, of course—showed gains of 25 percent *less* than the national average in reading, 22 percent less in math. Take two students with the same backgrounds, including the same test scores in the prior year, put one in an intellectually demanding classroom and the other in a typical classroom, and after just one year, the first student would do better by 32 points on the IGAP reading test and 48 points on the math test, translating into large effect sizes, 0.43 and 0.64, respectively (21). Both students with high prior achievement and students with low prior achievement learn more in classrooms with more authentic assignments. This is major impact.

If there is a proposition that most researchers would be willing to bet the farm on, it is the idea that if something is beneficial to students, access to that something is likely to be significantly correlated with the social status of students. High-quality assignments are rare, but at the elementary school level, neither the racial/socioeconomic composition of classrooms nor the students' prior level of achievement is clearly related to the quality of assignments. Teachers who make such assignments are an uncommon but equitably distributed resource. (The quality of assignments in the city improved somewhat between 1997 and 1999, but we don't know if the trend continued after that.)

Not only is the typical assignment in a Chicago elementary school devoid of intellectual challenge, but also students may have to endure it more than once. Smith, Smith, and Bryk (1998) ask readers to imagine a lesson on a parallelogram. At what grade level would you expect it to be taught? They saw introductory lessons on the parallelogram taught in second grade, in fifth, in eighth, and even in tenth. Across primary, middle, and secondary grades, "the same topics were being taught again and again, with little or no development in their content, depth and complexity" (3). Intellectually, the fifth-grade lesson on *Charlotte's Web* and the tenth-grade lesson on *Bless Me, Ultima* are pretty much the same. The Smith, Smith, and Bryk report is based on survey data from over 2,000 teachers in 384 schools. That was supplemented with two years of observation of 800 language arts and math classes in 15 schools.

They learned that instruction in the city is largely oriented toward review and repetition. In some schools, the situation is complicated by the fact that "faculty members lacked a shared conception of the instructional program overall, and of their own particular set of responsibilities for advancing it" (7). Students can contribute to slowing the pace of instruction by resisting difficult or unfamiliar material. The research team observed students telling a teacher they had never had a topic when the team knew otherwise. Also, the weak homework habits of many Chicago students mean that much of the review and practice that should be done after school takes place in class, further reducing time for the introduction of new material. Test pressure is a significant contributor. During each year of the research, the period of review for standardized tests began earlier and lasted longer.

The problem increases as students grow older. At the second-grade level, about half the teachers cover material consistent with grade-level mastery, and half of those are well above grade level, doing third- or fourth-grade work. In eighth grade, by contrast, three-quarters of teachers report content below grade level, with the bottom quarter of teachers describing work at about the third-grade level. Overall, less than half of the city's schools keep pace with the standardized test on which students will be judged.

Isn't it possible, though, that instructional pacing is fundamentally a reaction by teachers to the level of academic functioning their students happen to be at? Isn't it fundamentally just a reaction to an unfortunate reality? Apparently not. Even with prior achievement controlled, the percentage of low-income students in a school is correlated with instructional pacing. In high-poverty and high-minority schools, instructional pacing seems to flatten out around the fourth grade. After that, "The classroom life of these students appears to consist of repetitive cycles of basic skills instruction" (16).

Problems cluster, of course. Chicago's high-poverty schools tend to be larger schools. At the time of the study, the average elementary school with a 90 percent low-income student population served 676 students, over 200 more than the enrollment in more mixed-income schools. High-poverty schools also had a much more mobile student population than mixed-income schools, 34 percent to 10 percent. Even with student poverty and prior achievement controlled, school size and student mobility are significantly related to instructional pacing.

These data raise a significant moral problem, perhaps even more clearly than do some of the other instructional disparities. The city is clearly not providing all students with equivalent opportunities to learn, yet it is judging all of them by the same test scores. Access to the city's better high schools is increasingly determined by scores. This is a significant turning point in life, and some students, especially those who are poor or nonwhite, have not been given an opportunity to so much as see some of the material on which they will be tested. In the most troubled elementary schools, "little to no new material [in math] is introduced across the last several years of elementary schooling" (21). No one discounts their test scores because of that.

The study also had something to say about the factors supporting stronger instructional pacing. One factor was professional community: "Our results indicate that when teachers do not collaborate in their curriculum development and teaching, do not regularly confer with one another, and do not reflect on their practices and outcomes, slower pacing with more extensive repetition and review is likely to ensue" (18). The differences are dramatic, even in the poorest schools. In schools that have 90 percent or more low-income students, by the eighth grade teachers in the schools with strong professional community are teaching at the seventh-grade level. Teachers in schools with the weakest levels of professional community are teaching at the third-grade level. It is hard to believe that doesn't make a difference in children's lives. That is simply a staggering difference and one that flies almost completely below the radar screen.

Another important contextual factor is the degree of instructional coherence in a school. Within a given grade level in a given school, individual teachers may be covering very different material. A class might get the third-grade math curriculum two years in a row, while another goes from the third-grade curriculum to fifth-grade material. Even with prior achievement controlled, the more poor families a school serves, the more incoherent its curriculum is likely to be.

This is a segue to the larger, and underdiscussed, issue of programmatic and instructional coherence. One of the safest generalizations we can make about inner-city schools is that many of them are trying to do too much at once, the too-familiar pattern of lots and lots of motion with too little movement. Such schools would do well to heed the admonition of the Coalition of Essential Schools to do less but do it better. The current political climate, of course, not to mention the multiple needs of students, encourages the opposite; principals are being pushed into more and more frenetic behavior. The authors of the most important study on program coherence note that "Even when principals recognize that their teachers are stretched in too many directions, they seem unable to cut programs, believing strongly that they need all of these extra resources to help the children" (Newmann et al. 2001: 10). As commendable as the motives may be, it becomes a deal with the devil. Nothing we know about bottom-tier schools suggests that doing a lot of good things superficially is likely to have real impact on the lives of children and teachers.

Newmann and his colleagues take strong program coherence to include curricular coherence, but they go beyond it. They are talking about three broad conditions:

1. *A common instructional framework guides curriculum, teaching, assessment, and learning climate, something that combines specific expectations for student learning with specific instructional strategies, materials, assessments.* That is, teachers at a grade level talk about what to teach, how to teach, and how to figure out what's been learned; there is a logical progression of material from grade to grade and within each grade. As we know, attaining this level of coordination represents an enormous achievement in demoralized schools. It is not enough to provide common within-grade or across-grade planning periods. Where those structures work, it will typically be because "principals, school coordinators, other school leaders and external partners actively worked over a sustained period of time to coax teachers into collaborative activity around core instructional goals and strategies" (32; see Stevens 2006 for a more elaborate discussion).

2. *Staff working conditions support implementation of the framework.* That is, teachers and administrators have some clarity about what to expect from one another; teachers are hired (when possible) with an eye to where they fit into the overall program and evaluated on how they contribute to it; professional development is sustained and focused on

what teachers are actually expected to do, which is almost the opposite of what most professional development has been.

3. *Resource allocations—materials, time, staff assignments—are done in a way that advances the common instructional framework.* Teacher assignments reflect student need, rather than political considerations. Assignments would remain stable enough to give teachers time to learn to do them well. In incoherent schools, materials, if available, will be poorly used. "For example, several had purchased curriculum materials and computer technology they believed could help students perform better . . . but the materials were often purchased and delivered without training, or discussion of how to maximize or assess their benefits, and without a scheme for ensuring they were used in the manner intended. Only some teachers reported actually using the materials" (31).

We can add program coherence to our list of things that can have big pop. Ranking over two hundred elementary schools against a scale of coherence, Newmann and associates found that, over a three-year period, schools that increased their instructional coherence achieved test scores that were almost one-fifth of a year of learning higher than when they began (21). That's the equivalent of kids going to school an extra two months a year.

The Consortium has given us what is almost certainly the most authoritative sustained picture of teaching and learning in a big city that we have ever had. Their work offers large samples that we can have some confidence generalizing from, combines quantitative and qualitative approaches, and normally provides some basis for causal inference, at least to the degree of eliminating some alternative explanations. There are a few issues that seem Chicago-specific—length of the school day—but I assume that most of these patterns can be found in most large systems, with local variations on the themes.

Given the work of the Consortium and others, what overall picture do we get of teaching and learning in the big city? It is a picture of too many classrooms flat-out wasting huge amounts of time; too many classrooms where instruction is repetitive, undemanding, devoid of intellectual challenge or interest; a picture of a system where the neediest children are housed in large, unfocused institutions; places where adult mobility is high, where teachers don't communicate with one another, and where curriculum is fragmented and disconnected; and where a cloud of low expectations pervades everything and guarantees that adults will consistently underestimate what kids can do. We provide our neediest children with severely constricted opportunities to learn, and then we scratch our heads and wonder why urban schools don't work.

Our appreciation of the differences that opportunities to learn can make has certainly increased recently. Fifteen years ago, it was still intellectually respectable to talk about whether schools mattered or whether money made a difference. The research on opportunities to learn was accumulating simultaneously with the national movement to raise academic standards. Most states have already moved to ratchet up their high school graduation requirements, and more is yet to come (Achieve 2007). This is a welcome discussion in many respects, but it is worth repeating that the toughen-standards discussion has gotten ahead of the improve-the-opportunities-to-learn discussion. Pushing kids can have some value all by itself, but in the current context, it can mean punishing children for not learning what they had no opportunity to learn.

The case for putting the best possible level of human resources in front of the poorest children is compelling, but, again, we don't want to lose sight of how poorly the system uses the resources it has right now. What we know implies strongly that we could be getting much better results right now if, for example, schools were more respectful of instructional time, if programming were more coherent, if the teachers we have communicated more with one another, if schools deployed the best teachers they have now more intelligently and worked harder to retain those teachers, if they insisted that students work a little harder. We have good reason to believe it is possible to have larger impacts with the people we have on the ground right now. Part of what is distinctive about the current wave of reform is the degree to which it is founded on (and undermined by) disrespect for educators. In such a climate, we have to keep reminding ourselves that the nature of the ghetto school is that everybody is working below capacity, that present performance is a weak clue to actual capacity.

Seven times seventy, we have to keep reminding ourselves that we are talking about systemic problems which cannot be reduced to individual-level explanations. The idea that the fundamental problem is that teachers don't care—to which some urban parents subscribe—is exactly as useful as the idea that parents are apathetic—which many teachers believe.

In either case, the reaction to a situation that appears to be out of control gets confounded with what people really are and want. A young woman in her second year of teaching middle school in New York City's Washington Heights neighborhood applied for a grant from Donorschoose.org, a website where teachers submit requests for materials they need:

> In August I posted a request for five sets of thirty books of historical fiction. At that time, I didn't have textbooks and I had decided that I wanted to teach Social Studies through novels, not textbooks. The request totaled close to $1,000. In the following weeks I kept checking, but no progress. And then last Thursday I got an email that my project was suddenly fully funded! I was—and still am—so excited. The books came immediately, shipped from Barnes and Noble. I have handed out *I, Juan de Pareja* to one of my classes just to test out teaching through a novel . . . and the kids were thrilled about reading a book with me. They love the old-fashioned teacher reads, kids follow along method. I am now working with two English teachers on developing more interesting and activity-based lessons to accompany the unit.
>
> Of course, the frustrating part was that when I told my principal the good news all she said was, "Do you even have enough space in your classroom for all of it?" I was annoyed, but I can't let people like her dictate my enthusiasm.

What's sad is not that yet another principal doesn't have a clue about how to support creativity and initiative. What's sad is there is a fair possibility that the principal was once like the young teacher.

Chapter 4

Sympathy, Knowledge, and Truth: Teaching Black Children

Other things being equal, the mixed school is the broader, more natural basis for the education of all youth. It gives wider contacts, it inspires greater self-confidence, it suppresses the inferiority complex. But other things are seldom equal and in that case, Sympathy, Knowledge and Truth outweigh all that the mixed school can offer.

—W. E. B. Du Bois

The black child is different from other children because he has problems that are the product of a social order not of his making or his forbears.

—Septima Clark

Being a black teacher during the age of white supremacy demanded faith in the future when the present often seemed hopeless.

—Adam Fairclough

People continue to talk as if there were some great mystery about what kind of teaching would make a difference in urban schools. Actually, we know a great deal about that. No one has done more to broaden our thinking about what children of color can do than Asa Hilliard. One of his essays (Perry, Steele, and Hilliard 2003) gives us a way to organize our thinking about this with his suggestion that researchers need to spend less time worrying about every little thing that has some relation to achievement and concentrate on those things that have potentially large results, on results that smack you right between the eyes, interocular results, if you will. There are lots of things that make a difference, but when it comes to instruction, which have "Big Pop"? What produces large increments in learning, for large groups of urban kids, in a fairly short period of time? Figure 4.1 is one way to think about such differences.

Figure 4.1. "The Big Six"

**Characteristics of High-Impact Instructional Programs in
Urban Contexts**

1. Instructional time protected or extended
2. Intellectually ambitious instruction
3. Professional community (teachers collaborate, have a collective sense of responsibility)
4. Academic press combined with social support
5. Program coherence (i.e., institutional focus; are we all on the same page?)
6. Teacher "quality" / diagnostic ability

This is just one way to organize our thinking. One could do an equally reasonable list with fewer elements or with more, a sensible list with other elements.[1] My point is that this is one way to think about the problem that is empirically defensible, based on research that offers some grounds for generalizing and for at least rough causal inference. The various studies supporting these ideas use different metrics, but most of them give us reason to believe that each of these when reasonably well implemented can produce learning gains of one month or more. In many of these studies, the biggest gainers are African American or Latino boys, the biggest losers under business-as-usual. If we know a good deal about what would work, what we don't know is how to implement these things with fidelity at scale, within the operative resource limits.

Most of these points were discussed in the previous chapter and need not be elaborated here. With respect to the first element, however, extending or protecting time, let me note that there's growing discussion nationally about extending the school day or year (Schemo 2007), which can be a very expensive pathway to reform, and less discussion, so far as I can see, about making better use of the time we already have. Given our history, I would worry that in some cases, extending instructional time becomes a way of not thinking about the nuts-and-bolts issues of instruction, in which case I suspect its value would be less.

The idea that is new here is the idea of trying to strike a balance between academic demands and social supports. We will have a more extended discussion of this later, but for now suffice it to say that when children encounter classroom contexts in which they feel challenged, pushed, and simultaneously supported, the results can be little short of dramatic. All I will add here about teacher quality is that as much as I am trying to argue that we can get a lot more out of the teaching force we now have, I am struck by the way improving the teaching force seems to be an all-weather reform. That is, raising teacher quality can make a difference even when other things don't improve, even when leadership or school culture remains problematic (e.g., Boyd et al. 2007). When we don't know what else to do, we should be trying to put the best people we can find in front of poor children.

If this is true with the weak measures we ordinarily base discussions of teacher quality on, what would happen with more sophisticated measures? One important, and underdiscussed, theme in the literature concerns the power of teacher diagnostic ability. Paul Black and his associates (Black and William 1998; Black et al. 2004) have reviewed an extensive body of research that demonstrates persuasively that when teachers use formative assessments to diagnose student learning problems and adjust instruction accordingly, the effect is consistently large across different types of learners and situations. Effect sizes range from 0.4 to 0.7. These are whopping improvements. At the lower end of that range—the lower end—we are saying that diagnostic teaching moves the average student to the level of performance of the top third of students. Similarly, the Bay Area School Reform Collaborative has done an analysis of achievement patterns in 32 schools with comparable demographics, trying to understand why some of them were closing achievement gaps by race while others were not (Walsh 2003). They concluded in part that in the gap-closing schools, teaching was much more diagnostic, with teachers constantly assessing students and adjusting their instruction accordingly.[2]

We already know, then, quite a bit about what kind of instruction and what kind of organizational context can make a large difference. What we don't know is how to do these things at scale, with fidelity, given the social, organizational, and political deficits under which our schools labor. Still, we should be aware that all this reflects a fairly narrow, technical conception of what teaching is. Underlying much of this kind of discussion is the assumption that teaching can be reduced to the delivery of information and the development of skills. That way of thinking reflects little sense of teaching as a social activity. It may well be that in the grip of test-score hysteria, we have begun to think of teaching too narrowly, giving short shrift to its social dimension. That social dimension may be more important than we think and more important to some populations than others.

In her remarkable book on New York City high school students, Cristina Rathbone quotes a principal as saying, "You know as well as I do that the issues here are not academic, the issues are social and emotional and mental and spiritual" (1998: 145). The thought should give us pause. To the extent that the problems we are trying to solve are problems of connectedness, a strictly academic approach may not take us all the way.

Because this is a problem that I think needs to be framed historically and because different racial and ethnic groups have different relevant historical trajectories, I want to think about this problem primarily as it applies to Black students. One way to get at it would be to ask, when teaching worked for Black people, what was that teaching like? If you forget who you are, Bernice Johnson Reagon of Sweet Honey in the Rock once commented, you need to go back to where you were the last time you remembered.

Teaching with the Authority of the Race

However ironic it may seem, there is considerable nostalgia just now among Black Americans for the kind of education they had during the good old days of legal white supremacy. It is not hard to find Black people who think school desegregation was a deliberate plot to break the will and spirit of Black communities or others who think that, no matter what was intended, desegregation, when it occurred at all, almost always occurred on white folks' terms, which led to the undermining of an educational culture that Black people had been shaping since before the end of slavery (Anderson 1988).

Nostalgia is necessarily selective. The first chapter of Richard Kluger's *Simple Justice*, his history of *Brown v. Board of Education*, draws portraits of two South Carolina Black principals. One is the kind of dedicated, rooted-in-the-community educator around whom current nostalgia centers. The other is craven, incompetent, a servant of the white power structure, as corrupt as the day is long, stealing funds that should have been going to the children. The current longing for the good old days forgets the second type of Black educator—the people Du Bois (1935) called "ignorant placeholders." We can forget, too, that at times and places the sheer lack of resources must have overwhelmed good intent. The South, through the first half of the twentieth century, generally spent on the education of Black children about one-third what it spent on whites. Fairclough (2007) reminds us that some schools were theaters of class antagonisms, and in others the kind of treatment children got could depend on their complexion; many used a level of physical discipline that is discomfiting to read about, even now.

That said, there is still something about the education they received under these circumstances that many Black adults now wish they could give to their own children, and it clearly has to do largely with how they experienced teaching. Nostalgia should not be confused with history, but collective memories tell us much about how people understand the limits and possibilities in their environment, about what they think made a difference for them, and that can serve as the basis for hypothesizing, at least, about how teaching matters.

Vanessa Siddle Walker's (1996) rich and evocative portrait of North Carolina's Casswell County Training School reflects the themes one typically finds in these discussions. She sees the school as an example of institutionalized caring, caring that went beyond how any one individual felt about any other individual, caring that was reflected in high expectations and strict standards—teachers "didn't play," would "bless you out" if they caught you wrong. There was a heavy emphasis on extracurricular activity, with as much as 90 percent of the student body participating in something, as the school recognized the need of students to "learn to speak, to think, to perform" (204) as well as their need for explicit moral instruction. They were, as the principal liked to say, "building men and women" (204). Among other things, they took that to require implicitly and explicitly challenging notions of racial inferiority; they offered a counter-narrative, in Theresa Perry's terms (Perry, Steele, and Hilliard 2003). For them, "Teaching could not be reduced to a job or an occupation; it was a mission" (206). Apart from academics, as two other students of these schools have noted, the best of the segregated schools "addressed deeper psychological and sociological needs of their clients" (Irvine and Irvine 1983). One wonders how many of those clients had to memorize Paul Laurence Dunbar's "Encouraged" (Dunbar 1915):

> Because you love me I have
>   much achieved,
> Had you despised me then I must
>   have failed,
> But since I knew you trusted
>   and believed,
> I could not disappoint you and so
>   prevailed.

The poem captures much of what seems most important about Black schools in the South. Figure 4.2 is another way of summarizing collective memory.

Figure 4.2. Traditional Black Teaching Remembered

Thomas Sowell (1974, 1976)
- Schools were a blend of "support, encouragement, and rigid standards."
- Parents thought "The teacher was always right."
- The school "could do no wrong in the eyes of the parent."
- School "Would not let [them] go wrong."
- Teachers were demanding and took "personal interest" in students, often outside of school.
- "Some have a warm 'human touch' and others would have failed Public Relations I."

Faustine Jones-Wilson (1981)
- Teachers didn't give a choice between "learning and not learning."
- Failure "unacceptable to teachers, family, peers and the community."

Siddle Walker (1996)
- The segregated school is most often compared with a "family" in which teachers and the principal, with parentlike authority, exercised almost complete autonomy in shaping student learning and ensuring student discipline.

David Cecelski (1994)
- Teachers in Hyde County, North Carolina, created a "caring environment" and a "familial atmosphere."

Adam Fairclough (2007)
- "Many of those teachers [in Texas] taught with a zeal and commitment . . . as though they felt a personal mandate to compensate for the areas of lack in the lives of the students."
- Teachers in Columbia, South Carolina, "shared their lives with us, they made us feel like we were the most important people in the world, and they taught us pride and tradition."
- "For many women, teaching became a kind of sacred calling, rather like that of the celibate priest. . . . Either way, they acted as if God had called them to teach and expected their husbands to either help them or not interfere."

In many ways, this sounds like what we know about Catholic schools, just interpreted through a different historical experience. Teachers are seen as having a broad interest in children, in their character and in their future. There is a sense of mission, a moral compact between children and teachers. Children felt pressure to succeed; whether or not they are going to take school seriously is a choice that has been made for them by adults. They felt pushed cognitively and socially. There is some disagreement about whether teachers were warm and friendly but an overwhelming consensus that adults were all on the same page; teachers had the authority of the whole race behind them. If we were to abstract a teaching model from this, we might get something like figure 4.3.

Figure 4.3. Authoritative-Supportive Teaching

- High level of intellectual / academic demand
- High level of social demand
- Holistic concern for children and their future; sense of a larger mission
- Strong sense of teacher efficacy and legitimacy

Calling this model authoritative-supportive teaching would seem to capture its most salient aspects. If this is the kind of teaching that Black people remember as having worked for them, is there any reason at all to think it transfers to the contemporary ghetto? Actually, there are several interesting lines of thinking in contemporary research to suggest that a model of teaching very close to this can have unusually large positive impacts, even among today's rowdy youth.

One very instructive study tried to assess the relative impact of social support as against academic pressure (Lee et al. 1999), surveying 28,000 Chicago sixth and eighth graders and more than 5,000 teachers in 304 elementary and middle schools. To measure social support from teachers, students were asked whether their English and math teachers:

- related the subject to their personal interests (which, of course, implies that teachers know what students are interested in)
- really listened to what they say
- knew them very well
- believed they can do well in school

To assess support from parents, students were asked how often their parents or other adults in their household:

- discuss school events and/or events of interest to the student
- help with homework
- discuss with them things they had studied in class
- discuss homework with them

To assess social support from peers, students were asked whether most students in their classes:

- treat each other with respect
- work together to solve problems
- help each other learn

Academic press, as the study calls it, was measured by both teacher reports and student reports. The questions asked of teachers included whether their schools:

- set high standards for academic performance
- organized the school day to maximize student learning
- focused on what is best for student learning when making important decisions

The questions for assessing student perception of academic press asked students whether their English and math teachers:

- expected them to do their best all the time
- expected them to complete their homework every night
- thought it very important that they do well in that class
- encouraged them to do extra work when they don't understand something

This is very close to the authoritative-supportive model, capturing elements of social and intellectual demand, of holistic concern, of adults being on the same page. The main message from the study is that social support and academic press each independently made a meaningful difference, but when both are present at high levels, the results can be striking. In reading, children experiencing low levels of both support and press averaged a gain of 0.56 Grade Equivalents a year in reading, but students exposed to high levels of both improved 1.82 GEs, almost two years' growth in a year. Now that's interocularity. The numbers in math were even more pronounced. While low-support, low-press students improved 0.63 GEs, high-press, high-support students improved an eye-popping 2.39 GEs. The distribution of high-press, high-support schools is very much what one would expect. Racially integrated schools are three times more likely to exhibit both characteristics than predominantly minority schools; schools serving the highest-income-level students are four times as likely to exhibit both aspects than schools serving the poorest students.

These would be impressive numbers under any circumstances, but they are even more impressive considering the population under study—sixth and eighth graders. That's a tough crowd. By that age, many students have essentially given up on schools, and schools have given up on many of them. Something like that Old Time Religion, something like the traditional model of Black teaching, supportive but authoritative—still seems to work for a great many children. One might have expected that the sheer magnitude of the results would have attracted a great deal of attention, but this has actually been among the least requested of the studies done by the Chicago Consortium. We can only speculate as to why, but it is at least possible that the emphasis here on teaching as having an important component of social support does not fit comfortably with much contemporary discourse, with its emphasis on teaching as being about the delivery of material, the development of skills, and so forth.

Still, there is a growing research base on various aspects of the supportive-authoritative balance problem. For one thing, its helps us understand more precisely the nature of African American educational disadvantage. In Chicago, students attending predominantly African American schools are much less likely than students in integrated schools to be in environments where teachers trust parents (about 42 percent of teachers in predominantly African American schools report strong trust as against 72 percent of teachers in integrated schools) and less likely to be in places where teachers feel a strong sense of collective responsibility (Easton 2006). I think we can assume that in environments where adults are less cooperative with one another, they are less likely to be effectively supportive of students. Another Chicago study shows that in high schools where student-teacher trust is high (taking that to be an analog for teacher support), students average 2.3 percent fewer absences per term, essentially one additional week of attendance over the school year. In schools with the highest levels of academic press for the future, students averaged just under two fewer absences a year (Allensworth and Easton 2007).

At the elementary level, Ron Ferguson (2006) has found a relationship between how supportive the experience is for children and how they treat one another, taking us back to a theme in Helen Gouldner's (1978) work. If children don't think the teacher both enjoys helping them and holds them to a high standard—what he calls a "high help/high perfectionism" classroom—their engagement and behavior deteriorates, which includes children treating one another poorly.

There are some national data that reinforce the importance of social supports. Woolley and Bowen (2007), using a sample of over 8,000 middle school pupils, many of them with significant risk factors in their lives, have demonstrated that of the various variables they examined, social capital—the number of supportive adults in students' lives—had the strongest relationship to school engagement. Again, it is important that students have support across the various settings of their lives. Woolley and Grogan-Kaylor (2006), using a nationally representative sample of middle and high school students, have found that teacher support had the strongest association with academic performance, followed by neighborhood safety, followed by home academic culture. Significantly, when African American and Latino students received the same kinds of support across domains as others, they had similar academic performance.

Clearly, we want to think of support and demand in tandem, but my guess would be that demands are especially important for Black students and for any others who have been branded intellectually inferior. Part of my work at Westside High School involved trying to understand how students there understood their teachers and how that shaped student behavior. Thus, among other questions, I was asking, "What would a teacher have to be like before you said, 'That's a really good teacher'? How can you tell if a teacher is really concerned about students learning something in the course?" In response to the "really concerned" question, students stressed two things: The really concerned teacher works hard to make the material clear, and, less intuitively, the really concerned teacher is demanding. Clarity meant that the teacher should check notebooks, encourage questions, ask questions to see whether students understand, provide students with some indication of their progress. This is again a conception of teaching reminiscent of our authoritative-supportive model; it sees the good teacher as aggressive, as actively making sure students are learning, not just leaving it up to the students. Pedro Noguera (2005) found the same thinking among a group of students in Berkeley:

> They look first for people who care. . . . Second, they respect teachers who are strict and hold students accountable. Third, they like teachers who teach them something. When they found a teacher who was caring, strict and challenging, they responded really well [despite the fact that] some of these students had criminal records or missed more days than they attended. (17–18)[3]

When students at Westside said that the concerned teacher is demanding, they meant that the serious teacher will make students walk the straight and narrow, stay on their backs about homework and attendance, stop them from fooling around and wasting time in class. Even some shouting and cursing seem okay with the kids, but only if it is clearly related to getting students to do their best. Students talked in some detail about what made them think a teacher was "nice," but they clearly separated that from what made a teacher effective. In fact, when it comes to misbehavior, students thought that the teachers who were "too nice" were going to catch more than their share of trouble.

Asked to explain why they cooperated more with some teachers than others—worked hard, paid attention in class, came to class—about half the students said it didn't matter, they put out the same level of effort in all classes. The other students overwhelmingly saw themselves as working harder for those teachers who were both more serious about teaching and more insistent on appropriate behavior. It was clearly the perceived quality of teaching in combination with demanding behavior that had the most impact on student behavior. When demands were separated from good teaching, when poor teachers tried to put pressure on, that could be interpreted as a put-down. Students may respond to demanding teachers, but only if they have somehow legitimated their right to demand.[4]

Theresa Perry has provided what I think is the best context for thinking about this: "The task of achievement . . . is distinctive for African Americans because doing school requires that you use your mind, and the ideology of the larger society has always been about questioning the mental capacity of African Americans, about questioning Black intellectual competence" (Perry, Steele, and Hilliard 2003: 5).

Kids understand the Master Narrative; they know they are supposed to be dumb. In this sense, demanding behavior from a teacher, when it is understood as being for the student's own good, when it is legitimated, constitutes a counternarrative.[5] Whatever intellectual demands mean to everyone else, they mean something more to Black kids and other stigmatized populations because they are in dialogue with a different history. Demanding behavior, properly couched, welcomes you to the table; it signifies your membership in the larger moral community. Like the rest of us, kids may enjoy an undemanding environment if they can get it; once they get accustomed to it, it can be a real project to change their habits. At the same time, they can be sophisticated enough to understand, at some level, that it means somebody thinks they can't do better.

If data from Chicago can be generalized, youngsters in the inner city may have more trouble finding someone at school who will insist that they do their best than finding someone who supports them. Low-performing Chicago elementary schools in the mid-1990s were not much different from other schools in the level of teacher personalism that students reported. They were significantly lower in academic press (Sebring et al. 1996). This isn't to say that the number of caring adults isn't a problem; rather, in the lowest-performing schools, finding teachers who will insist on an appropriate level of demands is even more of a problem. Judging from my own experience, one part of the problem may be that some younger teachers—some young, white teachers in particular, I suspect—have a kind of "niceness" ideology. They think that what these kids really need is someone who will be "nice" to them. That's a poor (but unsurprising) reading of how the lives of urban children are constricted. I would ask them to see the problem through the eyes of W. E. B. Du Bois, whose first teaching experience came in rural Tennessee in the 1880s while he was still an undergraduate at Fisk. The students he taught there "found the world a puzzling thing: it asked little of them, and they answered with little, and yet it ridiculed their offering. Such a paradox they could not understand, and therefore sank into listless indifference, or shiftlessness, or reckless bravado" (1961: 60).

One of the most interesting groups of young teachers I know are the members of the Baltimore Algebra Project, a group of high school students who have been running a very successful afterschool program in which they tutor middle school students in mathematics. Researchers and adult teachers can only envy the level of knowledge they have about their clients, and we can be sure they bring all the determination of idealistic youth to their work. It is instructive to think about the kind of teaching styles they evolve. In the following interview excerpt (Payne, forthcoming), Mahogony Bosworth, Charnell Covert, Channell Parker, and Michele Shropshire talk about what they've learned about working with difficult clients:

BOSWORTH: At Lemmel [School] I had eighth graders. . . . They came when they wanted to. . . . They really didn't want to be there. I mean they learned. They sat there and listened but they really didn't want to be there.

SHROPSHIRE: The problem with the clients at Lemmel is that the clients that we got . . . were from a different program. And before we got them, they were working on easier math. So when they came to us, they didn't want to—really want to challenge themselves, so they were kind of reluctant to come to us. And that's why they were coming when they felt like it, or whenever.

COVERT: Anybody would have an attitude if they come from Baltimore City public schools. From my experience, it tends to be one or two attitudes: an attitude of, "Yes, I go to Baltimore public schools, but that doesn't determine my future. And I'm going to maximize that." Or it can be an attitude of, "Yes, I go to Baltimore City public schools, and that does determine my future. So I don't really care about learning because nobody cares about learning for me." Now, the people who are on the latter end, I think you just have to be understanding of where they're coming from. . . . I had some clients who had some real serious home issues. Like one of my high school clients was going in between homes. And it wasn't that he couldn't get it. He just was going through some things. And it was always that he would get put out of class and they would send him. And he would be upset because he needed to go to work because he needed to provide for himself. But he never felt comfortable telling his teachers because he felt like they were being sort of like, why sympathize with him? And he never really went to talk to them.

So he would like try to use that time as more of a venting time, which was fine. . . . And it would be fine for him but not so much pressure.

Where I'm not just like, sit down, do your work. . . . Who can do their work or focus on their work when you don't have anywhere to live? And he did make a choice to stay in school and he graduated and did fine.

But then also knowing, too, when people are trying to get over. Because there were a lot of people who would just say like, "Oh, my stomach hurts." And you'd be like, "Okay, well go home for today." And then you'll leave and see them in the parking lot with their girlfriend or something. And you're like, "Grrr, you tried to get over me." So it's just being stern and knowing, using judgment. Knowing what is what.

PARKER: I worked with these three boys and they were—they were like in fifth or sixth grade. . . . I wouldn't call them bad but it was really difficult. They were really difficult. And I would come in and they'd be like [in a disgusted tone], "Oh, here comes Channell." Because they worked with another guy who didn't really challenge them.

When I came and they knew that they were about to have a drill, a test, a quiz. And they knew they were about to work and they would come. And I would get there and they would be so mad at me. [But] after a while, it was to the point where, "I want to work with Channell. I want to work with Channell." And everyone would look at them as the bad boys. And that made them want to come to work even more.

These are Black Baltimore city kids and nobody believes in them. And they're all going to get in trouble every single day. I used to have to wait like ten minutes because they had been coming out of detention or whatever. And that made me want to come to work. Because I knew that they were smart. These boys were smart. I would, like, pull out my notebook and I would teach them some of the stuff I was learning [in high school] because it had to do with what they were learning. And they would learn it. And I knew they were smart and I knew they tried and they understood it. And I knew they was also the bad kids or whatever. . . . I'd be like . . . "I'm going to call your parents." And they would get their self together. Or, "I've got a dollar for the first one to get this question right." And they would get their selves together. I had to start pulling quarters out of my pocket and bring in [candy bars]. But it was worth it, because at the end of the day they understood what I was teaching them. . . .

They want to be big and bad. They don't want to learn. Treat them like you care—I would give them hugs and tell them I'd see them tomorrow, at the end of each session. After I treated them like I care, they'd start caring. And they wanted to come back. And they would go, "I'm working with Channell. Hey, let me work with Channell. You've got any candy today?" And everything made it worth it after that. So with difficult kids, treat them like you care and they'll be there every day. And they will want you to be there every day. . . . Challenge them. You've got to challenge them. Because if you don't challenge them they're not going to challenge themselves. And no one around them is going to challenge them. Not only do they score high on their MSA [Maryland State Assessment], but after a while—when I got there— they already had their books and pencils out. They already had their calculators and their blocks and all that. So after a while it wasn't me waiting for them. It was, they were waiting for me. It was to the point where I was meeting with their teachers, meeting with their parents, meeting with their friends who wanted to come in. They weren't getting in trouble. I want to see them in about five years, see what they are doing. Their friends were coming. I started with, like, two boys, and I ended up with, like, five. . . .

Shropshire: Sometimes [we gave out] candy or we'd throw a party and they weren't informed about it ahead of time. We would throw a party if like everybody did like super across the board . . . the incentives really helped out a lot. And for people I tutored specifically, like tutoring girls who wanted to talk about boys or anything else—well, once you develop a relationship with the client, it's like if you just look at them a certain way, they're like, "Okay, okay. We'll get back on task," or whatever. And that's all it really had to be. . . . Establishing the relationship is really just working with them every day. And when they come in, if there's like time between when they come in and when you start . . . you get them to talk about their friends or some boys. Or any other thing that's on their mind so you kind of know about them. And it builds on it like every day. So it's that in-between time. . . . And it kind of goes back to the conditions of the city schools. If you have 30 kids in class and one teacher, a teacher is not going to possibly be able to build a relationship. . . .

For a group of young people, this sounds pretty Old School, very much like what we are calling the authoritative-supportive model of teaching. There are differences of emphasis—one cannot imagine that many traditional Black teachers put this much emphasis on kids having fun—but the core themes of the model are here: Understand the social context of negative behavior. Push kids intellectually, challenge them. Be stern about the things that matter most. "Recognize" kids as persons. Convey a sense that they count too much to be allowed to mess up their own education. In the raggedy schools of contemporary Baltimore, a group of young people are evolving a style of pedagogy that would have seemed familiar to generations of African American teachers before them.

Reproducing Race

Suppose you live in an intensely anti-Semitic country. You yourself are not anti-Semitic at all, however. Indeed, you've never met a Jew, have no feelings about them one way or the other. Of course, you've heard what people say about them, that they are sharp, grasping, prone to cheat in business transactions. That's just stuff you've heard, not anything you personally believe. Still, those ideas are pervasive in your society. When you finally do meet a Jew, can you ignore them completely? Can you afford to, especially if the meeting is a business transaction? As you interact with the person, won't the things you've heard be in the back of your mind? Aren't you likely to watch the person just a little more closely, just in case? And isn't it possible that the other party will notice that, perhaps becoming more withdrawn and reserved, which you, of course, might interpret as a sign of his being up to something? If any little thing isn't exactly right, the saturation of negative ideas throughout the culture gives you an explanation ready-to-hand. We can get the beginnings of a negative spiral without anyone bearing anyone else the slightest ill will.

That example is from Gordon Allport's *The Nature of Prejudice*, first published in 1954. In some ways, that book reflects a more sophisticated understanding of race than does much contemporary commentary, scholarly and popular alike. We tend to reduce race to its more extreme interpersonal manifestations; that is, "racism" exists when a prejudiced person discriminates in some fairly explicit way. We want a smoking gun, somebody with a sheet and a hood. The privileging of this kind of overt discrimination paradigm over structural interpretations of race is one reason many Americans can think of racial problems as a thing of the past (Wellman 1977; Bonilla-Silva 2004). The idea that race isn't real because it is, after all, just a social construction, is another variant of that. The early- and mid-twentieth-century scholars who developed the ideas we now think of as the social construction of race—W. I. Thomas (1928), Robert Merton (1948)—were in fact trying to establish the utter reality of social constructions. The fact that their thinking has been turned on its head says something about the depth of contemporary confusion about what race is and how it reproduces itself.

This kind of confusion is so pervasive that it has come to affect the way we frame educational issues. One example is all the head-scratching over the poor educational performance of middle-class Black students, especially middle-class Black students in clearly liberal and progressive environments (as these things go), university towns like Evanston, Ann Arbor, or Chapel Hill. The assumption, of course, is that the social meaning of race lies largely in its connection to poverty; absent poverty and overt discrimination, Black students are pretty much the same as anyone else. That world doesn't exist yet. In this world, a world where ideas about Black intellectual inferiority are pervasive, shaping our behavior irrespective of whether we believe them, race presents barriers to development that may have nothing to do with either poverty or crude racism. Race is a social location, and where one is located socially determines how one experiences and interprets the world.

Consider something as basic as the capacity for trust. We have many years of data that suggest Blacks are less generally trusting of others than are whites. One recent study (Taylor, Funk, and Clark 2007) found 32 percent of whites in the lowest trust category as opposed to a full 61 percent of Blacks (and 53 percent of Hispanics). This has frequently been understood to be a function of vulnerability; the world over, more vulnerable populations are less apt to trust. "In virtually all societies, 'have-nots' are less trusting than 'haves'" (Putnam 2000: 138). The folklorist Zora Neale Hurston used to say that the motto of the rabbits is always "Make no mistake—Run every time the bush shake." At some level, the capacity for trust is a luxury attendant upon having a favorable social location. Those without power or resources cannot afford the consequences of misplaced trust, so they trust more sparingly. In schools, we have good reason to think that one of the ways we can rebuild trust is to reduce vulnerability (Bryk and Schneider 2002).

This research is about trusting other people, but it is also clear that Blacks have less trust in the future as well or, more precisely, less trust in their own capacity to shape the future. In many ways, the work that inaugurated systematic empirical analysis of educational inequality was James Coleman's mammoth *Equality of Educational Opportunity* (1966), at the time the second-costliest social science research project ever conducted. Some of his most instructive findings had to do with what he called *fate control,* an individual's confidence that he or she has some control over his or her own destiny. Students were asked whether they thought hard work or luck was more important for getting ahead; whether they agreed that every time they tried to get ahead, something happened to stop them; and whether they thought that if they really wanted something, they could get it. Fate control turned out to have a stronger relationship to achievement than all school-related factors put together. With the exception of Asian students, minority pupils had less confidence than whites in their ability to affect their own futures. Having that sense was especially important for Black students, accounting for three times as much of the variance in achievement among them as among their white counterparts. Glantz (1977) has confirmed both the strength of the correlation between fate control and achievement and the tendency of Blacks to have a weaker sense of their ability to control their environment. Kerckhoff and Campbell (1977), trying to explain levels of educational ambition among twelfth-grade boys, find that for Black boys the educational attainment of the head of household matters much less and the perception of the opportunity structure matters much more.[6] In some respects, then, it seems that Black students are more prone to seeing themselves as objects rather than subjects, a mind-set which militates against academic development.

Ron Ferguson (2006) notes that in his surveys of suburban students, Black students all through school are particularly worried about whether people think they are smart. It doesn't stop when they get to college. In the thirty or more years that I have been advising Black college freshmen, the most persistent difficulty has been getting them to seek help when they need it. Too often they are afraid that admitting they need help will reinforce whatever stereotypes the teacher or other students hold of them. The work of Claude Steele and his colleagues (summarized in Perry, Steele, and Hilliard 2003) has done much to help us understand the importance of stereotype threat. The work involves constructing experiments in which subjects, mostly college students, are led to believe that they are in danger of reinforcing some stereotype. Black students are led to believe they may be reinforcing notions of Black intellectual inferiority; white males are led to believe that they may be about to reinforce the idea that white males have less mathematical talent than Asians; white females to think they are being scrutinized for their mathematical ability compared to men; and, my personal favorite, white athletes are made to think that the activity they are about to engage in tests "natural athletic talent," something popular thinking sees Blacks as advantaged in. Even though the groups being tested have been matched for actual ability, the experiments reveal that stereotype threat consistently has a dramatic negative impact on intellectual performance. When a test is introduced in such a way as to get Black students thinking about notions of racial inferiority, for example, they will do less well than white students of equal measured ability. It proved to be very difficult to turn the tables and convince Black students that the tests they were about to take were "race-fair." What worked was implying that the research generating the tests had been done by Black scholars. When they believed that, "they performed well regardless of whether we had weakened their self-confidence beforehand. And when they didn't feel trust, no amount of bolstering of self-confidence helped" (123).[7]

It is important to note that the impact of stereotype threat seems to be greatest among the most achievement-oriented, most skilled students. Steele hypothesizes that one has to care about a domain of performance in order to be worried about the prospect of being stereotyped in that domain. Less successful students can protect themselves by withdrawing from academic competition, by deciding that it isn't important to them—which, again, presumably means they are more likely to seek their badges of dignity elsewhere (Sennett and Cobb 1972). This is a useful way to think about underachieving middle-class students. However much the ghetto may function as a tool of racial stratification, its very isolation also offers a measure of protection against some of the ways race can express itself. Where the White Gaze is more constantly present for students in integrated contexts, race and racial stereotypes may be more often consciously salient for them, and in a form against which it is particularly difficult to protect oneself.

It is not, to paraphrase Lorraine Hansberry, that Black youth got up one morning and decided they couldn't trust their environment. These predispositions are based on how they and people they identify with experience the broader society. They reflect real vulnerabilities. Black youth do not experience society as racially egalitarian and open in the way that many Americans assume it to be. Consider what we know about discipline patterns (H. Witt 2007). According to data collected by the U.S. Department of Education for the 2004–2005 school year, African American students nationally are suspended or expelled at nearly three times the rate of white students. In Minnesota, Black students are six times as likely to be suspended as whites, but that seems downright friendly compared to New Jersey, where they are almost 60 times more likely to be expelled. In 21 states, the percentage of Black suspensions is more than double their percentage in the student body. These disproportions affect middle-class as well as working-class Black students, and there is no reason to believe that they can be reduced to actual differences in student behavior. At least some of the discrepancy seems to be about teachers interpreting similar behaviors differently when they come from students of different races. Hispanic students, who also have to negotiate stigma in a variety of ways, seem to be suspended or expelled roughly in proportion to their population. We should think of teacher expectations as a stratifying device in themselves, a major part of the machinery by which social inequality is reproduced. Recall that Ron Ferguson's (2003) review of the literature concludes that race, ethnicity, and class all affect teacher perception and all affect teacher behavior.

We shouldn't be surprised to learn that African American students perceive school climate less favorably than white students or staff. A West Virginia study (Education Alliance 2006) of 2,900 middle and high school students found African American students gave their schools significantly lower ratings on seven of the eight dimensions of school climate examined, including academic expectations, quality of instruction, counseling about educational options, respect, mentoring and caring relationships, and fairness. Even when student academic performance and school demographics are controlled, Black students see themselves as being in environments where less is expected of them and fewer people care about them or treat students fairly.

At a broader level, we can assume that students understand the flow of resources to be racialized; ghetto students know their schools look like they do for a reason; they know that certain kinds of classes are reserved for them, they know that certain kinds of neighborhoods are reserved for them. Students in desegregated environments know that there is a reason so few people like them get the best teachers or wind up in the AP classes. They may not have a very precise analysis, but they know that access to resources and status honor are correlated with race. (And to focus on the fact that sometimes they will see race where something else is in fact operative misses the point entirely.) They cannot *not* see race in their lives. That this can be true and that we can still construct a national dialogue premised on the idea that middle-class Black youth underachievement is a great mystery can be regarded on the one hand as yet another testament to the power of self-serving thought or, on the other, as an indicator of how little weight the lived experiences of Black youth has in the national imagination.

Rumors of the death of Jim Crow are premature. What we know about the operation of race in our schools (and elsewhere) does not lend itself to either/or explanations. Again, it is not that Black students are coming to school with a bunch of negative attitudes that they just made up. I once heard John Hope Franklin, after one of his speeches, respond to a questioner who was bemoaning the terrible criminal behavior from young Black males by trying to get the questioner to see that youngsters like that had never been allowed to have a sense of equity in this country. That's a good metaphor for thinking about race outside the context of overt discrimination. There is a kind of mutual disinvestment going on, in which youth who are not made to feel that they are valued and welcomed members of the institution respond by disinvesting themselves in that institution and whatever it symbolizes, with ample room for misunderstanding and self-fulfilling prophecies on both sides.

Institutional disinvestment can take the form of outright and deliberate discrimination and its consequences, but it is more likely to be expressed in low expectations, low demands, listless teaching, and inequitable distribution of resources, human and social. We have already said that African American students in Chicago, for example, typically attend schools where there are lower levels of collective responsibility among teachers and much lower levels of teacher-parent trust. Add to that, those schools are less programmatically coherent, less safe, and teachers in them say they see less innovation going on (Easton 2006). (In all these respects, Latino students are in better schools, on average, than African Americans, but not as good as the schools serving more integrated populations.) That is, these institutions are just not making the level of effort we see in schools for other people; it's not the same level of investment. If the students are frequently lackadaisical and unfocused, they are only mirroring the institutional stance toward them. Everybody's half-steppin'. Saying that is not at all to deny that kids are bringing a whole lot of problems with them that have nothing to do with the school. It is merely to repeat Gouldner's point; by disinvesting in the child, the school exacerbates any preexisting problems and creates some new ones.

Consider, as a suggestive counterexample, the interesting research on the effects of small class size in the early grades on Black students (Krueger and Whitmore 2002). Tennessee randomly assigned over 11,000 students to either small (from 13 to 17 pupils) or large classes (from 22 to 25 pupils) for the first four years of schooling, after which the students who had been in small classes returned to regular classes. Smaller classes made a much larger difference to Black students. While they were in them, Black students in smaller classes performed 7–10 percentile points better than Black students in larger classes, while the advantage for white students in smaller classes over their counterparts in larger classes was 3–4 percentile points. When all students went back to normal-size classes, the effects of having been in smaller classes persisted, although it was smaller. When the students got to high schools, Black students who had been in smaller classes were much more likely to take the ACT or SAT, presumably a measure of preparing themselves for college. "Assigning all students to a small class is estimated to reduce the black-white gap in the test-taking rate by an impressive 60 percent" (29). It would be enlightening to know what factors mediated those outcomes (and to what degree they were social in character), but even without knowing that, this is enough to provide another example of how different investments in children can provide different outcomes. Less than 15 years ago, people were still publishing studies wondering if school resources mattered for poor children. We now know what a wrong-headed question that was. If anything, we should regard children from the social margins as being more school-vulnerable than others, more sensitive to whatever the school does or does not do.[8]

While this discussion has been framed largely in terms of Black learners, we could tell largely the same story, with changes of emphasis here and there, about other severely stigmatized and marginalized groups. In her study of West Side High, a school that reflected all of New York City's diversity, Cristina Rathbone (1998) discovered again and again that these kids, while they strove mightily to project an image of having it together and being above it all, in fact lived much of their lives on the defensive:

> Their self-sufficiency had its costs, of course. However much they seemed impervious, the kids at West Side knew where they stood in the general scheme of things. And although the incredibly scintillating, brisk, and charming exteriors they developed allowed them to survive the casual blows of day-to-day life, many kids ended up suffocating in the tiny emotional space they allowed themselves to hold onto. . . . [One teacher] asked her students to describe how West Siders were seen by the rest of the city: "lazy," "dropouts," "pregnant," "Puerto Rican sluts," and "kids who can't make it in the real world because they are too dumb and angry" were just some of the answers they gave. (116–17)

It is one thing to say that students on the margins understand the disregard with which the larger world views them and react to it, another to wonder how many of them internalize that disregard to some degree. Marc Elrich (1994), describing a sixth-grade class in which most students were reading two years below grade level, found that most of his Black students saw Black people as bad people. They saw Black people as dumber than whites or Asians, as not liking to work hard, and Black men as unreliable. "My students had developed a bipolar view of the world with whiteness and goodness at one pole and darkness and badness at the other." We don't know how widespread or deeply rooted such feelings are, but it may be that young people from stigmatized groups have their sense that they can control their environment and have their future compromised at one level by their awareness of the scornful gaze of the outer world, at another by their own capitulation to that scorn.[9]

Black learners have a different terrain to negotiate, terrain whose contours have been shaped by the constant and distinctive "recycling of the ideology of African-American moral, cultural and intellectual deficiency," to use Theresa Perry's words (Perry, Steele, and Hilliard 2003: 9). Many Black youngsters are trapped between what they understand as a history of collective humiliation and impotence and a set of contemporary social images that seem to confirm the idea that there is something fundamentally wrong with Black people. Based on their unreliable sense of history, on their own lived experience, based on how they understand the opportunity structure for people like them, past and present, Black learners may be prone to distrust, unsure of their ability to shape their own future and unsure of how schooling fits into that, uncertain how to structure the racial presumption they find all around them. Race problematizes the struggle for honor and welcome in ways that have direct implications for social and intellectual development. It robs children of the right to take their relationship to the larger society for granted.

This seems, then, to be an argument for a pedagogy of connectedness, one that in part connects students to a past that they may have rejected, a rejection that leaves them with fewer tools to fight racial stereotype in the present. To whatever extent children don't have confidence in their ability to affect the future, it is all the more important that they be connected to adults who can envision futures the young people cannot and keep them moving toward those futures. To whatever extent young people face more temptation toward destructive identities, they need connections to adults who are authoritative enough to draw some boundaries that take some negative choices away from them. The growing national mantra about instruction, instruction, instruction is a good thing; we need to be encouraging it. Still, we need to be wary of sliding into the trap of thinking that instruction is the whole battle. For some children, the mantra needs to be instruction and connection, instruction and connection.

Thus, extracurricular activities, one of the first targets of cash-strapped urban systems, may be especially critical for the population they serve. A growing body of research suggests that good extracurricular and community-based organized activities are associated with lower rates of academic failure, lower dropout rates, better school attendance, more satisfaction with the school experience, better rates of college attendance, especially for low-achieving children, and lower rates of various antisocial behaviors (Mahoney, Larson, and Eccles 2005; Eccles and Templeton 2002). Some of these effects seem particularly strong for low-income and at-risk youth, and some seem to persist well into adulthood. Of course, the youth who would benefit most are least likely to participate in these activities. Low-income Latino and African American youth have lower rates of participation than other students. It is particularly alarming that the proportion of African American seniors involved in academic clubs declined 36 percent between 1972 and 1992 (Pederson and Seidman 2005) and equally alarming that we have constructed a national dialogue about education that is essentially indifferent to that fact.

One institution that would not be indifferent is the Catholic school, which is probably the closest thing we have to an answer to the question about how one scales up effective education in the inner city. One review of the research on Catholic schools and African American students concludes that

> . . . family background variables such as income, parental educational levels, and parental educational aspirations seem less important in the achievement gains of African American students in Catholic schools than in public schools. . . . Individual characteristics such as intelligence, achievement, motivation, gender, religious affiliation, and race seem similarly less related to African American achievement in Catholic schools. (York 1996: 44)

Whenever one raises Catholic schools as a model, there is the objection that Catholic schools serve a different population and there are too many issues of self-selection for such comparisons to hold water. I don't believe that. Grogger and Neal (2000) have pulled together a good deal of evidence suggesting that that is not the case. I am very much affected by my own experience of talking with kids in Chicago who moved back and forth between Catholic and public schools, depending on the fluctuations in family income, and having them tell me, without exception that I can recall, that they worked harder and took school more seriously when they were in Catholic school. The most memorable was a boy who told me that when he was in Catholic schools, he went to school every day just loaded down with books, but when he was back in the neighborhood public school, "all I bring is my radio." I wouldn't go so far as to say selection effects make no difference, but my experience is that kids themselves describe dramatic changes in their own behavior depending on what they think the environment is asking of them.

We don't have enough examples of large-scale successful education in our cities that we can be ignoring any of them. Let's suspend disbelief for the moment and accept for the sake of discussion that there may be something we can learn from Catholic schools about what effective education at scale would look like in the inner city. Anthony Bryk and Valerie Lee (Bryk, Lee, and Holland 1993; Lee 1998) have probably been the two most influential scholars in this discussion. They put considerable emphasis on the Catholic school as an exemplar of the common school model. There is a common course of study that virtually everyone takes, thus avoiding the situation in public schools where students of color are particularly prone to "choosing" or being counseled into watered-down courses. Cognitive demand is structured in for everybody, which contrasts with public schools, most of which use some form of tracking at the high school, a way of telling students in the lower tracks they are officially stupid. There is a different level of personalism, built in part through shared experiences across the school community and high rates of participation in extracurricular activities. This is facilitated by a different understanding of the teacher's role:

> Rather than defining themselves as subject-matter specialists, teachers in Catholic high schools see their responsibilities as extending to any encounters with students: in hallways, the school grounds, the school neighborhood, and sometimes into their homes. Many teachers define their profession in moral terms—forming character as well as developing skills. (Lee 1998: 7)

Lee contends that the emphasis on moral community and human dignity is crucial to the kind of community Catholic schools form: "Besides imparting technical knowledge and skills to negotiate a complex secular world, students must be pushed to develop a moral vision toward which those skills should be pointed, and a conscience that encourages them to pursue that vision. In this sense, education is fundamentally a moral enterprise" (Lee 1998: 11). The more confused students are about their place in society, the more salient that moral conception of the educational enterprise can be. One can imagine any of the great Black educators of previous generations—a Charlotte Hawkins Brown, a Mary McLeod Bethune, a Benjamin Mays—uttering those words without missing a beat. Surely the hope of the charter school movement isn't this nonsense about how free-market principles are going to reshape other institutions, nor the idea that removing bureaucratic restrictions will make an enormous difference all by itself. The hope in the charter school movement is that some of these schools are attracting leaders and teachers with a moral fire, leaders who see their work as a calling, not a career, whose commitment to children goes beyond the merely professional.

What York (1996: 43) finds about teaching styles in Catholic schools—"highly traditional, unremarkable and structured"—would describe the teaching in a great many academically successful Afrocentric schools as well. Too many people cannot see past the racial ideology. If they could, what they would see in the strongest of those schools would be high levels of both cognitive and social demands for students, authoritative adults who also develop very personal relationships with students, a strong sense of a community with a moral mission. One such school in Chicago, the New Concept Development Center, posted very strong test scores for many years despite scraping along on very few resources, and now that it has evolved into the Betty Shabazz International Charter School, it consistently posts some of the highest scores in the city (C. D. Lee 2008).[10]

This is not at all to say that we shouldn't be trying to expose children to the most powerful forms of pedagogy we can identify. It is to say that students don't have to have that to learn at high levels. When children are committed to the task, they probably have a great many more ways of learning than we have of teaching. When relationships are strong enough, when teachers and students have a sufficient commitment to one another, teaching that is not very fancy may do just fine for a great many children. If the mother of all conservative sins is the reluctance to think seriously about redistribution of resources, the first of all progressive sins may be the fetishizing of pedagogy. Assuming that *how* we teach is the end-all and be-all may prevent us from getting to some of the questions our most marginalized youth are struggling with.

William Peters' video *A Class Divided* is still one of the best ways to teach what we should mean by "the social construction of race," both the artificiality of its creation and the reality of it as consequence. In the wake of Martin Luther King Jr.'s assassination, Jane Rice, an Iowa third-grade teacher, wanted to give her all-white students a visceral understanding of discrimination. She decided to create race in her own classroom, dividing the students by eye color and treating them accordingly. "What I mean," she told the class, "is that brown-eyed people are better than blue-eyed people. They are cleaner than blue-eyed people. They are more civilized than blue-eyed people. And they are smarter than blue-eyed people" (Peters 1971: 21). Whichever group was the superior group for the day was given special privileges—five extra minutes at recess, the right to go to lunch first and have seconds, the right to use the drinking fountain and the playground equipment. She also changed the way she taught:

When a brown-eyed child stumbled in reading aloud, she helped him. When a blue-eyed child stumbled, she shook her head and called on a brown-eyed child to read the passage correctly. When a blue-eyed boy, tense and nervous, rolled a corner of a page of his reading book into a tight curl as he awaited his turn to read, Jane displayed the book to the class. "Do blue-eyed people take care of the things they are given?" she asked. (23)

Within a few minutes, she has created an ideology of group difference, a system of privilege based on those differences and a system of selective perception and interpretation to justify both the ideology and the privileges. That's pretty much all you need to have something akin to "race." Watching the video forty years later, it is still striking how quickly and thoroughly the superior group buys into its own superiority. At one level, they understand it's a game; at another, it becomes real, real enough to break up solid friendships, real enough that "Blue-eyed!!" becomes a playground epithet strong enough to start fights. It is also real enough to make smart kids dumb. The inferior group had to wear a felt collar to make themselves easier to identify. The class regularly did a phonics drill with flash cards, while Ms. Rice timed them. Consistently, whichever group was the subordinate group for the day took longer. "We couldn't think with those collars on," one boy said. "My eyes just kept going around and around."

Jane Rice's collars are our Third Heuristic. They remind us that racial definitions are real in their consequences, and ignoring that fact only reproduces race. They remind us that race can interfere with the capacity to feel connected to a larger, worthy group, and one's sense of connection can profoundly shape intellectual and social functioning. If part of our job is just making a much higher level of instruction available to poor children, another part is helping them feel reconnected to larger social worlds, and the more stigmatized children have been, the more important and challenging our job becomes.

Chapter 5

"You Can't Kill It and You Can't Teach It": Bureaucracy and the Institutional Environment

Ask a question, but don't expect an answer. Ask for documentation, but don't expect it to be delivered. Ask for any piece of information from preschool classes to doctoral programs and be directed to one woman, [Department of Education] spokesperson Frances Marine, who gladly and repeatedly will refuse your call.

—*St. Petersburg Times* Editorial

How could it take two months to get stationery? Why were supplies for the beginning of the year showing up in November? What happened to the paperwork I had hand-delivered two weeks earlier? Why did we cling to an interminable, Byzantine hiring process while neighboring districts were grabbing some of our best teacher candidates?

—High School Principal,
Cambridge, Massachusetts

What do we do when big district problems are orders of magnitude larger than any superintendent's capacity to address them? When well-meaning people in a dysfunctional equilibrium can't break old patterns?

—Matthew Miller,
"The Super"

The fundamental pathology of the system, then, is the source of the problem, not just the incompetence of particular units or people.

—David Rogers,
110 Livingston Street

121

I have already said that it is a dumb question, but I still cannot help wondering, from time to time, which is the single most fundamental problem in urban schools. Some days I am quite convinced that it is deeply ingrained and deeply negative teacher attitudes. From San Diego to Philadelphia to Boston, promising reforms have been pulled down by teacher belief systems. Other days, I am equally convinced that the worst part of the problem is the rigid and incompetent bureaucracies that schools have to deal with. Urban schools exist in a larger institutional environment that is unstable, unsupportive, and undermining. Principals find their energies drained by protectionist and combative unions, by unfunded and often contradictory mandates raining down from Washington or the state legislature, mandates that, from the viewpoint of building leaders, often have a dubious relationship to education. Above all, there is the sheer confusion and incompetence that characterize the nominal leadership of many urban school districts. School-level leaders have to negotiate various forms of environmental turbulence that they can no more control than they can control the weather.

The Pathology of Bureaucracy

Written in 1969, David Rogers's *110 Livingston Street*, his analysis of the New York City Board of Education, may still be the most insightful look we have into the inner workings of the administrative netherworld of urban schools, a world where just figuring out who actually has power isn't easy. The titular authority of the board was undermined by its lack of resources and by the fact that it was normally engaged in a power struggle with the superintendent. There was a familiar reversal of roles between superintendent and board. The board itself, properly concerned with shaping policy, tended instead to get caught up in administrative minutiae. It wasn't unusual for the so-called informal board meetings to have 50–60 agenda items. One president of the board thought it necessary to have a daily meeting with the superintendent. Meanwhile, the superintendents, who should have been carrying out policy, found themselves making it because the board was otherwise occupied. Periodically, the board would bestir itself and try to reassert its prerogatives. The scuffling between the board and the superintendent gave increased leverage to the actors in the system least subject to public scrutiny—the system's administrative staff, the people who run and staff divisions, departments, and bureaus.

It was Rogers's main contention that the school system had evolved into a pathological bureaucracy, an organization whose traditions, structure, and operations subverted the organizational mission.

Nobody can make the system work if the bureaucratic structure is not radically altered. State education laws, traditions, rules, and interlocking administrative relationships victimize anybody who comes into contact with the system—parents with legitimate complaints, people applying for teaching licenses, city officials developing community renewal programs, publishers struggling to get their textbooks and readers into the classrooms even after the principals and teachers have accepted them, teachers and principals waiting months to receive needed supplies from headquarters. . . . To maneuver through the bureaucratic maze of the New York City school system takes more patience and political connections than most people can ever hope to have. (266)

The organizational characteristics that we ordinarily expect to contribute to efficiency—standardization, impersonality, large scale, a concern with the calculable (i.e., with bottom-line results)—are taken to such extremes as to do just the opposite, resulting in a world dominated by

(1) overcentralization, the development of many levels in the chain of command, and an upward orientation of anxious subordinates; (2) vertical and horizontal fragmentation, isolating units from one another and limiting communication and coordination of functions; (3) the consequent development of chauvinism within particular units, reflected in actions to protect and expand their power; (4) the exercise of strong, informal pressure from peers within units to conform to their codes, geared toward political protection and expansion and ignoring the organization's wider goals; (5) compulsive rule following and rule enforcing; (6) the rebellion of lower-level supervisors against headquarters directives, alternating at times with overconformity; . . . (7) increasing insulation from clients, as internal politics and personal career concerns override interests in serving various publics; and (8) the tendency to make decisions in committees, making it more difficult to pinpoint responsibility and authority. (268)

The fragmentation, unit chauvinism, and complexity of the hierarchy guarantee that information cannot flow smoothly from one part of the organization to another. As one school official put it: "It is known by everyone . . . that headquarters doesn't know what's going on. Information does not get back from the field and they don't even care. To some extent, field people don't even know what policy actually is. They get no help from headquarters, only a mass of paper directives" (279).

Part of what Rogers means by overcentralization, of course, is that their lack of knowledge about what is happening in schools doesn't prevent them from thinking they should make decisions about how toilet paper and lightbulbs (literally) should be distributed to schools. It is a system that has been shaped to serve the career interests of those who staff it, not anyone's educational interests. For that reason, it is necessarily a very inbred world, despite civil service regulations intended to prevent just that. Since the people inside the bureaucracy are responsible for enforcing the regulations, they do not find it difficult to find ways around them. To get into the system, to move up within it, one needs friends, sponsors, cronies to watch one's back, to mention one's name in the right places. (In pre-reform Chicago, one form that cronyism reputedly took, especially among Black administrators, was an emphasis on fraternity- or sorority-based networks. If you wanted something done in some offices, it didn't hurt at all to be a Delta, let's say.)

In a world dominated by cronyism, self-congratulatory talk about "professionalism" is everywhere, as if people were trying to convince one another. It is a universal tool for the deflection of criticism. No matter what outsiders to the system say, the response can always be "*We're* the professionals. We know. They don't. We have credentials. They don't." End of discussion. Presumably, all professions claim, with varying degrees of success, autonomy on the basis of specialized knowledge. What is different here is the absence of some countervailing power to insist on something akin to professional results. The result is a situation in which people can administer failure constantly and, again, not feel like failures, protected both by the complexity of the organizational structure and by ideologies of "professionalism."

These patterns do not, according to Rogers, originate in schools as much as in the larger sociopolitical environment. Rogers distinguishes between two ideal types of bureaucracy, the authoritarian and the professional (see table 5.1, below). Either can be an efficient means to governance. The Catholic Church or certain military organizations would represent efficient, authoritarian regimes. Given the context, urban civil service bureaucracies are likely to develop into perverted versions of

Table 5.1. Models of Bureaucracy

Authoritarian Model	Professional Model
High degree of centralization (even of routine operating decisions)	Flexible centralization (to set standards and provide leadership; but with many routine and non-routine decisions decentralized)
Authoritarian leadership ("boss rule")	Professional leadership ("collegial rule")
Hierarchy (many levels, "tallness")	Limited hierarchy (few levels)
Assumed omniscience of top officials	Flexible, consultative relationships with top officials
Hierarchical, "upward" orientation of field staff, with periodic tendencies toward widespread rebellion and noncompliance	Lateral, "collegial" orientation; no problems with rebellion; internalized professional standards regulate performance
Complete discipline enforced from the top down	Colleague groups informally enforce conformity to professional standards; administrative looseness; limited emphasis on authority based on office
Responsibility owed from the bottom up	Responsibility to live up to professional standards that one has internalized as inner controls
High degree of specialization (departmentalization, parochialism; separate units function by their specialist logics; fail to be concerned with the broader organizational implications of their actions and their politics)	Limited, flexible specialization (free, open communications; little separatism and departmental chauvinism)
Recruitment and promotion practices that reinforce adherence to traditional bureaucratic codes (inbreeding)	Regular recruitment of outsiders
Fragmentation of authority and power of top administrators, despite centralization (separate power blocs corresponding to major subunits—divisions, bureaus, separate levels); each bloc is a veto group, opposing changes that threaten its position.	Consolidation of power and authority at top; extradepartmental ties result in more commitment to organization-wide goals than to personal career- and empire-building

Source: David Rogers, *110 Livingston Street,* p. 525

the authoritarian model. On educational issues, the city is fragmented by divergent loyalties of community, ethnicity, race, class, and religion, leading to a politics of stalemate in which one group can often veto the initiatives of another. "There are no bases for the crystallization of large enough interest groups to press through innovation effectively. This permits encrusted, tradition-bound institutions like the New York City Board of Education to continue unchallenged, regardless of their many inadequacies" (523). The fragmentation of city agencies means that there is less coherent planning and more unevenness and inefficiency in the distribution of services. The scarcity of resources leads to more conflict as groups fight over what crumbs there are. Subject to constant cross-pressures and conflict, city officials tend to become cautious and vacillating. Leadership gets reduced to keeping the lid on and preserving what benefits there may be for itself in the situation. With no one to enforce adherence to the institution's main mission, the organization gets bent to serve the needs of various internal constituencies.

Rogers organized much of his discussion around the antagonism of the bureaucracy toward changes of any kind. Any innovation may be politically risky, may intrude on somebody's turf, may require the cooperation of units that just don't cooperate with each other. Rogers can also help us understand why support from central office personnel can sometimes be almost as frustrating as outright opposition.

Some of the more popular reforms of the past 15 years are built on a base of values that has limitless confidence in the ability of all children to learn; treasures collaborative and collegial styles of work; respects democratic process; honors traditional progressive values, including the idea that moral and social development are as important as academic development and the idea that intellectual inquiry is important as an end in itself. There are district officials being asked to support such reforms who have never been a part of a successful educational enterprise; who are not convinced that their teachers and principals are capable of learning, let alone their students; who have been trained to think of group process in terms of deference to superiors, responding to hierarchical structures, and sticking to procedure; who have never been encouraged to think deeply about any theory of learning; and who distrust goals they can't quantify. The very categories in which district officials have been accustomed to think can be so much at variance from those outside reformers use that even when both sides are sincerely trying to work with each other, even when they have learned to use the same language, they may not be able to actually connect.

Providing teachers with coaching from someone with stronger content or pedagogical skills has been associated with improved instruction in several cities, and Chicago has made a substantial investment in coaching, which doesn't mean that district mid-level leaders understand it. Some of them still understand professional development as a pullout process in which there isn't much need for coaches. You send teachers out to be trained someplace, and then you put them back in their classrooms and they do it. One observer noted that the district people are not developmentalists—they don't have a clear picture of how adults develop competence, and thus, for example, they don't see why coaches need to have some time to talk with one another or why part of a coach's job is building relationships or why coaches need to spend so much time in a given classroom to see results. The kinds of resources that seem barely adequate for reformers may seem completely extravagant to district officials used to doing professional development for a pittance.

Chicago school reform generated several projects which meant that district officials and community activists had to try to collaborate with one another. It was a predictable clash of cultures on several fronts, including the ways in which people thought about something as fundamental as time. Board people tended to think of the workday as having well-defined limits. If they put in a couple of extra hours, it felt like a significant sacrifice. Community activists, who live in a world where meetings may *start* at 9 or 10 p.m., could not abide this attitude. They had a more visceral sense of schools as being in a state of crisis, and one doesn't respond to crisis by making a big deal over working a couple of extra hours now and then.

People who spend their careers in failing institutions can have difficulty developing professional judgment. People with little exposure to strong instructional leadership may be overly impressed by a vendor who has but a little more. People who are used to implementing programs that have no impact on the classroom may see a program which affects a few teachers positively and think that's an acceptable rate of progress. Rome wasn't built in a day, after all.

Fifteen years ago, advocates of making schools smaller were outsiders in almost every city in the nation, trying to nurture enough good small schools to capture the attention of the powers-that-be. They've done a good enough job that in many cities they now have the official blessing of the hierarchy (partly because of the support of the Gates Foundation). For many veterans of the small schools movement, this is turning out to be a case of needing to be careful what you ask for. Several cities now have parts of the central office dedicated to the nurture of small schools. A number of people in the small schools movement think they may have been better off back in the day when they had to fight to get anything from the board. The various support offices get in one another's way; they seem to be jealous of one another; it is often unclear who is responsible for what; a "yea" from one office is often matched with a "nay" from another. District people, facing their own pressures, may want to develop schools at a pace experienced reformers think unwise.

When Rogers wrote, urban superintendencies tended to be stable jobs; one got into a good position and died in it. More recently, the average tenure of a superintendent has been less than three years. The tenure of superintendents is not clearly related to the quality of the work they do. When Diana Lam became superintendent in San Antonio, 45 schools, nearly half of all schools in the district, were on the state's watch list. Four years later, she had reduced that number to 3. A year later, she was to be dismissed, apparently because of friction with her board and a local teachers' union. The widely respected Ramon Cortines was forced out of the superintendency in New York City after a series of power struggles with Mayor Rudolph Giuliani. Subsequently, conflict with the good mayor—in part, this time over his support of school vouchers—helped speed the departure of the next chancellor, Rudy Crew, who had a strong approval rating from the public, was hailed by a *New York Times Magazine* article as the last best chance for public education in the city, and who had taken personal responsibility for some of the city's worst schools and had gotten many of them on what appeared to be an upward trajectory (albeit with controversial methods). He is now in Miami, where he again seems to have the lowest-scoring schools improving (Nagourney 1997; Gewertz 2007). After initiating an ambitious set of reforms in Charlotte, North Carolina, John Murphy found himself battling both school board members and school employees, leading to his resignation (Hill, Campbell, and Harvey 2000: 7–9). Anthony Alvarado is arguably the administrator with the most convincing record of large-scale urban turnarounds. After building New York's Community District

Two into one of the country's best-documented urban success stories, he became chancellor of instruction in San Diego, which saw a steady and substantial rise in test scores under his leadership. He ran into opposition from above and below, from teachers who didn't like his reforms and from other school officials, some of whom, apparently, just didn't like his style. The 1990s brought a cohort of superintendents who were dramatically more aggressive than the ones who typified earlier eras, but even the most respected among them found it difficult to negotiate the politics of their systems.

In most cities, policy is ephemeral, changing with every shift in the superintendency. While they are in office, superintendents tend to spit out reforms at a staggering rate, as if, knowing they are not long for this world, they decide to try everything while they have a shot at it. The most important study of policy churn is Frederick M. Hess's *Spinning Wheels* (1999), which looked at five types of reforms: proposals to change the school day or the use of time within the school, curricular reforms, professional development, student evaluation, and site-based management. In three years, the 57 mostly urban districts he looked at launched an average of 12 significant initiatives, which averages a new reform every three months. The process often had an almost arbitrary character, "with one district adopting innovative reform A to replace practice B even as another district is adopting B as an innovative reform to replace practice A" (5).

This is not so irrational if we understand it as a form of symbolic action. Each new superintendent needs to establish his or her reputation, and just continuing the programs of one's predecessors is not the way to do that. Better to get some things out the door with your own name on them. Professional reputation accrues to those who appear to be dynamic and proactive, not to good stewards of other people's programs.[1] A great many other actors in the system, insulated from the daily routines of schooling and the messy details of implementing reforms, aid and abet the process. "It is quite easy for the reform advocates, academics, consultants, and state and national policymakers to slip into the habit of encouraging superintendents to move quickly and to show quick results" (44). As one might expect, in those districts where leadership is more stable and where fewer reforms are attempted, reforms seem significantly more likely to be implemented well. Such districts are not the norm, of course. Ordinarily, "the great irony of school reform," concludes Hess, "is that the sheer amount of activity impedes the ability of schools to improve" (Hess 1998: 27).

Hess notes that the middle and lower levels of the central office have interests that run contrary to those of superintendents. They value order, predictability, and the security of their positions, which tends to make them much less entrepreneurial about reforms in general but especially so about reforms that threaten their own power in some way. These they may actively attack.[2] This, of course, was a major part of what Rogers saw in New York. Rogers described a world of checkmated power, so much so that it wasn't clear who, if anyone, had the power to get things done, and an organization subverted by its own internal contradictions, many of them driven by the fact that staff were bending the organization to their own needs. That continues to accurately describe most of the urban systems that we know. It is very much a picture of pre-reform Chicago, where the perceived incompetence and wastefulness of the professional bureaucracy during the 1980s angered Chicagoans from board rooms to the housing projects, unifying diverse elements of the city in a way that made the school reform act of 1988 possible. The general incompetence of the board was not open for argument. In their 1988 year-long series on the school system, the *Chicago Tribune* revealed that nearly 6,000 students each day went without a teacher because of the difficulty of finding substitutes, a fact of which the superintendent seemed completely unaware (and which illustrates Rogers's point about the disconnect between the central office and schools, resulting in part from too many intervening layers of hierarchy). In the previous three years, at least 200 children from the northwest side of the city had graduated eighth grade and not shown up for high school. The system couldn't find them, but a local social service agency did and convinced them to re-enter school. A leaking roof might take two years to repair, often the result of overcentralization plus cronyism plus compulsive rule-following. Libraries sat empty while new books sat in warehouses, often the result of the inability of various units in the system to communicate with one another (Staff of the *Chicago Tribune* 1988: 93–94).

Districts that tried to implement school-based management during the 1980s often found themselves in conflict with central offices that were uncomfortable with the idea. Since the decentralization of Chicago's schools was a much more radical break with the normal, it was inevitable that there would be conflict between schools and central office:

It was late October 1990, and schools across Chicago still waited for workbooks, computers, and thousands of other items authorized by local school councils. The authorizations all lacked the same thing: a signature from the system's central office. The administration had assigned only three peope to review proposals that filled a row of filing cabinets. (Vander Weele 1994: 29)

Whether things of that sort represented deliberate sabotage or just general incompetence was hard to say, given the plenitude of both. In the early 1990s, when the system budget was over $2.5 billion annually, one report estimated that $78–100 million of that was being wasted. They could have saved $7 million just by instituting procedures to monitor the contractors who did building repairs and were known to regularly overcharge. They could have saved a million just by eliminating publications that no one was reading; they were paying outside vendors for printing jobs they could have done themselves; a state court determined that they could have saved 15–20 percent on the health-care contract just by doing competitive shopping. That would have saved $96 million, this at a time when students at Morgan Park High were standing up because of a shortage of desks, when Dunbar couldn't buy equipment for its auto shop and carpentry classes, when Schurz High couldn't open its afternoon preschool or start its recreational reading program, while teachers and principals knew perfectly well that, no matter how stringent the budget cuts, money continued to flow to well-connected vendors and consultants (Vander Weele: 9, 31–35). After prolonged exposure to this level of irrationality, how could teachers and principals not become cynical and angry?

The 1988 *Tribune* series on the schools offered an unflattering portrait of the system's leadership. They seemed disconnected from the lives of teachers and students, uninformed about what was going on in their own system, and reluctant to accept any responsibility for the situation. When Manfred Byrd, the then-superintendent, was confronted with some of what the *Tribune* found, he "blame[d] past leaders of the system, a lack of money, the people who write the tests, the parents and the children" and just about anyone who criticized schools, since they were planting in kids' minds the idea that school was a bad place (Staff of the *Chicago Tribune* 1988: 104). Byrd took an equally broad view of the reasons for stagnant test scores. "Either we're not working on the right things . . . or we're not using the right materials, or we haven't prepared them the right way, or the kids are not coming with the right preparation and they're not getting the support they need from the community" (102). One might have hoped that after 34 years in the system, the person in charge could have offered a little more clarity than that.

Rogers devotes considerable space to discussion of New York's racial and ethnic politics, and Byrd's career illustrates a dimension of that. Beginning as a teacher in 1954, by 1968 he had risen to become the second-most important official in the system, a career that, according to the *Tribune*, had been helped by the desire of Black organizations for Black representation in the system's leadership. He was passed over several times for the top position in favor of white candidates or a candidate from outside the system. He got the job in 1984. His qualifications were at least comparable to those of most of his predecessors—but the fact that he got it when he did owed something to the fact that Black organizations felt it was "our time" and were politically positioned to make that stick.

The cry for leadership that "looks like us" is complicated in both its causes and its consequences. In the most cynical cases, relatively privileged people of color are using the oppression of the group to generate moral capital, the clearest benefits of which are going to go to relatively privileged people, not to those they purport to represent and serve. One would be hard-pressed to make a case that the post-1960s movement of people of color into higher administrative positions has been systematically associated with better service for—or just healthier attitudes toward—low-income children. Still, this cannot be reduced to just a bourgeois hustle. Groups that have traditionally been excluded from the councils of power need multiple assurances that they now have access, and having members of the racial community in visible and important positions can help do that.

In Chicago, Paul Vallas, who is white, probably understood racial politics much better than some of the city's left-wing reformers. While reformers were meeting with other reformers, reassuring one another that Vallas was an antidemocratic, authoritarian son of a bitch, Vallas would be all over the Black and Hispanic communities, hitting every pulpit and block club, handing out his home phone number. The reformers monopolized the rhetoric of bottom-up inclusion, but Vallas was much better than most of them at actually making people feel included, as befits a child of the Cook County Democratic machine. He made people feel like *we* were going to make things better for *our* children. He created a leadership team that very much looked like the city, including some people of color who had been among his severest critics. Now did any of those people of color in visible positions actually influence major decisions? It's not at all clear that they did, but, politically, that's not the point. Political capital accrues to those who can create the appearance of inclusion. On the other hand, Thomas Payzant in Boston has presided over an impressive improvement in that city's academic performance in elementary schools (Reville 2007), from which children of color and the poor have probably been the largest beneficiaries, but the nonwhite leadership of the city has never developed a sense of partnership with him.

In Chicago, some Black and Latino activists would argue that there is not that much difference between conservative and left-liberal reformers. Both are about the preservation of white privilege. Reformers on the left may present themselves as identifying with people of color, but when one looks at who makes decisions in their organizations, one sees white people. Same old, same old. When the well-funded educational advocacy groups or whole-school reform groups have people of color on staff, their job is to be seen, to lend an air of legitimacy. Left reformers tend to be colonialists, convinced that they know what's best for the natives. They are committed to certain theories of pedagogy and school governance in a way that nonwhite activists are not. When people of color don't share those theories, haven't read the sacred texts, don't speak the approved language of reform, left reformers feel entirely justified in excluding them from real decisionmaking. In some respects, white conservatives, like those from the Democratic party machine, with their clear focus on power, are easier to deal with.

As David Rogers describes it, one could write a history of the New York public school system in terms of the evolution of ethnic politics. Irish Catholics controlled the system at one point and tried to preserve its benefits against others, including the Italians, but that later gave way to Catholics in general trying to fight off the encroachments of Jews, and when Jews were finally in the ascendancy, they ran the system in a way that made it difficult for Blacks and Puerto Ricans to enter it or move up within it. As different outgroups come to power, the old patterns repeat themselves, and they become another important reason that so many decisions get made on political rather than professional grounds. If the pattern is ancient, though, it may still be, given that urban school systems have grown more dysfunctional and urban children have fewer supports in their lives than some earlier generations, that patterns of politicizing decisionmaking—whether for reasons of racial politics or for others—are more damaging than they have been in the past; this is a more vulnerable cohort of young people.

The Last Man Standing

In the *Tribune* series, much of the leadership in Chicago comes off as a group of genial lackwits; it is hard to read it and not think that *they* are the problem. The recent history of Los Angeles is instructive in that respect. They have had a very different type of leader. Roy Romer, who became superintendent in 2000, was a three-term governor of Colorado, a successful businessman, a lawyer, and the former chair of the Democratic National Committee. Even with that background, he says that it wasn't until he came to Los Angeles, with its 750,000 children (more than 27 states), that he learned what real politics was (Miller 2001). He was taking over a system in which two-thirds of third graders read below grade level, with a dropout rate double the state average, where half of all new teachers lacked the appropriate credentials, where half the new teachers would be gone after three years, and where multiple reports had documented the dysfunction of the central office. Romer's staff estimated that maybe 40–50 percent of elementary teachers had a good grasp of how to teach math.

He had hardly unpacked before union leadership started to demonize him. The union controlled many members of the Board of Education, so Romer found himself in the absurd position of trying to supervise people who controlled some of the people who supervised him. "Every time he tried to hang tough on issues of management authority over teacher assignment or training, for example, the union would get four members on Romer's seven-member board to pull the rug out" (Miller 2001). He got himself in hot water with the mayor by refusing to put people identified by the mayor on his advisory board, so the mayor started bankrolling his own people to run for seats on the Board of Education.

The desperate overcrowding in many schools led the system to put most of its students on year-round academic schedules, a more efficient way to use the space but at the cost of losing 17 instructional days a year.

Romer wanted to launch a mammoth building program right away, but his staff told him that wasn't in the realm of the possible. From the time a site was identified to the time ground was broken might take two and a half years, and actually bringing a new building on line was likely to take a full five years.

There were the usual impediments to addressing instructional issues. His predecessor, Ramon Cortines, had started a literacy program called Open Court in kindergarten and second grade. It seemed promising, and, unlike the incoming superintendents who are quick to dismantle the works of their predecessors, Romer wanted to expand the program to grades 3–5. Well, he was told, the Open Court books for those grades were not on the state-approved list, so no state money could be used for their purchase.

Over the course of the years, the district had bargained away significant management prerogatives. The union contract gave senior teachers substantial authority over the schools, grade levels, and tracks to which they could be assigned and even the power to select some administrators.

> That meant a senior teacher could get a first-grade class where the student-teacher ratio was (by law) 20 to 1 and the kids were younger and easier to control, even if she didn't know anything about teaching reading. Other senior teachers preferred grades 3, 4, or 5 precisely because they didn't have to teach reading, which was hard. (Miller 2001: 8)

Where most systems gave the least prepared teachers to the neediest students as a matter of practice, Los Angeles raised it to the level of official policy.

Los Angeles made quite respectable progress in the six years Governor Romer was at the helm. When he left, elementary test scores were rising faster in the city than in the state as a whole, presumably due in part at least to his emphasis on standards-based instruction. He had put in place a $19.3 billion construction program, arguably the largest public works project in the country, which has led to the opening of 65 new schools, with 85 more under construction or planned to open by 2012. The high school graduation rate was among the lowest in the nation; the political wrestling among the mayor, the state board, and the local board continued; and the new payroll system he initiated turned out to be a fiasco. As soon as he left, his successor was hit with a grievance from the union over class sizes (Trotter 2007; Maxwell 2006; Blume and Rubin 2006). In the context of discussions about whether Los Angeles should join the ranks of cities who have turned their school systems over to their mayors, Michael Kirst, professor of education at Stanford University and a student of mayoral control, noted that many of the cities which have chosen that route were in such terrible condition that there wasn't much downside risk, unlike Los Angeles, he thought, where even critics concede that Romer had brought stability and leadership and improved achievement (Boghossian 2005).

Roy Romer is a far cry from the inoffensive timeservers who dominated the leadership of urban systems for decades. I suspect he did pretty much what was doable in six years in Los Angeles. Perhaps the lesson of his tenure is that when leadership is talented, determined, and well connected, it may be able to make progress, but not perform miracles. Thinking that one person is going to quickly clean up political and organizational systems that have been dysfunctional for decades is, again, to forget how multidimensional and twisted the roots of the problem are. The same is true of thinking that unions are the basic problem.

Rednecks and Bourbons

> On the first day of school, back in September, Janice I. Solkov was the star principal for Edison, the private company hired by the state to manage the 20 lowest-performing schools [in Philadelphia]. . . . But last week she told her staff she was resigning. Dr. Solkov . . . said she had been exhausted, frustrated and finally defeated by the Philadelphia system's bureaucracy, which left her without enough teachers, and entrenched union rules, which kept her from even meeting with her teachers. . . . She wanted to hold staff meetings where everyone could discuss Edison's educational vision. But the union contract did not allow it. "The union suggests creative ways of meeting with the staff, such as dismissing the students early," Dr. Solkov said. She was not willing to do that. (Rimer 2002: 25)

It is almost certainly an exaggeration to say that the Chicago Teachers Union once was "the single most powerful force in the Chicago public school system" (Staff of the *Chicago Tribune* 1988: 77), but no serious observer doubts that, prior to reform, the union was among the most significant players. They had substantial clout in the state capital, with the Cook County Democratic machine, and with the local labor movement. Over the years, they developed a comprehensive contract that regulated areas ordinarily left to the discretion of management. They established a grievance procedure so broad that almost anything could be grieved, including curricular matters, and a sick leave policy so generous as to encourage teachers to take off. In the late 1980s, Chicago teachers were taking 11 sick days a year, nearly double the national average, with most people being afflicted on either Monday or Friday. It also seemed to be especially hard to find a healthy teacher in May. During the first two weeks of May in the late 1980s, more than 400 classes typically went uncovered, compared to a year-long average of 190. During Mondays and Fridays in May, that went up to 590 uncovered classes, or nearly 18,000 students without a teacher (Staff of the *Chicago Tribune* 1988: 77–79; 97–100).

Collectively, the various unions representing school employees did a great deal to hamstring principals. Prior to the 1988 reforms, principals weren't even in charge of their lunchroom or custodial staffs. They were not supposed to have keys to their own buildings; they were not supposed to be in the building without an engineer present. Worse, the "rules for hiring, firing, transferring and evaluating teachers [were] so cumbersome that they . . . eviscerated the power of the principal to choose and assign staff" (Staff of the *Chicago Tribune* 1988: 78). So much documentation was required to remove a teacher, no matter how manifestly incompetent, that principals felt they had to make that their main job for at least a year, and even then the odds were against their being successful. Between 1983 and 1988, principals tried to dismiss 139 teachers, but 99 of them were still in a classroom in 1988 (Staff of the *Chicago Tribune* 1988: 61). Rather than take their chances with a thankless process, the most determined principals found ways to make it worthwhile for their worst teachers to move on, most notably through harassing supervision. There were some issues, though, that principals just couldn't do anything about. The union's rigid enforcement of seniority prerogatives meant that, every fall, some students had their teacher "bumped" by a more senior person, completely without regard for the performance of the teachers involved or the needs of the children.

Unions drive principals to distraction in other cities. Nationally, one study of five districts found out that largely because of union seniority rules, 40 percent of vacancies were filled by teachers over whom schools had little or no choice, many of them people principals did not want in their buildings (Levin, Mulhern, and Schunck 2005). A New York City principal found himself with 200 more students than there were lockers in the hall. He didn't think it was that large a problem. He could just put lockers in the back of some classrooms and let students visit them at the beginning and end of the day. The teachers' union stopped him, arguing that he was making the teachers in those classrooms be administrators rather than instructors while students were using the lockers. "Finally, after five weeks of offers and counteroffers, he made a deal. Assistant principals, deans and security officers would monitor the rooms between classes. In turn, the teachers agreed to overlook a contract provision that says no open classroom can be without a teacher" (Holloway 1998). The same principal had to explain to his chorus teacher that he couldn't have 48 kids in the chorus. The union contract limited class size to 34 students, and there was little flexibility about it, even when a larger class made educational sense. The solution was to add another teacher. Tragicomedy gives way to plain tragedy. The principal of New York's School for the Deaf, where sign language is the official language of instruction, ran afoul of the union when he tried to replace 35 teachers who were not proficient in it with some who were. The union maintained that tenured teachers couldn't be removed by a principal and, besides, there were other ways to teach (Holloway 2000).

In New York, too, removing teachers is extremely difficult. In the year 2000, every day about 300 teachers reported to district offices and spent the day doing nothing and getting paid for it while waiting on hearings for misconduct or incompetence. Many of them just read the paper all day. Disciplinary hearings averaged 18 months and cost the system $100,000 in salary and benefits (Hartocollis 2000), not to mention the time it cost principals. Most cases involve misconduct like using corporal punishment, calling students names, or absenteeism rather than teaching competence, presumably in part because the documentation required for the latter is so onerous that principals just cannot find the time (Hartocollis 2000).

There have been progressive impulses inside the Chicago Teachers Union. During most of the 1990s, union leadership was much less aggressive than it had been, and the 1995 reform legislation stripped the union of the right to strike. In 2001 Deborah Lynch was elected union president on a reform agenda. The previous regime had been famous, according to the *Chicago Tribune*, for union leaders driving Cadillacs and Lincolns at union expense, for giving staff and officers lush expense accounts, for six-figure salaries, and for giving themselves better health plans than they got for their membership. Lynch reportedly put an end to that and tried to shape a union that both fought for better conditions for teachers and took the lead on educational issues. She gave strong support to the union's professional development center for teachers (of which she had previously been director) and entered into a partnership with the system that involved the union taking responsibility for ten schools in danger of being closed for low performance. In 2003–04 a number of cities that had been seeing progressive union leadership saw a resurgence of more traditional unionism, Chicago among them. In 2004 Lynch narrowly lost an election to Marilyn Stewart, a representative of the old guard, openly suspicious of the idea of unions as an instrument of educational renewal. "This is a labor union, not a university," Stewart said in response to a question about the professional development center. "A lot of our union funds have been funneled to this educational wing of the union at the expense of direct services to the members." Nor was she warm to the idea of the union taking on failing schools. "It is not the union's responsibility to run Chicago public schools," Stewart said. "That's the Board of Education's problem. If the school fails, who are they going to blame? The unions" (Editors of the *Chicago Tribune* 2004).

That kind of self-serving rhetoric invites criticism, but we have to be careful about making too much of this. There is a tradition in American thinking about social problems of blaming the redneck. If we don't blame the person at the bottom for the problem, we blame the person just above that (Payne 1984). If Blacks aren't to blame for racial problems, we are prone to reducing the problem to those hateful, poor white people. If parents and children aren't responsible for failing school systems, surely it is those uncaring teachers and their mendacious unions. Teachers are the rednecks in this story, either too unpolished to present their selfishness in socially acceptable ways or too unconcerned about outside audiences. Given their visibility, their apparent lack of interest in the welfare of children, and the militant ignorance of some of their leadership, it is easy to make unions the villains of the piece (e.g., Brimelow 2003).[3] They bear their share of culpability, but we would do well to remember David Rogers's analysis: the power of unions is symptomatic of larger institutional failures that leave poor and urban children vulnerable. Given the lack of institutional protection, a single-minded organization can have far more leverage than it ordinarily would. How is it that unions in many cities have amassed enough power to be able to negate initiatives to improve the quality of teaching? In many cities, part of the answer is a history of alliance between the union and Democratic city administrations, which leaves the powers-that-be unable to check the union. In many cities, boards of education, with no money to bargain with, have to make concessions around work rules. If we had been holding politicians accountable or increasing the resource base for urban schools, unions would never have gotten out of control. As usual, the role of the rednecks obscures the role of the Bourbons.

The Bottom of the Barrel

All things considered, what's the worst system in the country? It's probably impossible to say, but it's safe to say that any list of the bottom feeders that failed to include Detroit, New Orleans, and Washington, D.C., would be flawed. They are at least contenders. It doesn't matter how many examples of malfeasance and inefficiency one has seen; it seems that these systems always have something new to teach about the causes and consequences of deep dysfunctionality. New York City, prior to its last reorganization, may not have been as bad overall, but the sheer scale of the place makes it special, too.

When Kenneth Burnley took over in Detroit in 2000, he was the seventh superintendent in eleven years. An outside review of the system found a "persistent lack of urgency about improving itself" and "a culture of complacency" (Johnston 2001). As one result, the system had a backlog of 27,000 school maintenance work-order requests, beyond anything one experienced reviewer had seen previously. Burnley supporters credit him with getting a mammoth reconstruction project underway and two consecutive years of test score improvement. Still, in July 2004, Bill Brooks, the chair of the school board, called for Burnley's resignation, noting that Burnley had gotten the system on the right track but adding that "personalities were getting in the way of moving the district forward," language that frequently means someone hasn't paid his deference dues. Brooks added, "I think we have a plan and focus that we can change leadership and not lose that," Brooks said. "Four years is a pretty good run. You can't stay but so long when you become a caretaker" (MacDonald 2004). It is not clear whether it is more depressing that someone who can stimulate signs of life in one of the country's most moribund systems could be let go for such apparently trivial reasons or that someone in a position of authority can think that four years is a "pretty good run." Still, it is a comfort to know that Detroit had a plan and a focus. Presumably, they planned to consistently have the worst graduation rate among the nation's 50 largest cities, graduating a staggeringly low 25 percent of their student body (Editorial Projects in Education 2007), much lower than other troubled districts. The next worst districts, Cleveland and Baltimore, graduate about 10 percent more than Detroit. After that, a group of districts—Dallas, New York, Miami-Dade, Los Angeles, Milwaukee, Denver, Philadelphia—are clustered between 43 percent and 49 percent. All that focus Mr. Brooks spoke of helped the city earn the reputation of being the nation's fastest-shrinking urban school system, losing more than 60,000 students since the late 1990s, 14,000 of them in the fall of 2006 alone, many of them running to charter schools as fast as they could get there (Maxwell 2007).

Then again, all things are relative. If the leadership in Detroit is more invested in their power struggles than in serving children, it's not clear they have anything on the leadership in pre-Katrina New Orleans. Tony Amato became the superintendent in February 2003; by June 2004, there was a move afoot among some members of the board of education to force him out (Gehring 2004). Apparently, they believed he had been blaming them for the system's entrenched corruption and low academic achievement and working with the state legislature behind their backs. Not to be outdone, Amato seemed to be in the process of trying to get rid of the deputy superintendent whom he had hired just several months before. The state legislature, doubtless tired of the clown show the New Orleans board had been putting on, was trying to strip the board of its powers and hand some of them to the superintendent. New Orleans was starting to look like the limiting case of leadership instability, the case where everybody fires everybody else (Thevenot 2004; TheNewOrleansChannel 2004). Amato was pushed out in the spring of 2005, amid a growing financial crisis. Reflecting on the conversations among power-brokers around Amato's leaving, Mayor Ray Nagin commented that officials and administrators had been focused on the wrong things. "I am literally grieving for the children. In all the discussions we've been having, I have not heard anyone talk about the kids. It's always about the adults" (TheNewOrleansChannel, 2005). One can only assume he was new in town.

One nice thing about New Orleans is that one does not have to waste time ferreting out corruption and mismanagement; it's just there. As soon as Amato took the job, it turned out that paychecks had been issued to more than 1,600 people who should not have been paid, according to a consultant's report, while about 2,000 ineligible people were enrolled in the district's insurance program. Meanwhile, a former manager in the insurance department agreed to testify that local contractors paid him to steer contracts for repairing fire damage to schools their way. In one case, a review of system records "found a work order to repair fire damage that was filed several days before the date of a fire at a school" (Reid 2003). Anyplace else one would suspect chicanery, but in New Orleans, it may have just been magic.

Apart from whether anyone is stealing—and they certainly have been—the schools of Washington, D.C., should just be regarded as an out-and-out criminal enterprise. When the Council of the Great City Schools was asked to analyze the system's performance, it noted: "The instructional leaders from cities across the country who worked on this report were asked a simple question when we started our review. 'Why is student achievement in the D.C. schools not improving any faster?' Our answer is also simple. 'The district hasn't done anything to improve achievement'" (Council of the Great City Schools 2004: 10). According to the report, the district simply left the most important decisions to individual schools. "In short, the D.C. school district has abdicated its leadership responsibility. . . . The result is what one sees today: no plans for improving student performance, low expectations of students, no accountability for results, haphazard instruction, incoherent programming and dismal outcomes" (10).

Paul Vance was the superintendent who requested the outside study, one of six superintendents the system had in ten years. He resigned before the report came out, citing the uncertain future of the system's governance structure. The mayor was trying to acquire greater control of the system and advocating a voucher system. Vance left honorably, but four months later, another system leader, Barbara Bullock, former head of the teachers' union, was sentenced to nine years in prison for embezzling $4.6 million from the union, much of which was apparently spent on expensive clothing and furs. She had bipolar disorder, she explained, which accounted for her shopping habits (Blair 2004).

Bipolar disorder may be traveling south. As Washington's union leader was heading to prison, the attorney for the Miami teachers' union worked out an agreement to reimburse the union for $340,000. She along with other union officials had been accused of setting up a business to provide professional development services to the system—legal, if morally questionable—and then proceeded to siphon funds from it into their own pockets (Blair 2004).

Would that the corruption were confined to the union. In 2002 the *Miami Herald* examined a decade of school board spending, identifying a pattern of questionable contracts "that enriched favored lobbyists, contractors, and former board members" (Gewertz 2002). Millions were lost on shoddy construction projects; thousands of days of construction time were squandered by poor planning or builder error or inexperienced architects. One member of an oversight board contended that the district was "completely dysfunctional" and that the school board was committed to maintaining the status quo (Reid 2003). In suggesting that financial mismanagement was predicated upon a larger set of institutional issues, he was no doubt right. When he resigned in 2003, Superintendent Merrett R. Stierheim cited the difficulties of working for a divided school board in a "politicized" culture that is "highly resistant to change" (Gewertz 2003).

If that's true of Miami, pity Washington. Michael Casserly of the Council of the Great City Schools notes that the city "has almost got too much political power in too limited a space. Lots of actors are in a position of checkmating the actions of others. And, as a consequence, things often don't get done" (Reid 2004). The superintendent had to answer to the U.S. Congress in addition to the city council, mayor, the school board, and an independent finance authority. Each level of politics brings new opportunities for cronyism, and the general instability of the system strengthened the hands of the bureaucrats who outlasted regime after regime. "Favoritism and poor performance 'just went out of control,' according to Kevin Chavous, who once headed the city council's education committee. 'Friends of friends were getting contracts and jobs. They weren't doing the job. We paid more for services than we should have. . . . Our system morphed out of control, I think, largely because of the patronage history and the tendency to view the school system as a jobs system'" (A. Witt 2007). Incompetence and graft facilitated each other. "The school system relies on paper records stacked in 200 cardboard boxes to keep track of its employees, and in some cases is five years behind in processing staff paperwork. It also lacks an accurate count of its 55,000-plus students, although it pays $900,000 to a consultant each year to keep count" (Keating and Haynes 2007). In that context, "opaque school finances allowed corrupt officials to engage in bogus business deals, take kickbacks and create phony invoices and contract with fictitious firms to raid city coffers" (A. Witt 2007).

Lawyers were on the gravy train, too, billing the system outrageous sums. When superintendent Arlene Ackerman tried to cap the amount lawyers could bill at $80 an hour, "you would have thought that I was responsible for World War III. I started getting pressure—'we don't need a cap,' 'this is not fair.'" Mayor Anthony Williams called her in to talk about it, but she resigned before the meeting. Williams admitted later that he might have caved to political pressure (A. Witt 2007).

The system finally began making progress under Clifford Janey, who began to get a handle on curriculum and instruction, probably the first time in almost 25 years any superintendent could say that. He tightened graduation requirements and increased the number of students taking AP classes by a third. The city saw modest gains in NAEP scores between 2005 and 2007 and doubled the number of students enrolling in college since 1999. In the spring of 2007, Washington joined the ranks of cities giving the mayor control of the school. Mayor Adrian Fenty, citing the need for "dramatic," "radical" change in the system's basic operations, promptly fired Janey, leading many to worry that the progress made under Janey would be lost. Michael Casserly of the Council of the Great City Schools commented, "I really regret that we're about to start all over again. The impatience of the press and the politicians is going to mean that we're likely to start reforms all over again—not necessarily better reforms, just a new set of reforms" (A. Witt 2007).

Other cities add a regional flavor to system instability, power struggles, the politics of stalemate, backstabbing, graft, financial mismanagement, and overall ineptness, but New York is still New York. To the end of its miserable days, the New York City Board of Education did little to change the perception that it led the nation in organizational dysfunction.

When a new chancellor, Joseph A. Fernandez, arrived in New York in 1990 to administer the school district, he found it was not clear who was in charge, if anyone. His office windows were dirty, so he called an engineer to clean them. Sorry, he learned, by contract the engineers cleaned windows only once a year. When he asked his secretary to order highlighting pens, he was informed delivery would take four weeks. (Tyack and Cuban 1995: 78)

New York, New York. In 2002, when the future of the board was being debated, a former aide to the system chancellor wrote that he could find little purpose for the board except "as a forum where politicians can lobby for pet projects." The board, he contended, remained a remote entity to most parents and a major obstacle to the chancellor who

> spends an inordinate amount of time catering to the petty concerns of its members when there are more important things to attend to. I used to dread Wednesdays at Livingston Street, when the board met to vote on policy recommendations put forward by the chancellor. Without the support of a majority of the board, nothing got done.

At times the discussions that occurred in the board chamber were substantive. More often they were torturous, and they demanded days of preparation. What animated school board members the most was the stuff of local politics: a building plan here, a principal's job, or a favor to a community school board there. And of course the requests from friends in the legislature were incessant (Viteritti 2002).

When the board was finally killed by the state legislature, the *New York Times* offered end-of-an-era comments:

> Like the Kremlin, to which Mayor Michael R. Bloomberg compared it yesterday, 110 Livingston Street was more than a location. . . . It symbolized a state of mind, a failed system that was at once imperious and impervious. Rudolph W. Giuliani famously called for it to be "blown up." A former president of the Board of Education once suggested pulling a fire alarm there and then locking out all the administrators. One school chancellor who worked there used to call it "the puzzle palace." (Cooper 2003: 1)

The most dysfunctional districts, the "puzzle palaces," have some important lessons to teach us that go beyond the incessant power struggles, the shameless corruption, the normalization of incompetence (so that competent people get questioned all the time), the institutional impotence when it comes to doing anything for children. Their very starkness makes it easier to see that pathological bureaucracies encourage the degradation of civic discourse and erode the capacity for collective critical thinking; at the same time, they may also literally erode the moral faculties of decisionmakers so that good and decent people either do or allow the unconscionable.

One of the disturbing things about civic conversation in the worst districts is how frequently one encounters the idea that what we have now is so bad, the bureaucracy is so terrible, that just about anything would be better. While easily understandable, it is also easy to see that the more that idea gains credence, the easier it is to sell ideas that can be packaged as new, irrespective of their actual value. Any idea that can present itself as Bold!!, Visionary!!, Revolutionary!!—that is, as different from what we now have—can get taken seriously. In Washington, Detroit, and New Orleans, that means a flight to charter schools. Elsewhere, it means a push to close old schools and reopen them as new or to get rid of as many central office personnel as possible and replace them with MBAs. Charter schools, reconstitution of schools, and reorganization of central offices can all be done well, but that is most likely to happen when they are adopted in a critical atmosphere, not when they are just embraced triumphantly as the alternative to the past. When that happens, all the bright shiny ideas can actually become ways to avoid thinking about the hard questions of instruction, of human and social capital, of school culture.

The corollary to the idea that anything new is better is the idea that anybody would be better than the people we have now, who have, after all, failed and failed miserably. The general failure of the system taints everybody associated with it, the talented along with the twits, the dedicated and hardworking along with the placekeepers. So let's look for leadership anyplace but among educators. Let's have school systems run by army generals and corporate executives and lawyers. Anybody but those educators. Let's have teacher training done without schools of education. Let's recruit young people fresh out of college to teach, completely untainted by the old system. A plausible way to think about what happened to the small schools movement is that an idea nurtured for long years by progressive educators was taken over by corporate types unwilling to listen to educators, so they repeatedly did things those educators would have advised against, and the returns from small schools were significantly less than anticipated. The broad national contempt for educators functions as a parallel to the situation of children of color intellectually stigmatized. It is a kind of collar educators have to wear. It is not the absence of social capital but the presence of a kind of negative social capital, something that has to be struggled against before the problem at hand can be addressed.

In post-Katrina New Orleans, one can see a degraded civic culture in full flower. The *Boston Globe* ran an article with the modest subtitle, "How New Orleans could end up saving public education in America" (Peyser 2007). Just listen to some of the language:

> What has happened since the disaster, however, is redefining urban public education. Instead of simply rebuilding the old district, based on the old institutions, policy leaders in New Orleans and Baton Rouge decided to start from scratch, fashioning a public education system based on new ideas and promising models of reform from around the country. From the wreckage, New Orleans is emerging as a bold experiment in what a city school system can be. For decades, reformers have been pushing to change urban public education, but have been stymied by the entrenched bureaucracies and special interests that run the schools and control the money. . . . By the end of the last school year, New Orleans was back up to 26,000 public school students and 58 schools—only five of which were operated directly by the remnants of the old district. The rest are a mixture of state-run schools and independent charter schools, all served by a variety of new, mostly nonprofit, entrepreneurial ventures. . . . Although there are plenty of serious gaps and challenges, this "un-district" is being closely watched by educators across the country as a potential model for the radical transformation of city school systems. . . . Because of their position as monopoly providers of public education, urban districts invariably become overgrown bureaucracies that manage schools through elaborate, highly politicized systems of command and control that reward compliance with district rules rather than student achievement. . . . Change can be nearly impossible because of powerful teachers' unions, which hamstring principals. . . . Outstanding teachers and principals

are driven away. . . . In New Orleans, that dead weight of politics and bureaucracy contributed to truly dismal results. Three-quarters of eighth-graders scored "below basic" on the state's reading assessment in 2004. . . . [But] the system that is emerging in New Orleans puts authority where the students are, letting principals make more of their own decisions . . . about resources, personnel, and curriculum. Instead of relying on the district as the sole provider of support services, New Orleans is developing a variety of public and private alternatives. . . . New Orleans public schools are now largely union-free. . . . A number of other innovative ideas have taken root. . . . Such a real-life, large-scale example of a totally redesigned school system, developed under extraordinarily harsh conditions, promises to transform the debate about what is possible in public education.

So on one side, we have the old, politicized, bureaucratized, entrenched special interests. On the other, we have the bold, the radical, the promising, the potentially transformative, and so on and so forth. How's that for nuance? One would never guess from this kind of breathless caricature that, in the year before the storm, the system posted its best test scores ever. Even in the worst systems there are some things that should be built upon, not jettisoned without examination. One would never guess that some of the new entrepreneurs in New Orleans are old entrepreneurs in other cities, which they entered with the same kind of bold rhetoric and left with their tails between their legs. A Philadelphia task force report that looked at some of the same groups going into New Orleans concluded that the city's experiment with multiple providers is yielding disappointing results. "There is little evidence that the substantial investment ($107 million) . . . has produced sufficient academic success to warrant continuation," according to the task force. Indeed, schools managed by outside entities had much higher rates of suspension and higher rates of both teacher and student absenteeism (Snyder 2007a).

One would never guess that the new decentralized system is already showing signs of being more deeply segregated by race and class even than the old system. Resources, human and material, are being distributed in ways that are creating vast disparities among schools, and the charter schools seem to invariably get the better side of the deal. (In the spring of 2007, state-run schools could offer $4,000 more to beginning teachers than New Orleans Parish schools; a state-run website directed prospective teachers to charter schools if they were certified and to

New Orleans Parish Schools if they were not.) Selective admissions policies are being applied in ways that keep hard-to-serve students, including special needs and low-achieving students, out of the best-resourced schools. Of the first eighteen charters to open, fourteen established selective admissions policies (Dingerson 2007). It's becoming a system of choice for some people and a system of take-what's-left for others. National organizations, including some of those that have had such a poor record of achievement in Philadelphia and elsewhere, seem to be having more influence on the process of reshaping the system than people from the city's poor neighborhoods. "There was little concern that residents of New Orleans participate in the planning and rebuilding of their school system. It was as if *anyone* connected with the New Orleans Public Schools (NOPS)—whether a teacher or an administrator, a parent, student or crossing guard—was presumed to have caused the failure of the district prior to the storm" (Dingerson 2007: 58). Many schools are building faculties around young, inexperienced teachers, who, whatever gifts they bring, are unlikely to stay very long and who are, in many cases, contractually forbidden from criticizing the schools they work in. How's that for a basis on which to rebuild a civic culture? There are idealistic impulses, both conservative and progressive, behind some of what is happening in New Orleans, but there is also opportunism and political chicanery and garden-variety racism. An atmosphere of *anything-is-better* gives free rein to whatever forces are best organized to take advantage of it, good, bad, or indifferent.

Meanwhile, in Washington, where more than 25 percent of students now attend charters, there are serious concerns about their quality. In 2005–06, 30 of 34 reporting charters failed to make Adequate Yearly Progress under No Child Left Behind, which was actually a higher rate of failure than the DC public schools (El-Amine and Glazer 2007).[4] Certainly some of these schools are going to get better with time. Nonetheless, these numbers should give pause to anyone who thinks that anything is automatically better than the old systems. Maybe, maybe not. Ohio is another case in point. The state, responding largely to public dissatisfaction with its urban schools, made it easy and profitable to start charters, and 328 of them have opened since 1998. In 2007 half of them were graded D or F; 57 percent of charters were in academic watch or emergency, compared to 43 percent of traditional public schools in urban areas. Where disgust and impatience with the old system feed an uncritical search for alternatives and an uncritical disregard for everyone associated with the past, that disgust may actually help the old system reproduce itself in new forms, adorned with new rhetoric.

If it's important to understand what pathological bureaucracies do to general organizational functioning, it may be even more important to understand what they do to the capacity for moral response. Consider Washington again. It goes without saying that the system can't figure out how to get routine repairs done, but what should we make of the fact that even dangerous repairs are routinely ignored? In the spring of 2007, the central office had on file 1,100 "urgent" or "dangerous" repair requests that had been on file an average of a year. Of the 146 schools in the system, 127 had pending requests for electrical repair, some of which involved sparks or shocks. On average, they had been pending for two years (Keating and Haynes 2007). Violations of the health code might as well have been a matter of policy. Eighty-five percent of cafeterias had violations, and one-third of them showed evidence of rodent or roach infestation in the previous three years. A college student who taught at Bruce-Monroe Elementary was "initially appalled at the mice scurrying around the cafeteria and kindergarten classroom. They are so common, she said, that students have given them names and drawn their pictures" (Keating and Haynes 2007). There is not much one can say about this. Presumably, the people in charge are going right ahead getting their piece of the action, with their snouts stuck as deeply as possible in the public feeding trough, pausing long enough to blame somebody else for whatever problems the schools have. By no means is this a resource issue. Washington spends almost $13,000 a year per student, third-highest among the 100 largest school districts. Presumably, that's enough to ensure that children can eat lunch in sanitary conditions and still leave plenty to be stolen.

This kind of irresponsibility is so disgusting that there is a danger of particularizing, of thinking that there is something different about Washington or about the leadership of urban school districts. The sociologist Robert Jackall (1980, 1983) has done a study of similar behaviors among corporate leaders. How was it possible for Ford Motor Company executives to go on selling Pintos, knowing that they were a fire hazard? How do we explain the British executives who sold thalidomide after evidence indicated that it could be the cause of birth defects? Jackall, who, like

David Rogers, writes and thinks in the tradition of Max Weber, the preeminent student of bureaucracy, argues the problem is not morally depraved individuals so much as it is everyday sorts of people who are able to bracket their everyday moralities while at work, a process abetted by several features of the bureaucratic structures within which they work. Bureaucratic culture tends to reduce all decisions to the calculable, which means everything gets reduced to a kind of cost-benefit analysis, a calculus into which moral issues cannot fit. Bureaucracies also create neutralizing vocabularies to describe their work, thereby removing the emotional content of more accurate language, but the business leaders who call price-rigging "price stabilization" or who call lung disease "a symptom complex" could learn something from the school leaders who call school closings "system renaissance." As Rogers also noted, it makes a major difference that decisionmakers are separated from the consequences of their decisions. The many layers of hierarchy that intervene between decisionmakers and those affected by their decisions are a part of this, as is task segmentation and role specialization. The latter makes it possible, for example, for an engineer about to falsify data about the safety of brakes to say, "After all, we're just drawing some curves, and what happens to them after they leave here, well, we're not responsible for that" (Jackall 1980: 9), just as teachers at every age level absolve themselves of responsibility by focusing on the responsibility of others—the parents didn't do their job, last year's teacher didn't do her job, and even if I do mine, next year's teacher won't do hers. "In a social structure where the actual and symbolic interconnectedness of human action can be denied and where the faces of victims are unseen until it is too late, if at all, almost anything becomes permissible" (Jackall 1980: 13). Similarly, the sheer scale of organizations makes individual decisionmakers feel like their contribution to the overall enterprise is inconsequential. Every executive can think that if he or she doesn't go along with the program, the boss will just find someone else who will; the end result isn't going to change. The irony is that at this level, corporate executives sound exactly like those drug dealers who maintain that if they weren't selling drugs, somebody else would be; their role is inconsequential. For corporate executives, hardened criminals, and urban youngsters generally, the feeling that what one does, does not really matter, is an invitation to socially destructive behavior. One can easily see school officials thinking it isn't going to really matter if they steer this one contract toward their friends—if they don't do it, someone else will. In the larger scale of things, it isn't going to make a bit of difference. The end result of all these people thinking that their corruption doesn't matter is that children eat lunch with mice.

If the problem in urban systems were just incompetence, we would be immeasurably better off. When you are battering your head against one of these bureaucracies, it feels like you have found the bedrock of human stupidity, but that is best regarded as part of the system's camouflage, incompetence covering corruption, the James Gang pretending to be the Three Stooges. In Greek mythology, one version of the raising of Zeus holds that he was reared by the nymph Amalthaea, who fed him the milk of one of her goats. In gratitude, the adult Zeus broke off a horn of the goat, bestowed upon it the power to produce anything its owner desired in abundance without end, and returned it to his foster-mother. This is the original Cornucopia, the Horn of Plenty. This is what the bureaucracies running urban schools have tended to become, the Cornucopia, Amalthaea's Horn, pouring out contracts, sinecures, patronage, connections, and careers in overflowing abundance. The Cornucopia should be our Fourth Heuristic.

Chapter 6

Missing the Inner Intent: The Predictable Failures of Implementation

It is only with the heart that one can see rightly; what is essential is invisible to the eye.

— Antoine de Saint-Exupéry

I will not overpromise.
I will not disrespect teachers.
I will not do anything behind the principal's back.
I will not take part in any partisan or personal feuds.
I will not equate disagreement with "resistance."
I will not put down other programs.
I will not expect change overnight.
I will take time to study the history of reforms similar to mine.
I will not try to scale up prematurely.
If I am not in the field myself, I will take seriously what field workers tell me.
I will give school people realistic estimates of how much time and money it takes to implement my program.

— School Reformers'
Pledge of Good Conduct

It would have been a good idea if, at the beginning of the 1990s, some genie could have made every school reformer in urban America take the School Reformers' Pledge of Good Conduct. The disconnect between policymakers and reformers, on the one hand, and the realities of urban schools, on the other, is especially plain when we look at the assumptions in play when reformers try to put their ideas into actual practice. Thus far, we have said that the problems of urban schools are multidimensional, intertwined, irrational, and overdetermined. The worst schools suffer from deeply rooted cultures of failure and distrust; are politically conflicted, personality-driven, and racially tense; have difficulty learning from their own experience or that of others; have difficulty communicating internally; have difficulty following through even when they achieve consensus about what to do; tend to retreat from success even when it is within reach; have shallow pools of relevant professional skill, weak professional cultures, unstable staffs; and exist in a larger institutional environment that is itself unstable and unhelpful, at best, and ordinarily, dysfunctional and corrupt.

Now if this is the context, we should just assume that most reform implementations are going to be superficial, almost of necessity. Harried leaders are going to work on this for a little while, then that for a little while, unable to give most problems meaningful attention—perhaps too busy to figure out which problems are most meaningful. Thus, school reform in the 1990s brought forth a remarkable outpouring of activity, but many schools never got past the outward structures of the reforms they were trying to implement—the committees, the meetings, the materials, the specialized vocabularies. New educational programming was constantly being erected over weak social, political, and professional scaffolding. The inner intent of reform, to use Gary Sykes's phrase (1990), is consistently missed.

The only reason all this is even worth saying is that so many efforts continue to proceed in innocence, as if implementation were just a matter of bringing good ideas and clear thinking to the benighted. Some collective learning did take place, but whether we look at some of the popular whole-school reform models—perhaps the dominant models at the beginning of the decade; or the standards-based reform movement, certainly the dominant model at the end of the decade; or some of the other comprehensive reforms devised in the late 1990s—we continue to see the same basic errors. Whether they are working with individual schools or shaping statewide policies, whether we are talking about reforms of the left or the right, there is a recurring tendency to underestimate the rigors—the toxicity, if you will—of the urban environment, and thus the modes of implementation typically employed fail to be robust enough to have a chance. Like teachers who continue to teach in ways that fail, reformers have difficulty learning from their own practice. When such programs fail, observers, knowing little about the inadequacies of the implementation, may question the principles underlying the program.

Maybe some kids can't learn, after all. Maybe resources really don't matter.[1] Poor implementation is harmful not just to the particular teachers and students who are immediately involved; it also undermines the very idea that change is possible.

Whole-School Reform

Between them, the movement for whole-school reforms and the movement for standards-based reform, including No Child Left Behind, have probably been the two most important initiatives in urban education in the last fifteen years. The popularity of whole-school (or comprehensive) reform models resulted in part from the perception that reform initiatives which addressed only a particular grade or a particular subject matter or particular students seldom led to sustained change. Since 1965, Title I, the main federal program to support compensatory education, had been used mainly to fund pullout programs for at-risk youth, which had come to be seen as ineffective. By 1994, changes in federal law meant that schools with large low-income populations could use Title I funds for school-wide programs. At the same time, increasing numbers of educators and researchers were coming to see the school rather than the individual child as the appropriate level of intervention. (And now, of course, many would argue that the district, not the school, is the right level of intervention.) Thus, a different understanding of the problem and a new revenue stream were converging.

For a while, the whole-school movement generated new models about as quickly as Baskin-Robbins produces new flavors. By the end of the 1990s, we had at least 40-plus models nationally, reflecting as wide a range of focal concerns as one could imagine. Expeditionary Learning, which grew out of the Outward Bound project, emphasizes learning expeditions, long-term projects that combine academic learning, service learning, and physical learning in an egalitarian and collaborative school culture. The Accelerated Schools Program takes the position that remedial education is not the solution for at-risk students; remediation reinforces the low expectations that are such a potent part of the problem in the first place. Disadvantaged children need enriched and accelerated instruction. The School Development Program (or, popularly, the Comer Process, after Dr. James Comer of Yale, its developer) focuses on the dysfunctional social climate in schools and on child development broadly—that is, on moral and social as well as academic development. Unlike SDP, Success for All is instructionally based, a prescriptive approach to teaching literacy; it is also supported by a substantial (if still somewhat controversial) body of research. Core Knowledge is also prescriptive but in a different sense. It focuses on curriculum content, maintaining that there is specific information at each grade level that children need to master if they are to succeed in life. (See the Program Glossary for fuller program descriptions.)

The 1990s represented a boom period for the whole-school reform movement. The School Development Program, begun in the 1960s, had at least 100 schools around the country trying to implement it by 1990; by 1994, it was 300. It has since reached 800 (Haynes and Comer 1993; Sommerfeld 1994; Comer, Haynes, Joyner, and Ben-Avie 1996). Perhaps the largest program is Success for All, developed at Johns Hopkins in 1987, which had 1,800 schools by 2004 (Viadero 2001b). Not too far behind is the Accelerated Schools model, which, since its inception in 1986, has reached 1,500 elementary and middle schools (*www.acceleratedschools.net;* Bloom et al. 2001). Talent Development, another Johns Hopkins product, this one aimed at high schools, started in a single Baltimore high school; by 2004, it was working in 43 high schools in 15 states. That may seem modest compared to the others, but given what we know about the intransigence of urban high schools, it is actually a shocking rate of growth. In 1997 the spread of whole-school reform models was further encouraged and legitimized when Congress passed the Comprehensive School Reform Demonstration Program, which supported "research-proven" reform models in around 2,000 schools (Viadero 2001b). By 2005, say, several thousand schools, representing a few million students, were implementing a whole-school reform model (and, in some unhappy cases, implementing more than one).

Calling this a "movement" should not be allowed to obscure the level of partisanship. People tend to be advocates more for their program than advocates of the idea of whole-school reform. Attempts to get partisans of different programs to cooperate with one another have a notable history of failure, partly because everyone is so wrapped up in trying to demonstrate the superiority of *their* program. We actually now have enough research that we can make some reasonable judgments about program impacts, but that is not really the point. What we should have learned by now is that much of the energy which goes into finding the One Best Model is misplaced. What matters is that too many schools haven't the capacity to implement any of them with reasonable fidelity to the intent of the reform. Over a decade, we had thousands of schools trying to implement dozens of different change models under the widest variety of political circumstances. Had enough people begun asking the right questions at the right time, the situation was made to order for learning what it took to build the capacity to implement. Instead of that, we got more years of argument around simplistic versions of the great "What Works?" question.

The most important whole-school ventures would certainly include the wholesale conversion of the Memphis school system to whole-school models, the attempt by the New American Schools program to stimulate such programs nationally, and New Jersey's court-mandated effort to provide whole-school models to all its urban districts. Together, they can teach us much about both what has been wrongheaded about the whole-school reform discussion and what has, nevertheless, been instructive about it.

In Memphis, soon after assuming the superintendency in 1992, Gerry House required that each of the city's 163 schools adopt a comprehensive reform model from a list of 18 models approved by the district. An evaluation showed a pattern of improving test scores in the restructuring schools, and Superintendent House was named National Superintendent of the Year in 1999 by the American Association of School Administrators. Shortly thereafter she left Memphis, after which scores seemed to stagnate. In yet another example of policy/leadership churn, after an investment of about six years and $12 million, House's successor, Johnnie Watson, ended the initiative. (This might be thought of as poetic justice since House had begun her superintendency by dismantling some promising projects in site-based management.) Even those schools that wanted to hold on to their models were not allowed to do so. The Memphis experiment ended to applause from the teachers' union, which had long held that the models created too much paperwork and took up too much time for the results being produced. (Which makes one wonder whether teacher attitudes, especially after House was no longer in place to push, had anything to do with undermining the reforms.)

The impression that went out across the nation was that whole-school models had failed in Memphis. Lost in that story was the fact that there had been at least three different evaluation studies, and the two which concluded that reform was working were stronger methodologically in some respects. Two of the studies, which differed in their interpretation of how much score improvement there had been, agreed that those schools which adhered more closely to the program models tended to have better student-achievement outcomes than those that did not (Viadero 2001a). That is, if you actually implement the models, they can do something. One could imagine a world in which that finding would have led the system's leadership into an examination of what they had learned, in six years, about doing high-quality implementation. It is certain that in the course of that time, some leadership had been developed, some teachers and principals had grown passionate about the models they were working on. There were forms of capital in the system that did not exist at the beginning of the experiment. Instead of trying to think about whether they could build on that, the new leadership, classically, just looks at the (ambiguous) outcomes, throws up its hands, and starts down another path.

The Memphis story was even more of a blow to advocates of whole-school reform because the decision to drop whole-school reforms came just a few months after the RAND Corporation released a report that suggested that the several reform models being distributed by the New American Schools (NAS) program were showing mixed results. NAS was an even bolder experiment than Memphis. In 1991 President George H. W. Bush had asked a group of corporate leaders to get involved with the problems of schools—anybody but educators, of course. What they developed was something of a venture-capital approach to school reform:

> The core premise of NAS was that all high-quality schools possess a unifying design that allows all staff members to perform to the best of their abilities and that integrates research-based practices into a coherent and mutually reinforcing set of effective approaches to teaching and learning for the entire school. The best way to ensure that lower-performing schools adopted successful designs was to fund design teams to develop "break the mold" school designs that could be readily adopted by communities around the nation. After developing the design, teams would go on to implement their designs in schools across the country. (Berends, Bodilly, and Kirby 2002: 168)

They charged full-steam ahead, using 1992 to select designs (from 600-plus applicants), 1992–93 to further develop the best ideas, 1993–95 to demonstrate those ideas in practice, and 1995–98 to scale up. Seven teams went through the demonstration phase and into scale-up—ATLAS, Purpose-Centered Learning, Co-nect Schools, Expeditionary Learning, Modern Red SchoolHouse, National Alliance for Restructuring Education, and Roots and Wings, the latter an outgrowth of the Success for All model. By 1995, NAS design teams were working in 550 schools, not far behind a city like Chicago.

Implementation was necessarily uneven. Two years in, half the sample sites were judged to be implementing at a satisfactory level. The quality of implementation varied across districts, models, schools, and, especially, within schools. The NAS reforms had trouble getting teacher buy-in, and they found themselves competing with other reform efforts—reform overload, as the evaluators called it. District efforts to respond to the pressures of high-stakes testing undermined many programs; some schools didn't have the funds to continue; district and union policies got in the way, as did the instability of district leadership and the troubled relations among schools, districts, and unions—the usual suspects, as it were.

What helped was leadership on the ground. High-quality assistance from design teams significantly improved implementation and overall teacher satisfaction. Similarly, principals played an important role:

> Principal leadership (e.g., communicating expectations to staff, securing critical resources for the school, talking with teachers about instruction) proved to be an important contributor to implementation across all the studies. The survey analyses indicated that teachers' views of principal leadership were the most important indicator of the implementation level achieved. The teacher survey also indicated that teacher perceptions of students and their readiness to learn were significantly related to the level of implementation. (Berends, Bodilly, and Kirby 2002: 172)

Finding that student performance improved in NAS schools faster than in their districts in only about half of the schools involved, the evaluators concluded that the program failed to produce the widespread, dramatic increases in learning that NAS had expected.

> In general then, we conclude that NAS's initial theory of action was largely underdeveloped and unspecified in terms of ensuring a successful scale-up experience. The causal chain of events leading to strong implementation and outcomes has proved to be far more complex

than that originally considered by NAS and one that remained largely outside of its control and influence. This finding is in keeping with the literature on implementation indicating the complexity of the change process. (174)

Well, saints preserve us, truly. Didn't anybody know this literature before they started flinging programs hither and yon? Is it really necessary to spend a decade and $130 million to figure out that one doesn't have a theory of action connected to this world? That said, when one discounts the sense of corporate hubris and the fetishizing of "innovation" that seem to have surrounded this project from its inception, it is far from clear that NAS was in fact a failure. The notion that one can implement a program for two years and then not only scale up, but scale up to more than 500 schools almost at once, is just delusional, even if they were not still in the process of figuring out what the designs really were, and were not juggling the different political problems presented by more than a dozen school districts, and were not still trying to figure out what kind of supports schools need and how to deliver them. If a program as innocent in conception as this can achieve positive student results in "only" half its implementations, while at the same time changing teacher beliefs about children, that is cause for celebration. (In fact, comparing the NAS schools to their districts as a whole is probably not the first comparison to be made. The first comparison should be to non-NAS schools with similar demographics.) The next question should be how to deepen implementation, and unlike studies that focus just on outcomes, the NAS evaluation has a great deal to say about that, and what they have to say captures the experience of any number of other programs. Good implementation is more likely:

- in smaller schools and in elementary schools;
- in schools where teachers do not focus on their students' lack of skills, the lack of parental support, and student discipline problems;
- where teachers have a sense of efficacy;
- where there is a stable team of consultants from the design teams who could advocate for their model, provide ongoing training and support for the whole school rather than just a few teachers, and who help schools problem-solve; and
- where there is active, engaged support from principals and consistent support from the district in financial, regulatory, and political terms.

This is not far from saying that implementation is more likely when adults have not given up on one another or the children.

As places like Memphis, San Antonio, and Miami-Dade County were getting themselves out of the whole-school reform business, the state of New Jersey leapt in with both feet flailing. In 1998 the New Jersey Supreme Court ruled that the state was underfunding urban districts and ordered substantially more support for those districts, each of which was required to offer preschool for all three- and four-year-olds; to teach all students from a standardized state curriculum, reduce class size, and expand social-service supports; and to introduce school management teams and school-based budgeting and have every low-performing school adopt a state-approved (and "research-based") model of comprehensive reform. These 28 (now 31) districts were known as "Abbott" districts after the *Abbott v. Burke* funding equity lawsuit, and collectively they represented over 400 schools with 300,000 students. The models from which they could choose included Accelerated Schools, America's Choice, the Comer School Development Program, Community for Learning / Adaptive Learning Environment Model, Co-nect, and Success for All. The financial resources made available were not trivial. In 2006 Newark was spending $19,000 per pupil per year. On average, Abbott districts were spending $2,500 more per child than well-to-do suburban districts. Trenton now spends about $14,000 per pupil per year, which is actually a thousand or so more than some of the state's wealthy school districts (Fessenden 2006).

The court ruled in May of 1998; that fall, 72 schools started their partnerships—sort of. Rumor has it that the person who decided that 72 presumably low-capacity schools could be adequately prepared to start whole-school reform in four months is the same person who told the NAS movement that they could scale up after two years of demonstration and the same person who told the city of Memphis that it could simultaneously supervise 18 different reform models. In any case, it would have been amazing had these schools not run into implementation problems. After two years, a study reported that many Abbott schools were bedeviled by:

- inadequate support from the program developer;
- inadequate support from the state department of education;
- burdensome paperwork; and
- staff turnover in both the department of education and among the model providers.

In some schools, by the third year of implementation, only 10 percent of the original faculty was still in place (Erlichson and Goertz 2001).

All this was taking place in an atmosphere of considerable teacher skepticism. Two years into implementation—by which time teachers should be pretty familiar with the model and the people implementing it—only 48 percent of respondents in the first wave of schools believed their respective models were good for their schools. For schools that started the second year, that figure rose to 59 percent, presumably a reflection of lessons learned the first year and the longer lead time for planning. Nevertheless, even the second time around, substantial numbers of teachers continued to have doubts about the model, which almost certainly affected how faithfully they replicated it. Moreover, we know that some of the whole-school reform providers made significant compromises with the quality of their staff in order to scale up, and teacher resistance in a number of cases has been fierce (to the point of teachers walking out of training sessions).

Despite the rough start, a fair amount of progress has been made. Between 1999 and 2002 Abbott students improved 24 points on the state Elementary School Proficiency Assessment, compared to a 15-point gain from non-Abbott students. As has been the case in Chicago, some of the strongest results have been among the previously lowest-scoring students. In 1999, 66 percent of Abbott students scored in the state's lowest-proficiency category (compared with 30 percent of non-Abbott students). By 2002, that number had been reduced to 30 percent (Erlichson and Slavin n.d.; also Davis 2003; Mooney 2003). In fourth grade, language arts proficiency went up from under 30 percent in 1999 to over 66 percent in 2005. Test scores in Abbott districts are now improving more rapidly than those in the rest of the state. Improvement across districts is extremely variable, with some of the highest-spending districts having the least to show for it. Even in the improving districts, improvement seems concentrated in the lower grades. The preschool program seems to have been more consistently well implemented, and there seems to be no doubt that the Abbott districts are sending students into kindergarten with better preparation (Gewertz 2006; Hu 2006). Unfortunately, this is probably not a stable situation. The program has become the center of a political firestorm, amid allegations of inefficiency and waste—some of them almost certainly true—and growing resentment that 23 percent of the state's schoolchildren are getting 57 percent of state educational funding (Davis 2003; Gewertz 2006; Fessenden and Hu 2007). Even funding for the preschool component may be in jeopardy.

Whole-school reforms have been among the most controversial components of Abbott, but some observers credit them for part of the progress that has been made. James Lytle, former superintendent of Trenton's schools, has written an article that responds directly to those who question the value of whole-school reform. When he wrote it, Trenton had been working for four years with seven models, usually at a cost between $50–70,000 per school annually. Lytle makes it clear that working effectively with model developers is almost a job in itself. They tend to be disinterested in practitioner knowledge, they frequently fail to appreciate the range of demands on teachers and principals, they often fail to keep the central office adequately informed, and the consultant services they offer are inconsistent in their quality. In New Jersey, part of the problem was that many model developers did not have the internal capacity to rapidly expand their support capacities when faced with the opportunities that Abbott brought. This is a crucial issue, since "We have found that successful implementation is at least as dependent on the quality of the consultant as it is on the design of the model" (2002: 166). Lytle's experience has been that none of the programs is as comprehensive as they think they are; all of them need to be supplemented in some way. Moreover:

> In our experience, developers are often overly attached to their models, overly concerned about implementation "purity," and not adequately respectful of the need for mutual adaptation in successful program implementation. Further, several developers we work with seem slow to learn from the experience of implementation . . . and don't give sufficient consideration to local context. (166)

That thorough and trenchant critique notwithstanding, Lytle remains strongly committed to working with the national reform models, not because they are the answer but because they can help organize the search for answers. They give him a kind of natural experiment, a chance to learn from different approaches to the problem and to identify the program elements that matter most. "For example, with Success for All, the process of reviewing student performance at eight-week intervals and reformulating instruction based on this analysis might conceivably be a more important element of the program design than the reading materials" (165).

For us the benefits of being involved in whole-school reform extend well beyond learning and implementing the model. For the first time our teachers are engaged in national and regional networks of practitioners. . . . Their conversations with colleagues from across the country have helped them become less parochial and more open to change. . . . We have become much more focused on student performance and on evidence. . . . Our teachers have accepted leadership roles in improving instruction, in part because most of the models require teacher facilitators who provide collegial coaching and support. (165)

Lytle's approach may be the most strategically sensible way to think about the role of whole-school reforms in the future—they can be tools for increasing district capacity rather than vehicles for raising test scores in individual schools. Urban districts must get better about supporting instruction, but that isn't going to happen overnight. In the interim, in districts that are capable of forming real partnerships, whole-school models can help schools refocus on the work and begin rebuilding their human, social, and organizational capital. At the same time, Superintendent Lytle's criticisms of reform organizations, which have been echoed across the country, suggest that these organizations need grounding in the life of districts to keep them from drifting into self-absorption.

Nationally, we have a growing body of evidence about the possible effects of whole-school models. In one of the more authoritative impact studies, Borman and his colleagues (2002) reanalyzed 232 studies of 29 comprehensive school-reform (CSR) programs and found that the overall effects are "statistically significant, meaningful and appear to be greater than the effects of other interventions that have been designed to serve similar purposes." Students in CSR schools consistently outscored students in control schools (Borman et al.: 34). The data also suggest that the best rewards come to those who wait. They found a relatively strong initial effect and a slight dip the next few years. After the fifth year, effects began to increase substantially. "Schools that had implemented CSR models for five years showed achievement advantages that were nearly twice those found for CSR schools in general" (27). After seven years, effect sizes were two and a half times greater. One suspects, of course, that schools with the building-level leadership and the political capital to stick with a program for seven years are relatively unusual.

Just how unfortunate that is is made clear by another recent study that essentially replicates Borman and his colleagues. The American Institutes of Research looked at 650 elementary and middle schools, half of them implementing one of eight whole-school models and the other half without any prepackaged program for whole-school improvement (Viadero 2007). As it happened, though, the schools that were not formally implementing a reform model were often implementing program elements similar to those advocated by the whole-school reform models. This may mean that certain ways of improving schools, including some ideas that were once pretty much the preserve of certain reform groups—data-driven decisionmaking, professional learning communities, instructional teams, close monitoring of instruction—have simply become pervasive.

The major finding is that while the schools with reform models and those without look pretty much the same in terms of achievement for the first couple of years, they begin to differentiate after the third year. Between the third and fifth years, those schools with reform models that continue to implement them with fidelity begin to do significantly better. Success for All produced the strongest academic gains, and more of its schools implemented faithfully over time. ATLAS and Accelerated Schools produced the strongest gains in collegiality, instructional collaboration, and developing a shared sense of school mission, all of which might have important long-term payoffs.

To consider another example, the America's Choice model has served over 500 schools. In an evaluation of their work in Rochester, New York, where over half the schools were using the model, the Consortium for Policy Research in Education found students in America's Choice schools learning 17 percent more in grades 4–8, 26 percent more in math, even though the America's Choice schools had larger numbers of disadvantaged students. The program reduced achievement gaps between white and nonwhite students and had its strongest effects on bottom-quartile students (Supovitz, May, and Perda 2004).

The evidence accumulates, then, that whole-school models done with fidelity and sustained over time can have significant positive effects. Unfortunately, if not surprisingly, the evidence accumulates too late in some respects. The Comprehensive School Reform Demonstration program, which provided funding for whole-school reforms, was allowed to die a quiet death in 2006; that is, no new grants were awarded. At least part of the problem seems to be that the whole-school reforms don't do enough fast enough in the current political climate.

The literature on whole-school reform effects would be even more useful if we had a comparably strong literature on the likelihood of being able to implement a given program in the first place. Right now, we can only make rough guesses about the success rate of different models, but the little we do know is suggestive. Ted Sizer of the Coalition of Essential Schools says that his biggest disappointment is the small number of schools that have broken through. Gibboney (1994), a sympathetic observer, isn't sure that by 1993 any of the coalition's schools had achieved thorough, whole-school reform, despite many cases of excellent work in some parts of the school. His standards may be too stringent, but Sarason (1996) comes to essentially the same conclusion, partly on the basis of the detailed ethnographic work of Muncey and McQuillen (1996), who note that all the change efforts they studied contributed to "increased political contentiousness within faculties and between teachers and administrators." Given the literature we have right now, it's not clear that even 10 percent of the coalition's implementations in urban areas during the 1990s produced sustained change in schools by any of the usual measures.[2]

As originally conceived, the Essential Schools model may have been an especially difficult model for dysfunctional schools. On the one hand, urban schools in the coalition have adopted some good policies—lower teacher-student ratios, more reading and writing requirements, more active learning activities, and generally higher standards. On the other, the coalition has traditionally not had a clear model of implementation. Gibboney (1994) thinks the major weakness in the coalition's approach is that "it severely underestimates the quality and depth of supportive education that teachers, administrators, school board members, and key community leaders require to mount and sustain their fundamental reform initiative"; the support offered is "too thin and too superficial" (68, 70; see also Sarason 1998: 100). The lack of a support structure was deliberate to some degree. According to Muncey and McQuillen, "the Coalition central staff does not offer member schools a model or even a starting point for change but rather emphasizes local control and autonomy" (8). While it is easy to appreciate the philosophical basis for that position, in the inner city it can be an invitation to disaster. Some schools have enough leadership talent and other infrastructure to make something out of the vision, but in general one would think that bottom-tier schools need a great deal more support in the early stages, and without it, even if they start moving in positive directions, they are especially likely to founder. In the late 1990s, the coalition reexamined its implementation style and began putting more emphasis on making a "coach" available to schools and providing other implementation supports.

James Comer (1997) has expressed some frustration with the fact that, in his opinion, after three years, typically "only" a third of the schools he works with are demonstrating significant gains. As compared to the coalition, the Comer program has a fairly clear implementation process. The facilitator gives it an on-site person with a deep understanding of the program who can help problem-solve. In some districts, facilitators clearly speak with the authority of the district superintendent, giving them substantial leverage. In the early phases of implementation, much of their problem-solving has to do with social and political issues. There is also the team structure—a leadership team, a parent team, a team for the delivery of social services—with pretty elaborate guidelines for how teams ought to operate and a series of New Haven–based trainings for building and district leaders. They offer some follow-up support nationally, but that is clearly one of the weaker areas of implementation, and the program has begun working out a series of partnerships with universities under which the universities will be able to offer some of that support. The curriculum component is still evolving. The mode of implementation is not static, but there is a clear framework of implementation in place.

Other programs go well beyond a general framework. Early childhood reading programs—Reading Recovery, Reading One-to-One, Success for All—seem to be among the most replicable programs we have, and some of them have very precisely articulated implementation procedures. Success for All (Madden et al. 1993; Slavin et al. 1995; Progrow 1998), for example, has its own reading curriculum featuring both phonics and literature-based instruction along with cooperative learning. Student progress is assessed frequently. Weaker readers have tutors, certified teachers given additional training by the program. There is an ongoing staff-development program that conforms in some respects to what we know about good development. A family support team offers parenting education programs, tries to get parents more involved in school, and helps solve problems concerning individual students. All this is overseen by a facilitator who is at least half-time, who supports teachers, coordinates the various program components, and generally troubleshoots. If early versions of Essential Schools represent one end of the implementation spectrum, Success for All represents the opposite end. The program comes with curriculum, pedagogy, new staff roles, professional development, social supports, and lots of troubleshooting capacity. It imports so much infrastructure of its own that the organizational and cultural weaknesses of schools should matter less.[3]

The best guesstimate that we can make is that for most of the 1990s, any program that had a 30–50 percent hit rate was probably at the upper end of the distribution, and that's leaving out the issue of long-term effects. There are bits and pieces to suggest that the rate may have improved later in the decade as programs learned—slowly, as Dr. Lytle notes—from experience and beefed up the way they supported implementation.[4]

An optimistic reading of the whole-school movement over the last fifteen years might go something like this: In a world where it looks like everything has to be tackled at once, reform models can give schools a reasonable number of focal points to concentrate on. An encouraging variety of whole-school approaches can work, if we actually implement them, which is largely a matter of the quality of the follow-up support and the quality of the leadership at the building level. It also helps greatly if the district is at least symbolically supportive. Under optimal conditions, we may have an even chance of implementing a given program. At a cost roughly equal to adding one and a half to two professional staff positions to the school, programs can show measurable results in two to three years, but the strongest results are likely to show up in the third through the seventh year or beyond. We should plan on schools getting at least five years of substantial support, and much of this support should be focused on developing long-term capacity, which includes changing negative teacher beliefs. Previously lowest-achieving students are likely to be the largest benefactors of change. Rough going in the early years does not necessarily preclude an ultimately successful implementation. We have good reason to think that as we improve program implementation, positive effects should be stronger and should be achieved sooner.

A pessimistic reading would just dismiss all of that. Might be true, might not. It misses the point. From a pessimistic viewpoint, this has too frequently been a history in which programs have been oversold and under-thought-out, adopted with exaggerated hopes, expanded at unrealistic rates, and then jettisoned for reasons as specious as the ones for which they were adopted. The politics which drove that process are still operative, now strengthened by top-down government mandates. Just as we are learning to do whole-school reform reasonably well, No Child Left Behind, for example, is likely to encourage the weakest schools to adopt quick-fix solutions that are likely to dead-end, taking us back to where we started.

The Standards-Based Movement

The 1990s saw several different approaches to the idea of "systemic" reform. A word of caution here: Anytime anyone in this discourse invokes the magic word *systemic*, the wise will gesture as if to ward off evil; garlic has been known to help. If the word means anything in these conversations, it seems to mean "Let's pretend to do on a grand scale what we have no idea how to do on a small scale." Some uses of the term have been more thoughtful than others, of course. For many, the standards-based reform movement, the most influential policy approach of the last ten years, represents the maturation of the discussion about how to approach schools as systems, a summing up of decades of experience.

The idea behind standards-based reform is that if states or localities set high standards for curricula; develop assessments that measure student performance against the standards; give schools the flexibility they need to change curriculum, instruction, and school organization to enable their students to meet the standards; and hold schools strictly accountable for the outcomes, then student achievement should rise. Accountability may mean that schools will be publicly evaluated and ranked, they may be reconstituted, or students may find themselves unable to graduate. The idea is to institutionalize high expectations for everyone, motivate teachers without stifling their professional discretion, and create tools for administrators that will let them know more about what is going on instructionally in their buildings. Standards signal the end of laissez-faire curricula and do something of an end run around the problem of weak instructional leadership at the building level. To the extent that states or districts provide clearer goals, it should be easier for building-level leaders to mobilize their resources around them.

Sensible as most of this sounds, putting it into place can be more than a notion. In 1996 the Pew Charitable Trusts funded seven districts around the country, all of them serving largely low-income populations (San Diego; Christina, Delaware; Community District 2 in New York

City; Fayette County, Kentucky; Pittsburgh; Portland; and Yonkers, New York) in support of their efforts to implement standards-based reform. In their evaluation of the project, Jane David and Patrick Shields (2001) concluded that the theory behind standards-based reform did not stand up well against the realities of low-performing school districts. In addition to the usual environmental turbulence—changes in top leadership, shifts in state policy—just creating appropriate assessments frequently proved more difficult than expected, partly because the process became politicized, with different constituencies pushing their own priorities. Accountability did motivate educators, but it motivated them to avoid sanctions by raising test scores, "which typically results in less ambitious teaching, especially for low-performing students. Only when the assessments encourage more ambitious teaching—for example, by asking for written arguments or applications of knowledge—did we find teachers attempting changes beyond practicing test-like multiple-choice items" (ii). Deeper district-wide changes in instruction happened when district leadership gave teachers not just standards of what students should learn but also a clear sense of what effective instruction looks like, supported by intensive professional development and ongoing support for implementing it. Providing extensive support for improved teaching, however, required major shifts in budgets and staffing, shifts that would move more of the available resources to previously low-achieving children. The financial and political ramifications of such shifts were hardly comfortable for district leaders.

All other problems were complicated by the hard rock of teacher belief. First, teachers tended to see the reforms as yet another in a long line of "here-today, gone and forgotten tomorrow" policy changes. Above all, "Promoting teaching practices designed to help *all* students reach ambitious standards runs counter to widely held shared beliefs about the nature of learning and about the abilities of many students, especially poor and minority students" (i). Two other observers, Charles Thompson and John Zeuli, make the same point:

> The alignment of curricular materials, assessment, accountability systems, teacher education requirements, initial and continuing teacher licensure requirements, and other system components may reduce impediments to reform, send a coherent message supporting reform, cre-

ate incentives for reform, and make available some useful tools for reformed practice, but even if it could be achieved and sustained, such
alignment by itself cannot change teachers' fundamental ideas about
subject matter, teaching and learning. (1999: 366)

It is not that standards have not made a contribution. If all the movement had done was move us away from the laissez-faire curriculum and
laissez-faire attitude that traditionally dominated urban systems, that
would have been a significant help. I would agree with those who attri-
bute some of the recent national progress in test scores, including some
small progress on the NAEP for urban districts (Cavanagh 2007), to the
standards movement, as well as some of the more substantial progress
made by cities like Philadelphia. David and Shields note some promising developments, including the use of more class-based diagnostics,
more support for principals as instructional leaders, more professional
development for teachers, increased attention to data in school planning,
attempts to provide more instructional time, and more challenging instruction for the weakest students.

Still, this has been more difficult than many of its proponents expected. Many of the models produced by the whole-school reform movement—certainly, the Algebra Project, the Coalition of Essential Schools,
the Comer Project, Expeditionary Learning—are in the tradition of the
Progressive movement; the standards-based movement is generally seen
as a program of the right. The standards movement reflects some of the
traditional preoccupations of the right, at least in its faith in centralization and standardization. Nevertheless, when it comes to underestimating the salience of teacher belief, underestimating the importance of
sustained and intensive intervention into the teaching process, and misunderstanding the resources needed to support change, programs evolving from these very different roots make similar errors, a blindness more
fundamental than ideology.

Scaling Up Failure

A listing of some of the most common errors made in program implementation might yield something like figure 6.1. Most of these points
have already been illustrated, but a few deserve further elaboration:

Figure 6.1. Impediments to Program Implementation

- Tendency to discount the social, political environment
- Lack of time, including time for training, for planning, for reflection, for key people to exchange information in a timely fashion; competing time demands made by different programs
- Inappropriate pace and scale of change; tendency to try to do too much too quickly
- Not enough leadership; tendency for everything to fall on the principal and the faithful few
- Narrow base of support; lack of ownership / false buy-in
- Generalized belief in program failure; tendency of teachers to comply in a minimal way
- Absence of realistic assessment, consequent inability to make midcourse corrections; tension between desire not to hurt anyone's feelings and honest assessment
- Ambiguity of roles introduced by new programs
- Leadership's lack of deep understanding of particular innovations; lack of comparative knowledge regarding innovations
- Instability of key personnel
- Interference / lack of support from district offices
- Lack of program coherence
- Absence of follow-through

When people who have led a reform effort are asked what they would do differently given the chance, perhaps the single most common answer in my experience is "Take more time." Not more money, not more administrative support, not different teachers—although all of those come up—but more time: time for professional development, time for key relationships to develop, time to change teacher belief, time for midcourse assessment. According to Ken Rolling, director of the Chicago Annenberg Challenge, which worked with over 200 schools, "Whenever the Chicago Annenberg Challenge partners discuss their plans, the first reaction from teachers is always, 'We don't have time to learn, plan and assist each other.' Lack of adequate—even minimal—time is the number one barrier facing teachers who want to learn and improve their teaching" (Smith 1998: 14). James Lytle, who has worked with several reform models in Trenton, notes:

Some models are unrealistic about the time requirements for implementation. If a school uses Success for All and its related components, Roots & Wings and World Lab, there isn't enough time left in the day for art, physical education, or world languages. Modern Red SchoolHouse requires an enormous amount of teacher time to work on curriculum articulation. Some models deal primarily with instructional design and give little attention to curriculum; other models give extensive attention to curriculum and very little to classroom instruction. (Lytle 2002: 166)

It is left to building leaders to find time to address whatever important issues the models leave out. Of course, some districts still expect teachers to donate the time for professional development, always a morale booster.

Perhaps the safest generalization one can make about urban schools or school districts is that most of them are trying to do too much too fast, initiating programs on the basis of what's needed rather than on the basis of what they are capable of. During the 1990s the National Science Foundation launched several waves of "systemic" initiatives intended to transform science and math teaching in this country. They didn't quite do that, as it turned out, and in retrospect, it might have been wiser to choose, say, one city and try to have real impact there before going nationwide. Being "systemic" at the local level is challenge enough right now. One of the consequences of the early round of school reform in Chicago was the creation of a much more entrepreneurial attitude among principals, which frequently led to them bringing in programs at a pace that made no sense for their level of organizational development. It was not at all remarkable for a school with no track record of successful implementation to be trying to implement three or four new instructional programs simultaneously. The worst such schools came to be known as "Christmas tree" schools, adorning themselves with program after program (Bryk et al. 1993).

One of the problems at the local level is that the foundation community frequently beats the drums for scaling up quickly. In Chicago, foundation executives used to say they had to see some bang for their buck. The more schools you had in your program, the happier they were. Rapid growth became a kind of interim proxy for success. When Dr. Comer, with 25 years of experience behind him, decided to bring the School Development Program to Chicago, he wanted to start in two schools and to delay expansion until he saw how those schools did. Local foundations, unburdened by experience, wanted him to start in 16. The compromise reached was that the program started with four schools the first year and added four more the second year, and even that proved to be too many. They were moving into new schools before they completely had a handle on what was going on in their old ones. Similarly, the Coalition of Essential Schools made a decision to expand rapidly because they found that foundations would only take them seriously if they were growing (Muncey and McQuillen 1996: 9–12).

The continuing tendency to push the pace, to start scaling up half-implemented programs, tells us that the absence of social capital in urban schools is still not adequately appreciated by decisionmakers. In bottom-tier schools, the first year or two of any new initiative may be more about rebuilding the social infrastructure than about them actually implementing anything. Even those leaders who do understand such needs come under a variety of political pressures that may force them to move more rapidly than they would like. Within a few years of its founding, the Chicago Annenberg Challenge was funding 220 schools, a much larger number than it could have an impact on. Part of what drove the process was a politics of fair distribution. If schools supported by this community organization got funds, then schools supported by *that* organization had to be funded. If a Latino neighborhood got funded, a Black neighborhood had to be funded, and so on. This point should give pause to proponents of fixing urban schools by vesting essential control in the mayor's office. The fragmentation of power in urban systems has to be addressed, but doing so by just abdicating to mayors is to put everything in the hands of those who, typically, know least about the life of classrooms and are likely to add to the bigger-faster-sooner clamor. Political leaders typically want to convey an appearance of bold, aggressive leadership, and, with an eye ever on the next election, they are under pressure to appear to be doing something for all their various constituencies, pressure they are likely to pass on to educators.

To the list of villains pressuring schools to do too much too soon we can add parents. Where parents are positioned to affect school programming, they are likely to be on the fast-growth side. Good programs may take time to develop, but time is something their children don't have. If parents learn of something that sounds good, they want their children to have it *now*. Even educators who are willing to resist hurry-up pressures from other sources find it hard not to respond to moral urgency from parents or community groups.

It is not clear what long-term impact the rapid expansion of various reform initiatives in the 1990s had on the quality of their work. Even when they have adequate resources, it can be difficult to find the quality of personnel needed. This was clearly a problem in the early years of the Abbott districts in New Jersey. Similarly, the small schools movement has been driven largely by concern with relationship issues, but as the movement has grown into the nation's primary tool for the reformation of urban high schools, we may be running out of the teachers who function well in that kind of environment.

In the larger whole-school reform organizations, a split often develops between field staff and national staff, with field people feeling overwhelmed each and every day and likely to understand talk of expansion as a sign of lunacy, while national staff are positioned to better appreciate the strategic advantages of growth and may be tempted to write off the cautious attitude of those in the field as the usual griping from people who can't see the big picture. Tensions of these sorts were very evident in the early years of the Abbott districts in New Jersey.[5]

On these issues of pace and scale, we should probably be speaking out of both sides of our mouths, trying to respect both the complexity of the problem and its urgency. We should advise schools and districts to implement carefully and cautiously, assuming that there are always more alligators in the swamp than the ones you can see. At the same time, we must recognize that this just isn't always going to be practicable. Between the pressures of moral urgency and those of political expediency, many systems are just not going to be able to resist the temptations to try to do everything at once. Thus, like it or not, part of the task is going to be helping school systems figure out how it is possible to move quickly on multiple fronts without shooting oneself in the foot while proclaiming victory.

Along with the issues of pace and scale, the issue of teacher buy-in is among the most difficult to negotiate. There is no real disagreement on its importance and desirability. Generalized belief in program failure means that teachers have already bought out of everything, even before they encounter it. Some programs—the Algebra Project, Accelerated Schools—require that teachers vote before the programs come into a school. That doesn't always work, though. A few strong personalities may unduly influence the voting, or the principal may twist arms or teachers may agree in good faith to a program only to learn that they had no idea what they were getting themselves into. A traditional math teacher may get very excited about training in inquiry-based math but not be able to really understand what the transition entails until he or she has tried it for a substantial period of time. Bob Moses of the Algebra Project thinks that it takes a year of trying it before a teacher can make an informed decision. As a part of that process, it is very useful for teachers about to implement a new program to have substantial contact—preferably including classroom visits—with other teachers who have implemented the same program. In practice, urban principals rarely have the resources, including the substitute teacher support, to make this practical, so teachers continue trying to implement programs that they understand primarily through the presentations of the program's developers.

In their metanalysis of comprehensive school reforms, Borman and colleagues found that whether a program requires a majority of the faculty to vote in favor of it is *not* associated with better student outcomes (36). We know from other research that teachers and principals adopting reforms often feel uninformed and that the decisionmaking process is rushed (Datnow, Hubbard, and Mehan 2002: 21). The New American Schools evaluation found that those schools which went through a well-informed choice process reported higher levels of implementation than those that either felt forced to accept a design or felt that they did not initially understand the design (Berends, Bodilly, and Kirby 2002: 172). Their data also confirm the commonsense notion that genuine teacher buy-in is in fact related to higher levels of implementation.

This poses a dilemma for leadership in the most demoralized schools, where there may not be much possibility of getting buy-in, since teachers have decided in advance that all programs will fail. If buy-in is made an absolute requirement, these schools are left out. Perhaps all the leadership can do in these situations is build as much support as possible before a choice is made but treat building additional support as a priority even after implementation has begun.[6]

During the implementation process, shifts in key personnel can undermine promising initiatives. One of the ironies of success is that it makes the people who are associated with it more marketable than they had been previously. After he became CEO of Chicago schools in 2001,

Arne Duncan started appointing principals who had had some success in tough schools to some of the most important positions in his administration. Leaving aside the issue of whether having been a principal adequately prepares one for citywide responsibility, this sends a wonderful message. Moving ahead in the system was now going to mean demonstrating the capacity to do something for children; cronyism, butt-kissing, and time-serving were no longer good enough. Nevertheless, it turned out that some of the schools those principals left were not yet strong enough to stand without their leader. Test scores fell off immediately.

Lack of time, the hurried pace of change, the absence of assessment, false buy-in or no buy-in, and the ambiguity of some of the new roles introduced into school by reforms (what exactly is an instructional coach? what's a facilitator?) all contribute to one of the most important characteristics of bottom-tier schools: their inability to follow through. A school will set clear priorities at the beginning of the year and then never talk about them again after December; the priorities get lost in the daily shuffle, pushed aside by crisis or by new initiatives. In the early years of school reform in Chicago, a number of schools decided they would have children wear uniforms, but having decided it, had difficulty actually getting that done. The idea of uniforms was normally met with considerable enthusiasm by parents, teachers, and administrators. It's a policy that requires no extra resources and no professional skill. It doesn't challenge the core beliefs of any important constituency. It does require that the adults in a school-community be able to collectively follow through on something they've agreed to. The fact that something that appears to be so simple to do turns out to be difficult for some schools underscores how little implementation capacity they have.

When troubled schools do manage to put something worthwhile in place, we have to worry about how long they will be able to hang on to it. The Chicago Comer program learned that even when schools develop high-functioning teams, they may not be able to sustain them, often because of personnel changes. Other schools found that teachers who experience success with a given instructional program do not necessarily want to go back to that program the next year. The Coalition for Essential Schools has found that even when teachers have invested a great deal of effort into transforming their teaching style, "by the third, fourth or fifth year a lot of teachers slowly started reverting back to their traditional ways of teaching." They also find their efforts undermined by high turnover among administrators (Viadero 1994). Dr. Comer feels that at least a third of Comer schools make gains but then have difficulty sustaining them (see also Muncey and McQuillen 1996; and Payne 1984: 59–67). We have a very adequate basis for expecting that our toughest schools will have as much trouble sustaining successful initiatives as they do establishing them. Reformers typically expect that once teachers have had some success using new methods, they will buy into those methods. We will revisit this in the next chapter, but it certainly looks naïve. If schools continue to improve, positive synergies may develop at some point, but they take longer than most of us suppose. These schools have been failing for so long that little bits and pieces of success don't immediately take root. The law in bottom-tier schools is that what it takes to get you there won't necessarily keep you there.

The difficulties of sustaining positive momentum once it has been achieved remind us again that a great many inner-city schools are trying to do too much at once. Such schools would do well to heed the admonition of Essential Schools—to do less but to do it better. The current political climate, of course, and the multiple needs of students encourage the opposite; principals are being pushed into more and more frenetic behavior. We noted earlier that in their very important study of the coherence of schools' instructional programs, Newmann and his colleagues (2001) find that, over a three-year period, schools that increased their instructional coherence achieved test scores that were almost one-fifth of a year of learning higher than when they began. Schools cannot achieve coherence if they are trying to do everything at once. Yet the authors note principals often feel they must do just that: "Even when principals recognize that their teachers are stretched in too many directions, they seem unable to cut programs, believing strongly that they need all of these extra resources to help the children" (10). Mess up for good reason, mess up for bad; the consequences are going to be the same. As great as the needs are, as understandable as it is for school leaders to want to fix everything at once, nothing we know about bottom-tier schools suggests that doing a lot of good things superficially is likely to have real impact on the lives of children or teachers. To implement in the ghetto, you have to come strong, as kids say on the playground, or don't come at all.

Implementation and the Politics of Contempt

The Edna McConnell Clark Foundation is about to stop giving grants to support school reform. Why? Because the foundation has come to the reluctant conclusion that large-scale school reform might not work. Clark Foundation president Michael A. Bailin questions whether the millions his foundation has spent on large-scale reform programs have had lasting impact.

—Education Week, April 4, 2001

The essential problem in our schools isn't children learning; it is adult learning. It is embarrassing to contrast figure 6.1 with something like the 1978 Berman and McLaughlin findings about factors determining the success of educational innovations. After more than a quarter of a century, their examination of nearly 300 federally funded educational innovations stands up very well against contemporary experience. Berman and McLaughlin concluded that one-shot, pre-implementation training was ineffective; that training should be concrete, teacher-driven, and extended; that teachers should be provided assistance in the classroom; that they should observe similar projects in other schools; that there should be regular project meetings focused on practical problems; and that principals should participate in training and teachers in project decisionmaking. High schools were harder to change than elementary schools. Veteran teachers were *less* likely to implement successfully. Teachers' sense of agency was strongly related to positive program outcomes; teachers' verbal ability related positively to student achievement. The quality of relationships among teachers, the active support of principals, and the effectiveness of project directors all strongly affected the quality of implementation. That is, Berman and McLaughlin conveyed a strong sense of how difficult it is to make lasting change, a sense of the importance of leadership, of teacher attitudes, and of the social issues involved in making change, a sense of the need to make substantial investments in teacher development and support. There is a strong sense of the need for implementation to be intense.

We could argue with this or that point, but clearly much of what we "learned" in the 1990s about institutional intransigence was clearly available in the record much sooner than that.[7] Two experienced observers of urban schools note that "the history of education during the 1960s and

179

1970s is replete with examples of superior curriculum and instructional programs, developed in and for urban schools, that were rejected one by one by urban school cultures in favor of more traditional approaches." Even when schools were changed, "Transformed schools do not have long lifespans. They appear on the scene, bloom, and rather quickly revert to the old school culture" (Parish and Aquila 1996: 303). In 1965 Lawrence Cremin argued that one promising reform after another failed because we were not developing a teaching force capable of the kind of pedagogy reform requires. In 1971 Seymour Sarason (1996) cautioned that we should expect little or nothing from school reform efforts because reformers so consistently failed to understand schools as organizations with their own cultures and their own power arrangements. In a recent retrospective, he notes that for fifteen years, he kept a file of letters from people who had mounted failed reform efforts. One of the strongest themes in those letters was that reformers "had vastly underestimated the force of existing power relationships and had vastly overestimated the willingness of school personnel to confront the implications of those relationships" (1996: 340). Even before that, as we saw in the last chapter, David Rogers (1969) produced a thorough analysis of leadership in the public schools of New York and its profound inability to promote change. All apart from what they said about the processes of change, Berman and McLaughlin were very explicit about the usual consequences: successful implementations were rare, they had difficulty sustaining their success over a number of years, and their replication in new sites usually fell short of their performance at their original sites. Most of the innovations they examined were in less troubled environments than the inner city. Much federal spending on educational innovation, they concluded, was being wasted. A few years later, Larry Cuban (1984) took a detailed look at high school pedagogy and concluded that it has hardly changed over the last century, surviving wave after wave of school reform (see also Gibboney 1994).

How, then, is it possible for successive cohorts of school reformers to be innocent of all this? How is it possible that each new group of reformers can be surprised at terrain that has been so well mapped? Even reforms led by experienced and dedicated people tend to assume more social and organizational infrastructure than exists in fact in the bottom-tier schools. James Comer of the School Development Program and Ted Sizer of the Coalition of Essential Schools have both indicated that they initially underestimated the difficulty of making real change. Noting that it took eleven years longer than he expected to reach certain program goals, Comer explains: "We did not anticipate the multiple and complex problems we encountered in and beyond schools" (Comer 1997: 72). Similarly, Sizer, reflecting on 12 years of reform work, writes: "I was aware that it would be hard, but I was not aware of how hard it would be, how weak the incentives would be, how fierce the opposition would be." He now has a finer appreciation of the salience of school culture and governance (Miller 1996: 4). "Implementation is much harder than any of us expected," he has added. "I think this is probably just a long, slow process, and too much was claimed for it too soon" (Viadero 2001b).

After more than a decade of working in leadership positions at the Coalition of Essential Schools and the Annenberg Institute for School Reform, Paula Evans became principal of Cambridge's Rindge and Latin High School, only to quickly learn that assumptions which seemed "so logical and commonsensical" when she was with the reform organizations failed to mesh with the realities of a large, urban high school: students who didn't want to be reformed, preferring to keep things safe and comfortable; faculty who didn't want to collaborate, no matter what the research said; white parents who thought that all the new programs were going to take resources away from their children; African American parents who were just as sure that the same programs were really just meant to get more white kids into Ivy League schools; a central office that was mind-boggling in its inefficiency and managed to undercut her authority even though they essentially agreed with what she was doing (Evans 2003).

Virtually all reformers tout their work as "research-based."[8] The term has been so debased that it is no longer clear that it refers to anything at all, but it clearly does not refer to research on the history of past reforms. In the article that made "scaling up" a part of the professional language, Richard Elmore (1996) points out that school reforms tend to be either short-lived or shallowly implemented, in part because "curriculum developers proved to be inept and naive in their grasp of the individual and institutional issues of change associated with their reforms. They assumed that a 'good' product would travel into U.S. classrooms on its own merits, without regard to the complex institutional and individual factors that might constrain its ability to do so" (14). Interestingly, with the exception of extensive references to Cuban, Elmore cites little of the history of this discussion, and much of the commentary stirred up by Elmore proceeds as if he is saying something new. In their valuable study of the Coalition of Essential Schools, Muncey and McQuillen conclude that "research on educational reform often rediscovers the wheel, finding out what has already been learned in previous studies" (288). As much as the schools they are trying to change, the reform community seems to have some institutionalized inability to learn from experience. Sarason argues that part of the reason we learn so slowly is that many reformers act as if they don't have anything to learn. Engineers, Sarason points out, think of "models" as learning devices. You implement a model with the expectation that you will learn from the attempt, not with the expectation that it will "work":

> Why should any effort at innovation be expected to be other than a first approximation of what needs to be done? . . . What permits an advocate for such an effort to assume that his conceptual rationale and implementation strategy will not be found wanting in some important respects when they run up against institutional realities? . . . The educational reform movement has been almost totally unaware that its initial models never should have been regarded as other than just that: first approximations that would be found wanting in very important respects. On the contrary, each discrete effort at change seemed to assume that its rationale was the model, not an initial one that would lead to better ones. (1996: 354–55)

Sarason is almost certainly right to suggest that part of the problem is the professional culture of school reform groups. Reformers can simply come to take their own models too seriously, get too invested in their own ideas to think critically about their implementation. They come to be communities of true believers (Gibboney 1994: 71), forever reassuring themselves of the rightness of their model and sneering at every "competing" model.

Smugness easily crosses over into contempt for school people. In Chicago, groups who could agree on little else had a high degree of consensus that educators were at the root of the city's educational problems. The businessmen who created Chicago's corporate-supported inner-city demonstration school and the left-of-center community-based activists who advocated the 1988 reforms were both prone to seeing the problems in terms of teachers and principals who didn't care, weren't trying, weren't smart enough. The implication always seemed to be that once *we* come to power, we'll be able to set things to right quickly.

James Lytle, the former Trenton superintendent, notes that model developers typically don't give much credence to practitioner knowledge and adds that not one of the developers Trenton has worked with—not one—thought it necessary to strategize with school leaders before starting to work.

> Too many of the developers take the "McDonald's" approach: the significant thinking and planning are done at corporate headquarters and the franchise holders are expected to adhere to corporate policies and regulations. . . . Developers have both idealized and simplistic notions of educational leadership. When one reads their promotional literature and training documents, the rhetoric of the principal's "vision" for his or her school is prominent, but vision quickly becomes translated to mean internalizing the precepts of the model and facilitating its implementation. (Lytle 2002: 166–67)

One could envision taking the position that, well, these problems in urban schools have been around for a long time despite the fact that lots of smart and dedicated people have tried to do something about them, therefore they must be really tough problems, therefore I should think carefully about how to "ruggedize" my little program before I throw it out there, I should think carefully about how to learn from them. If one assumes the people working on the problem are uncaring jerks, then there is no reason to inquire further into their experience. So we continue forcing underdeveloped reforms on already overburdened teachers and then blaming those teachers when reforms fail to produce the promised miracles. Just as teachers are too quick to conclude that their teaching is fine (it's just that *these* kids don't know how to appreciate it), reformers come to think that the reforms they advocate are right, they will work—just not here, not in this school, not with this particular group of hard-headed teachers and untalented administrators. As noted earlier, the widespread and uncritical contempt in which urban educators are held functions as a pretty exact parallel to widespread assumptions about the intellectual deficiencies of Black or Latino children. It functions as negative social capital; not just the absence of advantages others may have, but also the presence of obstacles others might not have to struggle through.

The situation has certainly not been static. Reformers do learn. As whole-school reformers get more experience, they tend to deepen their approach to implementation in recognition of how difficult it is—adding coaches, strengthening follow-up support, allowing more time, toning down their promises. Comprehensive programs tend to become more comprehensive over time. They often become less ideologically rigid as well. Advocates of staunchly progressive programs come to feel that it's okay to mandate teacher participation sometimes; advocates of traditional programs learn that there are advantages to not living and dying with worksheets. Foundations learn as well. By the mid-1990s, Chicago's MacArthur Foundation, which had once been perceived as equating growth with success, was letting its grantees know that it was interested in "deep change." When Arne Duncan became CEO of the system in 2001 and laid out his various programmatic visions, the foundation community, wiser after many defeats, generally advised, "Go slow, young man, go slow" (although apparently to little avail).

Framing this as a learning matter captures only part of the problem, however. Reformers now have a clearer understanding of the difficult character of the environments they are working in and of what good implementation requires in such environments. Whether that ever translates into a sense of partnership with urban teachers is still an open question. Contempt operates here as self-serving; that is, it operates as an ideology, and as noted earlier, ideologies don't easily yield to experience.

It is now a familiar cycle. Reformers develop morally compelling visions of what we could do for children if only (and only if) we commit to Program X. Program X will be well supported with intellectual rationale and will offer a trenchant critique of existing practice. It will also be underconceptualized with respect to the day-to-day realities of inner-city schools and how to work through them. The reformers have some early successes, perhaps in smaller schools or in schools where there is particularly good leadership or in situations where the program founder is actively involved in implementation. They sell the vision on the basis of those early successes ("It's research-based!!") and expand, cheered on by the funding and political establishments. As they go into more and tougher schools, they find that their earlier experiences did not fully prepare them for dealing with the array of problems urban schools present. They may outrun their supply lines, finding themselves unable to replicate the quality of personnel that made those early implementations successful. With dozens of schools—or hundreds—they cannot adjust to problems the way they could with a few. Program results become more mixed. Some of the original success stories start to deteriorate. The same people who encouraged rapid expansion—the policymaking community, the foundations, the media—become disappointed. The intellectual and humanistic premises of reform are called into question, and we go spiraling off on another round of collective despair about how awful inner-city schools are.[9]

Standards of Implementation

We know now that one of the main impediments to improving instruction in urban schools is the fact that teachers tend to be isolated from one another. Similarly, the fact that reformers are isolated—by ideology, attitude, cohort, geography, and multitudinous tribalisms—from one another makes larger-scale change much more difficult. Each group learns implementation the hard way—or fails to learn. It might help if we could invent a process to codify and make widely available the rich body of practitioner knowledge. In the 1990s, many states and cities made substantial progress toward articulating standards for curriculum content. They might have been even better served had they simultaneously developed standards of implementation, standards that used accumulated practitioner knowledge to address the *how* of implementation rather than the *what*.

Different types of reform would require different types of standards, but formalizing clinical knowledge need not be terribly difficult. One could envision a process that brought together a group of experienced practitioners for extended conversation about the commonalities and differences in their experience. Whatever guidelines emerged from such a discussion would have to be adapted to each local context, but simply having a set of standards should encourage subsequent waves of implementers to ask more sophisticated questions about their own work and how it needs to be supported. Such standards might have two categories. Where a rough consensus can be hammered out—and "hammered" is undoubtedly the word—they would take the form of actual guidelines with suggested minimum resource levels. Where even rough consensus is not possible, we may know enough to frame some issues as strategic dilemmas.

Consider reform mathematics. The National Council of Teachers of Mathematics, along with the National Science Foundation, both advocate teaching mathematics in a way that emphasizes genuine understanding rather than rote memorization. They would like to see much greater use of inquiry and problem-solving in teaching and much less didactic instruction. Given the experience of those who have already tried it, what should a city have in place to give itself a reasonable chance of implementing a reform mathematics program at the elementary level?[10] A plausible answer might include:

- at least five full days of pre-implementation professional development for teachers, and at least half that for principals
- at least another five full days of professional development during the school year, for the first two years
- at least one common planning period a week for teachers on the same grade level, and at least one such period a month for teachers of contiguous grades
- at least two hours per week of principal time to address individual problems and opportunities in their buildings, meet with coaches, etc.
- biweekly contact (at least one class period) with a highly trained coach (five years' experience teaching math or a master's in math, in addition to twice as much training in the project being implemented as given to teachers—training for coaches should start a year before implementation). Teachers in the lowest-achieving schools should have weekly contact with a coach. Coaches should have two days a month of professional development or planning / problem-solving time.
- at least two full days per year of professional-development time for principals, to deepen their knowledge of the program, assess progress, strategize about mid-course adjustments
- for every five teachers in a building, one teacher-leader with at least two freed-up periods weekly, to help solve problems, find materials, mentor younger and lateral-entry teachers, coordinate grade-level meetings. (Training for them should also start a year before full implementation; five days of professional development for them for the first three summers)
- some method for tracking the level of actual implementation at the classroom level
- a plan for dealing with mobility among students and staff (that is, what happens when a child transfers from a school doing traditional math to one doing reform-math? What happens when new teachers are hired after pre-implementation training is over?)

Not all that we know can be reduced to a set of guidelines for resources. Sometimes we can only identify choices that seem likely to have important implications for how a project develops. For example,

- What should be the unit of intervention? Is it better for coaches to work with individual teachers or with grade-level teams or whole departments or some other clustering of teachers? Does the latter approach make possible more efficient use of resources, or does it simply dilute the process?
- Should coaching be authoritative or collegial? That is, should coaching be associated with the possibility of sanctions for teachers, as when coaches are a part of the formal evaluation of teachers, or are coaches just there to help those teachers who want to be helped?
- Is it better to give teachers a period during which they can choose whether to use reform or traditional math, or to simply mandate that everyone will implement the reform curriculum?

Standards of implementation should also include guidelines for data-gathering. Too many projects get three or four years into implementation before they figure out that they aren't keeping information in a form that would be useful. Again, each type of reform will be different. In the case of reform mathematics, the challenges will include the following facts:

- That the shift to reform math always involves an increase in the amount (and probably, usually, the quality) of professional development. Any increase in outcome measures can as plausibly be attributed to the fact that teachers just know more math as to the particular way they are teaching it. Thus, school systems need data that will allow them to estimate the level of actual implementation of the new program by classroom and schools, which can then be compared to outcomes.
- That one of the goals of reform mathematics is to increase significantly the numbers of youth taking advanced math courses, and it is very important for school systems to track that. Unfortunately, some teachers and principals believe so strongly that only a few kids can do advanced math that, when they see different kinds of kids in those classes, they may assume the classes are being watered down. Even if scores are good, it may still be assumed that teachers are teaching to the test. It is important that systems have multiple outcome measures to make such charges less plausible. SAT or ACT scores are generally

more persuasive than scores on the state or local assessment test. Ideally, a district should be able to say not only that SAT scores are rising faster among students who had reform math, but also that they are rising even faster among those students who have had the most exposure to classrooms where there has been high implementation. Many districts, unfortunately, don't gather data in a way that allows them to follow students over time.

- That reform mathematics is sometimes perceived by the parents of successful students as operating to the disadvantage of their children. Thus, it is not enough for districts to have data showing that the average child is doing better; they should also put themselves in a position to say that the kinds of kids who used to do well continue to do so, as indicated by SAT score trends for upper-quartile students, or something to that effect.

Again, this is only illustrative of what standards of implementation might look like for one category of school reform. The idea of implementation standards is not to produce an exhaustive checklist. The hope is that standards of implementation can function as a consciousness-raising device, encouraging richer conversation and debate about implementation by institutionalizing respect for the experience of one's predecessors and institutionalizing recognition of the overdetermination of failure. That people encounter the standards and debate them is more important than "following" them. The standards identify some of the factors that consistently undermine promising reforms—failure to allot enough time for professional development, failure to provide adequate follow-up support, the disengagement of principals, leaders who understand the reform only superficially, the absence of problem-solving capacity, the inability to do ongoing assessment.

More broadly, such guidelines could encourage districts to think more realistically about what is possible with the resources they have. Most districts would find out that what they normally do to implement new instructional programs does not compare well with what experienced reform leaders think is appropriate. Knowing that may help districts think more carefully about the pace and scale of change. Having such standards become a part of our collective discourse might also help move our conversation beyond "It worked / It didn't work." When we encounter programs trying to do staff development by stealing a few hours from teachers after school and trying to provide support by having one coach cover an unreasonable number of schools, we know we should take disappointing outcomes with a grain of salt.

Several months after hurricane Katrina, I was in New Orleans with a group that included Warren Simmons of the Annenberg Institute. We found ourselves in conversation with Jerome Smith, a hero of the Civil Rights movement and a longtime community activist and educator in that city. At some point, one of us asked him what he thought of the plan to make New Orleans a virtually all-charter-school city. His response was something like, "Depends on the hearts of the people running it." Warren and I laughed simultaneously. Both of us were reasonably conversant with the large and sometimes contradictory literature on charters, but Jerome Smith's comment cut through that to a more profound way of thinking. The Big Magic isn't in the charters themselves so much as in the thinking and understanding of the people who implement them, in the approach they take, in the values they hold dear.

More recently, I had a long conversation with an official who heads what we can call the Office of Making Autonomy Work in her city. As we sat in her office, she made wondrous claims about the great good that would come from granting autonomy to more and more high schools. To no avail, I kept pushing her about the evidential base for her optimism, and she kept right on reciting the party line. I knew perfectly well evidence didn't have anything to do with what she was saying; this was ideology, a worldview enshrined as public policy. I could find no evidence whatsoever that either she or her bosses had spent any time thinking about what teaching should be like in these schools. Indeed, it sounded to me like the autonomy fetish was partly a way to avoid thinking about teaching. I left thinking that the city was going to pour resources into these newly autonomous schools and then turn around and say, "Look what autonomy does!!" I am not in principle against the idea of freeing certain schools from bureaucratic oversight under certain conditions, but I don't see any Big Magic in autonomy itself as opposed to the way it's implemented. To the extent that we keep implementing reforms with the idea that there is some one program that is going to make all the difference; to the extent we keep implementing reform without adequate support or without a spirit of persistence, a determination that we are going to give the work a fair chance to take root; to the extent that we keep implementing good ideas in a spirit of contempt for the practitioners who have to make them work; to the extent that we keep implementing reforms without any capacity for mid-course corrections, without any understanding of the relevant historical context; to that extent we can expect to get implementations that continue to miss the point. How we do this may be as important as what we do, arguably more so. One of the foundational studies of the current discussion on successful urban districts (Snipes, Doolittle, and Herlihy 2002) found that successful districts and unsuccessful districts say they are doing the same things; the difference appears to be in the way they do what they do. "It ain't the shape of the ship," a bit of street doggerel goes, "it's the motion of the ocean." It ain't the thing that you do, it's the way that you do it. We can let that be our Fifth Heuristic.

Chapter 7

A Curse on Both Their Houses: Liberal and Conservative Theories of School Reform

The students [of color] are quite used to being "tolerated." . . . At the same time, many were not used to being stretched or challenged; they resented it. Many didn't understand that high standards are for everyone; they were content with poor grades.

—Principal, Cambridge Rindge and Latin

It seems like you're insisting that everyone here learn.

—Indignant student,
Cambridge Rindge and Latin

I am what time, circumstance, history, have made of me, certainly, but I am also much more than that. So are we all.

—James Baldwin

They do not understand that our historical experience has been speaking to white people, whether it be begging white people, justifying ourselves against white people or even vilifying white people. Our whole context has been, "That is the man to talk to."

—Walter Rodney

If we think of the serious discussion of urban schools as something that has ebbed and flowed for 40 years, more or less, since the publication of the Coleman Report, I think we must say that we have learned a great deal, especially in just the last few years. Yet, and still, it is disheartening to think about how long it has taken us to get to this point. We have functioned as a learning-disabled community. Some of our disabilities have been mentioned earlier, but I want to concentrate now on just one of them: the disability of ideology and the way it distorts much of the discussion among academics, reformers, community leaders, and politicians. We have too often been more invested in our paradigms than in solving the problems they address. Progressives—among whom I count myself—are as culpable as conservatives. Each side has a set of cherished beliefs about which they cannot think critically. I want to sketch that large problem, but then I want to concentrate on a subset of issues, what I have come to think of as the Bill Cosby problem—the always ticklish problem of how we should think about the responsibility of the poor for their own condition.

Cosby, of course, famously accused the Black poor of failing to live up to their end of the bargain; admonished them to stop blaming everything on racism and discrimination; to get their priorities straight; and to stop spending everything they get on clothes (Cosby 2004). More recently, Oprah Winfrey made similar remarks. When asked why she did so much to support a school in South Africa, she was quoted as saying, "I became so frustrated with visiting inner-city schools that I just stopped going. The sense that you need to learn just isn't there. If you ask the kids what they want or need, they will say an iPod or some sneakers. In South Africa, they don't ask for money or toys. They ask for uniforms so they can go to school" (Samuels 2007). Again, people in the inner city just don't have the right priorities, a point confirmed by Herman Badillo, our first Puerto Rican congressman, who criticized Latino parents for not taking the education of their children seriously. "Hispanics have failed to assume responsibility for their children's welfare. . . . Hispanic parents rarely get involved with their children's schools. They seldom attend parent-teacher conferences, ensure that children do their homework or inspire their children to dream of attending college" (quoted in Cortes 2006). Criticisms of this type, especially coming from people one might expect to be sympathetic to the poor, are difficult for progressives to process, a problem to which we will return after we think a little about the ideological character of educational discourse.

The Dance of Ideology

What I think of as the conservative theory of change (e.g., Chubb and Moe 1990; Finn 2000; Thernstrom and Thernstrom 2003) says, basically, that if you want institutions to change, you need an effective incentive structure; you have to reward somebody or hurt somebody. In practice, conservatives have put much more emphasis on the hurting part. If there is a penalty for failure, they say, people will put out more effort. What we have allowed to develop is a situation in which people feel it's okay to fail with urban kids and are allowed to get away with it. We need accountability. We need high-stakes environments for teachers and kids. At the same time we need to remove the bureaucratic impediments that keep professionals from doing their jobs. No Child Left Behind draws primarily from this school of thought, and in that sense this is the most dominant theory behind educational policy at the moment.

Liberal or progressive thinking (e.g., Anyon 1997, 2005; Kozol 1967; Meier 2002; Kohn 2000) finds this morally abhorrent and technically inefficient. What I think of as the progressive position is that you get change by changing people, by developing them. People have to be convinced that there is some value in what you're asking them to do. People must have ownership over change, and that means change must be largely a bottom-up process, a voluntary process. You cannot simply issue mandates from on high and get real change in institutions as complex as schools. You issue mandates, you get compliance, and that's on a good day. This is pretty much the dominant theory at American schools of education.

From the broad theories, we can extract some cherished ideas that, I think, bear rethinking. For progressives, those ideas include the following Holy Postulates:

1. Thou Shalt Never Criticize the Poor. It is okay to imply that the poor have agency but agency only to do good. If the poor do anything that's counterproductive, it is only because of the inexorable weight of oppression, which leaves them no choice. We do not talk about poor children or parents as part of their own problem.

2. The Only Pedagogy Is Progressive Pedagogy and Thou Shalt Have No Other Pedagogy Before It. Drill and practice is everywhere and always bad; Distar (a highly structured instructional program) is the devil's handiwork, but anything that suggests centralization or standardization of instruction has the taint of evil. Context is irrelevant—teachers in a given building may have questionable content knowledge, there may be no support structure for teaching, teachers may not believe in their own efficacy or in their students. Doesn't matter. Real teaching is always inquiry-based, student-centered, constructivist.

3. Leadership in a Community of Professionals Is Always Facilitative, Inclusive, and Democratic. Again, we advocate this without regard to the context, without regard to the degree of social capital in a school or the degree of organizational coherence. This is part of the larger set of ideas which holds that real change must be voluntary; you must have buy-in from the bottom before you can do anything.

4. Test Scores Don't Mean a Thing. They don't reflect the most important types of growth, it's easy to cheat, easy to teach to the test. Tests take us away from the real business of education. On the other hand, if test scores rise in the context of progressive instruction, then they are further proof of the superiority of that method of teaching.

The errors of the right are presumably more dangerous at the moment because the right has institutional power. Conservatives proceed from a reductionist set of sensibilities: a reductionist sense of child development, a reductionist sense of teaching, of research, and of human motivation. (Sign on a Chicago principal's desk: "The floggings will continue until morale improves around here.") These sensibilities translate into a contrasting set of postulates:

1. Money Doesn't Matter. The mother of all conservative sins is refusing to think about resource reallocation. The popularity of vouchers and charters is due partly to the fact that they present themselves as revenue neutral. Look at Washington, D.C., they will say. Lavish spending and terrible results. Look at the Abbott schools in New Jersey. . . .

2. It Only Counts If It Can Be Counted; Only the Quantifiable Is Real. This applies to everything from children's growth to teachers' credentials. This is actually just one reflection of the next point.

3. The Path of Business Is the True Path. Leadership, decisionmaking, and organizational functioning should all mirror what is found in the American business community, renowned for its efficiency and hardheadedness. One result is the fetishizing of privatization, often without any regard to context or process or attention to the instructional core.

4. Educators Are Impractical. Another corollary of the romanticizing of the business model. In contrast to the practical, get-it-done businesspeople, educators are seen as losers, dreamy, if not out-of-touch whiners.

5. Change Is Simple If You Do It Right. "Doing it right" often comes to mean equating change with the changing of structures. There is very little sense of social process. If we organize schools as charters, that's assumed to mean something fundamental has been changed. Big Magic.

These are only ideal types, and both camps have moved some, over the last decade especially. Still, this does capture some of the central tendencies of the two camps. For now, I want to think a bit more about some of the problematics of the progressive side, which, however well intended, may in fact blind us to opportunities. We can get so busy "speaking truth to power" that we fail to address people who are more likely to do something with it.

Iwo Jima and the Problem of Voluntary Change

There is just no doubt that one of the central problems in improving urban schools—arguably *the* central problem—is the problem of teacher resistance, or teacher skepticism, if one prefers. I've noted before that in my experience, veteran teachers are among the most prone to be skeptical about reforms, and the opposite ends of the teaching spectrum seem overly represented. That is, most of the weakest teachers and some of the strongest teachers are especially hard to bring on board.

How should reformers respond to the reluctant teachers? Among progressives, I think the dominant response for perhaps the last two decades is that we should not push the reluctant, we should not confront them, we should not mandate participation. Real change has to be incremental and voluntary. If you force them, people will go through the outward motions as long as someone is there to watch them, but you can't get real change in an enterprise as complex as teaching by bullying people. Instead, accentuate the positive. In every school, there will be at least a handful of teachers open to change. Reformers should cultivate them, work with them. You want to go in and demonstrate that if kids are taught differently, taught in a way that is more engaging, taught in a way that reflects their interests, they'll learn more. Other teachers will see kids learning more, and they will willingly adopt the innovation of their own volition. Teachers, after all, want to be successful. Once the culture of the school changes, the hard-core holdouts will either come around or get out and find a place where they are more comfortable. We will create pockets of excellence, as people used to say, until we have a whole garment.

This is the Iwo Jima model of school change. Reformers are the Marines hitting the beach, establishing a beachhead, and fighting their way inland, one classroom at a time. Today the kindergarten, tomorrow Manila. One can find examples of schools that have in fact changed this way, but it's a dicey process. We find a great many schools where, three or four years into the process, reformers are still pinned down on the beach, still working on with the faithful few and still waiting on the rest to come to the light. I don't see how we can continue to think of this as a viable way to change school districts. If there is enough instructional leadership in a building, if there is more than a threshold level of social capital, maybe, just maybe. As a model of scaling up among the neediest schools, almost certainly not.

In retrospect, there are at least two overarching problems with the voluntary-change model. First, it assumes that teachers and reformers are working with the same epistemologies. What is success? If test scores rise, is that success? Or is it better students this year, or that we are teaching more to the test, or that we've stopped teaching biology and art to spend more time on tested subjects? Teachers and reform advocates may differ on the answers. Or teachers may feel that the tests just don't measure what's most important: "These kids need life lessons more than they need a few more points on a test. . . ."

The second obvious-in-retrospect point is again something we noted earlier. To the extent that teachers have an ideological investment in believing in program failure, it may be difficult for any level of evidence to convince them they were wrong. A stressful, low-reward environment predisposes people to construct an affirming worldview, one that tells them they are already doing everything that's possible under the circumstances. Admitting that improvement is possible is an invitation to self-critique.

More broadly, the voluntary-change model does not take into account what we know about the social and political character of urban schools. We know that our toughest schools are demoralized. They have weak organizational infrastructure; infrequent professional interaction among teachers; low levels of teacher agency, conditioned by a set of negative ideas that many teachers hold about urban children—ideas tinged, at least, with racial and social-class stereotypes. If those are the social conditions under which we are working, it seems very strange to think change can be entirely voluntary. We cannot go into schools where many, if not most, of the professionals have come to believe the job is impossible and expect to make change by asking for volunteers. Under these conditions, if everything is voluntary, some people will opt out, and their nonparticipation will demoralize others. Change requires a demand of some kind, requires some form of pressure, and the question is how to apply it in the least destructive manner. Any naked use of power, I understand, is very disturbing to those of us with a preference for purely democratic vehicles of change. In fact, demoralized institutions are unlikely to yield to anything less.

The story of District Two in New York City is widely understood to be a story about intensive professional development and elaborate instructional support, one of the earliest examples of large-scale coaching. That it is also a story about demands is often missed, but in fact District Two encouraged people who couldn't go along with the program to find employment elsewhere, which means that 40 percent of the principals left in the first five years of Anthony Alvarado's administration. A substantial number of teachers transferred out at least partly because of the new pressure (Wolk 1998; Burney and Elmore 1998). Similarly, Boston's improvement in literacy scores during the 1990s is widely attributed to their increasing professional development by an order of magnitude; it is less well known that Boston, too, removed 40–50 percent of the least successful principals. These are two of the more important stories of progressive, large-scale school improvement in the last couple of decades, and in both cases, the narratives that get constructed around them downplay the role of top-down pressure.

For some time now, the official leadership model of progressives has been some variant of the facilitative, democratic, inclusive model. That model as usually presented is certainly ahistorical and decontextualized. In schools where distrust between teachers and administrators or between teachers and their colleagues has built up for many years, over the short term including more people in the decisionmaking process gives them new weapons with which to carry on their old vendettas. There may come a point in a school's development where democratic leadership can lead to major improvements in school functioning, but that is far from saying that all schools can profit from it at all points in time. By the same token, we have to consider more authoritative leadership styles in context as well. Just putting pressure on people without making sure they have the resources to do their jobs, pressuring people in contexts where the leadership has not established basic legitimacy, seems likely to be counterproductive.

In his Chicago period, Paul Vallas helped me rethink my position on some of these questions. Vallas was the paradigmatic top-down leader, putting pressure on everybody. If he didn't get what he wanted, he was going to facilitate your exit from the system. Few observers doubt that he generated a higher level of effort throughout the system. The progressive reformers who had been very influential during the pre-Vallas period generally openly loathed him and his style. Nevertheless, I heard many of them say that their reception in the schools changed after Vallas took the helm. Teachers started paying more attention to reformers and the kinds of help they could offer. Vallas's style generated a sense of urgency, and in that context schools considered tools they had sneered at earlier.

No one thinks that pressure alone leads to deep change. We certainly know that the opposite tack, purely voluntary change, has a dubious history. At this point, it may be irresponsible for progressives to continue clinging to the Iwo Jima model, hoping for a breakthrough one fine day. We are probably better off thinking of severely damaged schools as needing different types of leadership at different points in the process. In the same way that we think of individual children as needing a blend of both support and pressure, it makes sense to think of schools as needing both.

The gradualism implicit in the voluntary-change model recalls another call for gradualism. In post–World War II America, the gradualist position on race would have held that the racial situation had to change, but it couldn't change faster than attitudes. Gradualism had no more famous proponent than Dwight David Eisenhower, who said, "I do not believe that prejudices . . . will succumb to compulsion. Consequently, I believe that Federal law imposed upon our States . . . would set back the cause of race relations a long, long time" (qtd. in Patterson 2001: 81). With the wisdom of hindsight, we can appreciate both the tenacity of attitudes and the fact that much of the progress in racial inequality we have seen in the last half-century wouldn't have been made if we had waited on attitudes to change. Similarly, waiting on teachers who have been beaten down and demoralized to change voluntarily is likely to be a long wait.

We have to give conservatives credit for managing to create a sense of urgency around the issue. NCLB makes finding a solution to the problem of underachievement within a few years a public priority. The legislation may reflect a silly sense of how to do it, but asserting that it can be done and must be done quickly is a step forward in public discourse. Partly, no doubt, because of the voluntary-change model, progressives have been predisposed to the idea that real change takes time. It would be very useful at this juncture for the left to construct a conversation that reflected a left sense of urgency, something that recognizes both that change takes time and that children don't have it. How, without sacrificing the core progressive values, can we shorten the time it takes to make positive change? How, to paraphrase Rochelle Nicholls Solomon, do we balance urgency with complexity? A part of the answer to that may be that we have to stop being apologists for the poor.

Apologists for the Poor

The left has traditionally been reluctant to think about the role of the poor in creating their own problems, and for very good reason. That idea has probably been the dominant theme in American thinking about social inequality in the twentieth century and has normally been used against the poor, used to deny any structural roots to inequality, used to let the privileged off the hook. The last thing we want to do is contribute to the victim-blaming that constitutes so much of what passes for social discourse among us.

In this context comes Mr. Cosby, shooting off his mouth in an uncivil, apparently mean-spirited way. The reaction was not just a reaction to what he said. It was a reaction to the historical context, a sense that destructive stereotypes were being legitimated, a sense that the ideological enemies of the poor were being handed a weapon with which to flog the most defenseless. Many of us reflexively rushed to attack his motives, his reasoning, and his Momma. Nevertheless, the heart of what he was saying was not only true but unremarkable. Is it possible for inner-city parents to do a better job of supporting their children's education? Indeed it is, and we really shouldn't have to have a debate over it. Almost anyone who works with urban children, no matter how sympathetic to parents, can recite the litany of counterproductive parenting habits. Some of the strongest critiques of parenting in the inner city come from those inner-city parents who are active. It would be unwise to write all of that off as false consciousness—poor people who fail to understand the realities of their position.

There is an obvious element of the self-serving in the way some urban teachers stress the shortcomings of parents and children. A Chicago teacher commented: "Let's tell the truth here. . . . The school has everything but the labor pains. A teacher cannot take Mom and Dad's place. What am I going to accomplish when mom doesn't take the time to pick up a can of peas and say, 'Green! Round! Peas!'?" Taken literally, this is demonstrably false. We know that there is a great deal schools can do, even in the face of parents who do not cooperate, and that what they can do is potent enough to dramatically change the lives of most children. We cannot allow educators or comedians or anyone else to use the limitations of parents to excuse the limitations of schools.

Still, saying that something is ideological or an exaggeration is different from saying it has no truth value at all, a possibility that, in our rush to align ourselves with the poor, we may not be willing to examine, and in a given case that may mean we fail to give ourselves a chance to think about levers of change that have more potential than the politics of image. Of course it does make sense to speak to The Man, to challenge dominant ideology, but sometimes it makes sense to speak to The People too, and doing that usefully requires more than telling them that nothing is their fault.

Whenever we allow ourselves to become merely apologists for the poor, we are accepting the framework of the debate, the legitimacy of the question. You can turn your back on Mishnory, as the expression goes, but you're still on the Mishnory road. Rush Limbaugh shakes his finger at the poor, and we immediately jump to their defense. They've had bad experiences with schools in the past, their work doesn't leave them with the time to attend to school affairs, they are culturally oriented to deferring educational decisions to professionals, their lives are just too stressful, and so on. There is considerable truth in these defenses. As an important case in point, consider the Minnesota Family Investment program (Gennetian, Miller, and Smith 2005), which gave monthly cash payments to supplement the wages of low-wage earners, typically increasing income by a few hundred dollars per quarter. While the increase in cash earnings was not large, it had a significant positive impact on children's academic achievement in single-parent families, compared to children in a control group, as measured by test scores, teacher reports, and parent reports. The small group of children in the experimental group who were ages two to five at the time of entry into the study doubled the number performing at grade level in math and reading when they reached fifth grade. Overall, the income supplement raised achievement from around the 25th to around the 30th percentile, although there is reason to think the numbers actually understate the impact. If poor parents had more resources, many of them could be better parents.

Thus, we need to continue to make these kinds of arguments in part just because they are true, although we should do so with an appreciation for the limited power such defending-the-poor arguments will usually have in the halls of the influential. We should also have an appreciation for the fact that all we are doing is producing a more nuanced answer to the fundamentally boneheaded question, What is the matter with these poor people? We should also not allow ourselves to lose sight of the fact that, in the short term, defending the image of poor parents doesn't do one bit of good for their children. It may be nice to know that there are compelling reasons for what parents do or do not do, but that doesn't change the consequences for children. It was my grandfather who liked to say you can mess up for good reason, you can mess up for bad; the consequences will be exactly the same. Urban children need better teaching, but many of them could use better parenting, too, and just acknowledging that poverty presents very real impediments to better parenting doesn't help us think about how to get it.

Typically, several different ideas get conflated in these discussions. There is the idea of causation, which should be understood to have, minimally, both structural and individual aspects, both historical and contemporary aspects, both indirect and proximate aspects. Then there is the issue of change, and while academics like to pretend that we can change the world if and only if we can understand root causes, that is not necessarily the case. The way you get into a situation, as Ron Ferguson likes to say, is not necessarily the way you get out. Root causes are not necessarily amenable to manipulation by social policy. Over the course of the twentieth century, this country has spent substantially less money on the education of Black children than on white children. This certainly affects the kinds of relevant social capital that Black parents can pass on to their children, but it is not something that can be fixed easily by public policy. Fortunately, social patterns that have been generated by one cluster of factors can be changed by others. If we want to know how to make change, it is often going to be more efficient to address that question directly. Instead, we allow ourselves to be suckered into a sterile debate about whether parents are the "cause" of the problem, using "cause" in a narrow, ahistorical sense. We should be much more interested in how parents can become a part of the solution. If we are afraid to look at that, we will miss one of the possible levers of change and, potentially, a lever easier to move than some of the others.

In the early years of Chicago school reform, there was an increase in parents acting as volunteers in schools. Many observers credit them with making schools safer and with improving the climate of some schools—that is, doing something about the frequently harsh tone of interaction between teachers and students. Parents playing roles in governance also deserve some of the credit for opening schools up to outside expertise. They created an atmosphere in which principals wanted to look active, which encouraged them to bring in outside programs and experts.

I followed some of the Chicago Comer schools in which all those patterns were evident. These were all bottom-quartile schools at the beginning of the decade, and almost none of them had anything like a coherent parent program, typically with fewer than a dozen parents participating in any identifiable way. The Comer project fairly quickly, within a year in most cases, was able to build parent programs of 30–100 regular participants and could call on two to three times that number for particular events. Parents were patrolling hallways and playgrounds, acting as classroom aides, doing lunchroom duties, and in some cases even taking over classes while teachers did professional development. It was very clear the children felt good about having their parents involved. We were caught off guard by how much the parents themselves were affected by their own participation. They took pride in what they were doing and developed more confidence in their own abilities. This was especially true for those without prior job market or organizational experience. (Several volunteers used their volunteering as springboards to real jobs, in most cases the first jobs for the individuals involved.) It is important to note that this was in a context in which parents were strongly stigmatized by school professionals, who could be quite inventive in the ways they found to put parents down.

The point is that, prior to the Comer intervention, a potentially important resource was going unused. What did it take to mobilize it? Persistent outreach to parents, in a socially appropriate way, and ongoing support for them. Building the parent programs probably took less than a third of the time of facilitators over a one- or two-year period, although it almost certainly helped that the facilitators in Chicago were experienced social workers. Still, if we compare what it took to move parents with what it sometimes takes to move teachers to a higher level of practice, it seems, in this case at least, to have been a relatively modest investment. Yes, there are parents who have been too beaten down by life in poverty to support children adequately, but there are others who aren't and just need to be challenged and supported.

There is another reason for thinking more about what parents can do. Not doing so breaks faith with teachers. Teachers confront problematic parental behavior on a daily basis. They certainly perceive parental behavior selectively; they certainly underestimate the role that they play in driving parents from schools; they certainly give up on parents too quickly. But with all that said, they aren't making it all up, and if we are to respect teachers, not to mention the parents who do struggle to do what they can, they need to know we acknowledge that.

Our determination to defend the image of the poor may be especially poorly timed right now. I don't see the right stressing victim-blaming quite as aggressively as is normally the case. For all the faults of free-market fundamentalism, it recasts the problem as not being one of the character of the poor but of the characteristics of institutions, which is something of a sea change. To see the problem in terms of inadequate incentive structures is very different from the traditional culture-of-poverty explanations. I'm not sure the left has fully appreciated the change. In some ways, we are expending a lot of energy fighting yesterday's battle. (I expect, though, that we will see the pendulum swing again. As more and more voucher programs and charter schools yield dubious results, we may see a resurgence of traditional victim-blaming theory.)

My guess is that raising a child in the inner city is a different proposition from what it was even a few decades ago. The decline of extended families, increases in residential mobility, the outmigration of jobs, the secularization and criminalization of inner-city communities, and the increasingly problematic definitions of masculinity in such neighborhoods are only a few of the factors that have made it more difficult for even the best parents to respond appropriately to the environment. Obviously, when poor parents do exactly the same things as wealthier parents, they cannot expect the results to be as favorable; when they make mistakes, the consequences are likely to be more drastic for them and their children. I'm pretty sure that the payoff for being a good parent in the inner city now is smaller than previously, but there is still a payoff. If so, it still makes sense to assume that the poor, like the rest of us, have within their collective selves contradictory tendencies, tendencies constantly reinforced by life circumstances and exposure to the broader popular culture, that can reinforce and deepen their poverty, but also tendencies that would give their children a better chance.

We cannot be certain, of course, how large an impact parents can have on the larger problem of underachievement. We should be mindful of the fact that the cases we have of relatively large-scale positive change— Manhattan's District Two; Boston's literacy efforts; Wake County, North Carolina; San Diego in the late 1990s—are not cases that relied on any dramatic changes in parent behavior. They seem to be based on the political stability of the system, the strategic distribution of resources (including human resources), extensive and intensive professional development for instruction, and ongoing support for better teaching. I do not know of anything that looks like a major turnaround that has been built around changing parent behavior. We don't know how powerful a lever parent behavior can be, but there is some reason to think it can make some difference, and we are still at the point where we cannot ignore any tools that might matter. (Then, too, most of the examples we have of large-scale change are proving unstable, and it may be that parents can play a role in stabilizing change when it happens.)

The fact that maintaining that the poor have a role to play in changing their own lives has come to be thought of as a conservative posture, while defending the image of the poor has come to be the liberal, sometimes even the radical, position is a measure of the impoverished character of the conversation. From Marx through Gandhi through Martin Luther King, liberal and radical theorists have been comfortable with the idea that the oppressed ordinarily—some would say "inevitably"—reinforce their own oppression. One example of what Marxists mean by the "unity of opposites," for example, would be the tendency of workers, in ordinary times, to support the economic systems that exploit them. Marxists who study contemporary education contend that the authoritarian values by which many working-class populations raise their young militate against the intellectual development of their children (Bowles and Gintis 1976). The difference is that they do not separate the values of workers from the social structure which shapes those values.

William Hinton's *Fanshen* (1966) is an analysis of the Chinese communist revolution at the ground level. Part of what is most striking in his analysis is the ability of the early communist leaders to see the peasants they worked with in three different time frames. They could see them in the present—dangerously ignorant, superstitious, individualistic, fatalistic. They could also see the past—the arrangements of Chinese social structure that virtually guaranteed peasants would develop this way. Obviously, they did not think that either the past or the present had to define the potential of the peasant. The peasants' future depended on what kind of developmental pathways could be opened for them, and that was the job of the Communist Party.

Consider the problem from the viewpoint of community organizers. Think about SNCC (Student Nonviolent Coordinating Committee) workers going into small Mississippi towns in the 1960s and organizing voter-registration drives. Their position was that the poor had to be a part of the process of fighting for their own inclusion into American society, that no solutions could be trusted if the poor were not involved in their crafting. The idea that they therefore thought of the poor as the "cause" of the problem would have struck them as being past absurd.

In college, I knew a very religious student who didn't enjoy the debates the rest of us were having about how to end poverty. His position was that the poor serve a necessary function. Without the poor there would be no one to whom people like himself could act charitably, thus demonstrating their faith. It seems to me that some of us are doing the same thing—using the poor as the means to position ourselves on the side of the angels and dumbing down the discussion to do that, pretending that social marginalization does not do anything negative to people. I don't see it as our job as scholars, educators, and advocates for children to pretend that the negative isn't there. It is our job to not let public discussion reduce people to their negatives, to insist always on seeing the larger context, to continue looking to augment the strengths and possibilities that low-income parents and their children bring with them.

Epilogue

There is one thing still wanting, and that is a suitable house of our own, located in a more central part of the city than the one where our school is now being taught, and one sufficiently commodious to enable the teacher to carry out more fully his plan of systematic teaching, and where the colored classes may also receive their instruction designed for them without mingling so much with the whole school, which to the minds of some is not a very pleasant reflection, and also to the teacher is oftentimes very annoying and causes him, generally speaking, more trouble than three times the same number of white children would do, placed in the same position (owing to the peculiar temperament of the African race).

—James Kennedy, School Superintendent,
Cape May Ocean Wave, March 21, 1861

When I was a boy, I thought all Black men recited poetry and prose. When my father got together with his boyhood friends, it was not at all unusual for someone to start reciting Shakespeare and for someone else to follow that with some quatrains from the *Rubaiyát*, which might be followed by bits of Paul Laurence Dunbar or James Weldon Johnson. These were yard men, delivery "boys," dockhands, truck drivers, casual laborers, and factory workers. My father's contribution, delivered with expression, was likely to be Kipling's "If," most likely the opening lines:

> If you can keep your head when all about you
> Are losing theirs and blaming it on you,
> If you can trust yourself when all men doubt you
> But make allowance for their doubting too,
> If you can wait and not be tired by waiting,
> Or being lied about, don't deal in lies,
> Or being hated, don't give way to hating,

Or the ending:

> If you can fill the unforgiving minute
> With sixty seconds' worth of distance run,
> Yours is the Earth and everything that's in it,
> And—which is more—you'll be a Man, my son!

207

I learned "If" and the Gettysburg Address by heart because my father knew them. At some point, I figured out that not all Black men were like Payne and his running buddies. They were students of the legendary William J. Moore, which made them different in more ways than one.

William Moore was the grandson of a fugitive slave and the son of parents who were emancipated by the Civil War, but he grew up a child of privilege. His father was the church sexton for the First Presbyterian Church in West Chester, Pennsylvania, and William grew up a tight confederate of the very well-to-do boys who attended the church. He says he felt almost no color line. For the most part, their education, in school and out, was his education. He had the run of their libraries, he had access to university extension courses, attended lectures at the American Philosophical Society. He built boats with his friends and learned to sail. They collected rocks, birds' eggs, leaves, butterflies, and insects, identifying their specimens with the help of books or the many professional adults they knew. His interest in astronomy he attributes directly to his grandfather, the escaped slave, who, when William was eight or nine years old, took him out in the yard one night and showed him the Big Dipper, the North Star, the Pleiades, and Orion's Sword, the constellations slaves had used to find direction at night. His mother, a seamstress, taught him to read before he entered school, but the most important thing he got from his family educationally was probably an attitude toward school: "My parents utterly failed to understand how I should fail if other students succeeded" (Moore 1999: 9).

In 1895, after graduating from Howard University—"There I not only had the best academic training but was also inspired by contact with the great men of my race" (34)—he went to West Cape May, New Jersey, where most of the Blacks worked supporting the tourist trade in the neighboring shore resort of Cape May. He planned to teach one year there in the segregated elementary school, mostly to please his mother, before striking out for Texas, but "After I became acquainted with the situation . . . and found conditions that fitted in with my ideas, I resolved to stay for a while and work out some theories I had for a first-class elementary school" (12). The area was well known for racial prejudice, but Moore was pleased that the local board of education seemed willing to provide him with whatever supplies he needed, and he felt he could count on the parents, most of whom had only three or four years of education themselves and wanted better for their children. He ended up spending 53 years in that little school, starting out with eight grades in one room and ending up as the principal.

"All during my teaching career," he has written, "I had two main objectives. First, to make the school so attractive that the children were happy to be there, and second, to make the school a sort of community center" (15). There was more than a bit of whimsy in his teaching. One of his sons remembers him as liking to say, "A boy ain't hardly much good without a piece of string in his pocket." Along with the regular curriculum, he taught weaving, carpentry, bead work, carving, and toy-making, reserving the most fun things for inclement days to encourage attendance. The pupils wanted to be there because "Mr. Moore will have something new today and I'll miss it" (15). Reminiscent of the many long days he spent as a child studying the flora and fauna near the Brandywine River, every spring he took his class on the two-mile walk to Cape May Point—he believed in children walking—where they studied the many unusual forms of plant and animal life caused by the confluence of the Atlantic Ocean and the Delaware Bay. He also kept school interesting "by utilizing our inherent love of music." That meant a great deal of singing in class, but it also meant finding ways to use the children's interest in popular music, which led, among other things, to the formation of a mandolin and guitar club, "which became locally famous and played many engagements at schools, lodges, community meetings and parades" and was even broadcast on the radio (15).

I have a picture of my father, at the age of 15 or 16, holding his guitar in a very pensive sort of way. My father used to say that no student came away from Mr. Moore unchanged. He also believed that Mr. Moore could teach anything to anybody and could master anything himself. If he didn't know something, he went and got some books and studied them until he could teach it. The most famous example was his not learning the game of tennis until he was in his thirties, when he had to learn something about it because of his summer job at the local tennis courts, and eventually learning the game so well he wrote a manual on teaching tennis to beginners and became for decades the preferred teacher for many of Cape May's summer visitors. I wonder if the refrain I heard so frequently from my father when I was growing up, that I could learn anything anybody else could learn, was my father echoing Mr. Moore, who would have been echoing his own parents.

His teaching of Negro history seems to have been largely a response to a student, who asked, after reading about how proud some white people were of their lineage, what Negroes had to be proud of. In response, he wrote a kind of prose-poem for that student and others, outlining what Negroes had contributed to the making of America, which became a theme in his teaching. My mother, who went to school at the other end of the county (and was also in a pretty good school system by the standards of the area), had never heard of some of the Black writers my father could talk about when she met him and recalls being particularly surprised that my father knew the Black national anthem; outside of West Cape May, Black kids in the county had never heard of it and frequently refused to believe there was any such thing.

We have numerous comments on record from West Cape May students of that era, white and Black, suggesting that they didn't give much thought to segregation. It seemed natural to them; they didn't worry about it or think they were missing out on something. The Black and white schools were right next to one another, sharing common play space. Children played with one another before and after school and at recess and then went their separate ways when the bell rang.

The high school was integrated, and one of the problems that presented was that West Cape May kids couldn't afford the kind of clothes other kids could. At some point, Mr. Moore had his eighth graders make a list of the clothing they would need the next year and the next day brought in a bunch of mail-order catalogs so they could find out what their new wardrobes would cost. Once they had an estimate, he told them that it was their responsibility to save that amount from their summer jobs. At the end of the summer, he would take the children on the train to Philadelphia, where they could purchase their school clothes. The kids got a lesson in budgeting and savings, and they also didn't have to look like the poor kids all year. Actually, travel was a prominent part of the school program. The lower grades regularly visited museums and cultural institutions in Philadelphia. Every year, the community raised funds for the eighth-grade trip to Washington. Well into the 1950s, they couldn't stay in D.C. hotels, so they stayed with families from Cape May who lived in the area.

My aunt, Mildred Payne Moore, class of '29 at West Cape May School, remembers that one of his favorite songs had the theme:

If you can't get in the big front door,
Go over the garden wall.

She also remembers that one of his favorite sayings was "You have to measure up!" And he meant it—children had to be recommended for high school then, and if you didn't meet his standards, you didn't get recommended. The students who got by him typically had little trouble competing academically in high schools. As far back as the 1930s, West Cape May seems to have established a reputation for producing strong students. Many West Cape May kids knew algebra and Latin before they got to high school; some skipped grades and entered high school early. They regularly won academic awards. In the 1920s, two West Cape May students—Cornelius Johnson and Weaver Howard—were valedictorians. Soon after, Cordelia Howard would have been valedictorian, but the school told her they were doing away with that award and just designating some students honor students. Many people were sure the school just didn't want to give the award to another Black person. For decades, West Cape May seemed to send more Black students on to college than the whole rest of the county. It probably goes with the territory that, among Blacks in the rest of the county, there was some suggestion that West Cape May students were different somehow or held themselves apart.

Reflecting back on his students' achievements, Mr. Moore commented that "they won many honors and were acclaimed by principals and teachers as well-prepared students. All this as a result of teaching that we, as Americans, could do anything that any other American could do. That it was a disgrace to fail or quit when studies were hard, and that parents and community expected West Cape May students to succeed" (Moore: 13). The story of West Cape May Elementary illustrates what Kevin Gaines (1996) meant by the ability of Blacks to transform segregation into congregation. Mr. Moore and his school were a kind of counternarrative, daily giving the lie to the narrative of Black intellectual inferiority.

At first glance, the issues of contemporary urban education seem far removed from the world of William Moore and his children. I'm not sure that's really true, though. The search for prescriptions can be dangerous if we let it, but I don't know that all our work has given us a better model for educating children from the social margins than William Moore seems to have had in 1895. Give them teaching that is determined, energetic, and engaging. Hold them to high standards. Expose them to as much as you can, most especially the arts. Root the school in the community and take advantage of the culture the children bring with them. Pay attention to their social and ethical development. Recognize the reality of race, poverty, and other social barriers, but make children understand that barriers don't have to limit their lives; help them see themselves as contributing citizens of both a racial community and a larger one. Above all, no matter where in the social structure children are coming from, act as if their possibilities are boundless. I don't know that all our research and work and experimentation have given us any more clarity than that.

Program Glossary

Accelerated Schools Project

The Accelerated Schools Project was designed by Henry Levin in 1986 as an antidote to reforms centered on instructional remediation. It tries to treat every child like a gifted child, which means developing accelerated-learning environments. Its guiding principles include unity of purpose, empowerment plus responsibility, and building on strengths. For each accelerated school, the program trains a five-member team comprising the principal, a designated coach, a school staff member who will serve as an internal facilitator, and two other school staff members. *www.acceleratedschools.net*

Algebra Project

The Algebra Project was founded in 1982 by civil rights leader Robert P. Moses. Its premise is that mathematics is the key to full participation in modern society and that algebra is the key to learning higher-level mathematics. In its original form, the project intervened in the middle school mathematics curriculum, using children's everyday experiences and language as a bridge to abstract mathematical ideas. *www.algebra.org*

America's Choice School Design (K–12)

America's Choice School Design (formerly known as the National Alliance for Restructuring Education) benchmarks its work against international standards. The program emphasizes an aligned, standards-based curriculum, leadership development, professional learning communities, close monitoring of instruction, and early intervention. The program can be implemented in elementary, middle, and high schools. There is a focus on literacy at all levels. Leadership generally consists of the principal, a design coach, a literacy coach, a math coach, the heads of subject-area departments, and parent community outreach. *www.ncee.org/acsd*

ATLAS Learning Communities

Authentic Teaching, Learning, and Assessment for All Students is a partnership developed in 1992 from four different reform programs: James Comer's School Development Program, Howard Gardner's Project Zero, Theodore Sizer's Coalition of Essential Schools, and Janet Whitla's Education Development Center. Its work is structured around pathways, the feeder patterns from elementary to middle school and from middle school to high school. ATLAS works to make the entire K–12 experience more coherent. Instruction emphasizes depth over breadth, and basic skills are taught in the context of problemsolving. Whole-faculty study groups within and across schools meet weekly to examine classroom practices. The program insists on strong family and community involvement and a culture of organizational self-assessment and reflection.
www.atlascommunities.org

Audrey Cohen College: Purpose-Centered Education (K–12)

Purpose Centered Education was developed by Audrey Cohen College in the 1970s. It can be adapted for any grade from kindergarten through graduate school. The premise of the program is that students learn more when learning is connected to a clear, complex, socially useful, and meaningful purpose. Students might spend a semester studying ways to improve transportation systems and the next studying ways to make the workplace safer. The college has identified 24 essential abilities that are needed for achieving a purpose and that operate as standards students are expected to reach by using their knowledge and skills to plan, carry out, and evaluate a constructive action.

Chicago Annenberg Challenge

Operating from 1995 to 2001, the Chicago Annenberg Challenge used its share of Walter Annenberg's gift to public education to leverage school change by focusing on the time eduators had available to work on reform, on the size of schools and classrooms, and on reducing the isolation of schools and educators. At its height, it supported 220 schools. It is credited with sponsoring professional development across the city at a time when that was not a system priority.

Coalition of Essential Schools

The Coalition of Essential Schools was founded by Ted Sizer of Brown University in 1984. Their ten common principles include the ideas that school should focus on helping young people learn to use their minds well; that each student should master a limited number of essential skills and areas of knowledge; that the school's goals should apply to all students, while the means to these goals will vary as those students themselves vary; that teaching and learning should be personalized to the maximum feasible extent—no teacher should have direct responsibility for more than 80 students in the high school and middle school and no more than 20 in elementary school; that the governing practical metaphor of the school should be student-as-worker rather than the more familiar metaphor of teacher-as-deliverer-of-instructional-services; that teaching and learning should be documented and assessed with tools based on student performance of real tasks; and that the school should demonstrate nondiscriminatory and inclusive policies, practices, and pedagogies. The coalition imposes no specific curricular innovations or instructional techniques on member schools. *www.essentialschools.org*

Co-nect Schools

Co-nect was established by members of the Educational Technologies Group at BBN Corporation in 1992. Co-nect offers comprehensive school-wide and district-wide capacity-building programs that include planning for continuous improvement, data-driven decisionmaking, and such alignment strategies as curriculum mapping, technology integration, benchmarking, and leadership training. Co-nect partners with districts to identify the unique root causes of student underperformance in schools and to design a solution to address their gaps, support existing initiatives, and reflect specific focus areas, school demographics, and budget realities. *www.co-nect.net*

Core Knowledge

Founded in 1986 by E. D. Hirsch Jr., Core Knowledge is a reform centered on curriculum content, arguing that there is a specific body of knowledge and group of skills that students need to acquire at each grade level. It offers a progression of detailed grade-by-grade topics in language arts, mathematics, science, history, geography, music, and fine arts, so that students build on knowledge from prekindergarten through eighth grade. The Core Knowledge Sequence typically comprises 50 percent of a school's curriculum; the other 50 percent allows schools to meet state and local requirements. *www.coreknowledge.org*

Direct Instruction

Direct Instruction evolved from a theory of instruction designed by Siegfried Engelmann at the University of Oregon. Direct Instruction emphasizes very detailed and carefully planned lessons designed around small learning increments and clearly defined and prescribed teaching tasks. The degree of prescription leaves little room for teacher innovation or flexibility. There is no tracking; every student receives the same instruction. This is a particularly controversial model, much disdained by progressives, but its research base is substantial. *www.nifdi.org*

Expeditionary Learning Schools Outward Bound

Currently being implemented in 140 schools, Expeditionary Learning Schools Outward Bound (ELOB) is based on the principles of Outward Bound. Curriculum, instruction, assessment, school culture, and school structures are organized around producing high-quality student work in learning expeditions—long-term investigations of important questions and subjects that include individual and group projects, field studies, and performances and presentations of student work. *www.elschools.org*

Knowledge Is Power Program

The Knowledge Is Power Program (KIPP) began in 1994 when two former Teach for America teachers, Mike Feinberg and Dave Levin, launched a fifth-grade public school program in inner-city Houston, Texas. There are currently 57 KIPP public schools enrolling more than 14,000 students. The program offers a structured, no-nonsense, no-excuses learning environment in high-need communities. Instructional time is extended—as much as 60 percent more learning time than is available in typical schools. KIPP principals have substantial autonomy with respect to budget and personnel. *www.kipp.org*

Modern Red SchoolHouse

The Modern Red SchoolHouse (MRSH) was established in 1992 by the Hudson Institute. The MRSH design builds on the strengths of the schools and develops a customized implementation program. MRSH provides the school with the tools to design a standards-driven curriculum, develop personalized instruction informed by timely access to data, establish effective organizational practices, use technology to improve communication, and develop parent and community partnership programs. The MRSH design involves teachers, administrators, paraprofessionals, and a family and community task force. *www.mrsh.org*

Paideia

Mortimer Adler's Paideia program is probably best known for its emphasis on promoting critical thinking through Socratic dialogue, much of which takes place in seminar settings. The program generally discourages didactic instruction except when it is being used strategically. Paideia schools offer the same integrated core curriculum for all students, including fine arts, music, foreign language, and the manual arts, giving students the opportunity to explore these areas as they relate to the core academic subjects. *www.paideia.org*

Reading One-to-One

Developed by Dr. George Farkas in 1991 as an affordable alternative to higher-cost reading intervention programs, Reading One-to-One uses trained volunteers, many of them college students, to provide low-cost tutoring in reading and writing skills to at-risk elementary school children. Forty-minute tutoring sessions occur three to four days per week.

Reading Recovery

Founded in New Zealand over 30 years ago, Reading Recovery targets the lowest-achieving first graders. Individual students receive a half-hour, one-on-one lesson each school day for 12 to 20 weeks with a teacher who has been given training in the Reading Recovery methods. There were more than 12,000 Reading Recovery teachers for the 2006–07 school year. *www.readingrecovery.org*

School Development Program (The Comer Process)

In 1968, reacting to the assassination of Dr. Martin Luther King Jr., Yale University child psychiatrist James Comer began developing what is now known as the School Development Program (also known as the Comer Process), which improves schools by improving the social climate among the adults in schools. Much of the work is done through three teams: a parent team, a planning and management team, and a student and staff support team. All three teams are expected to follow three guiding principles:

1. No Fault, in that people should focus on problem-solving rather than fixing blame.

2. Consensus Decisionmaking, which attempts to avoid creating winners and losers in the decisionmaking process.

3. Collaboration, which includes encouraging collective work among constituencies that are ordinarily at odds with one another.

www.comerprocess.org

Success for All

Robert Slavin, Nancy Madden, and a team of developers from Johns Hopkins University founded Success for All in 1987. Its teaching approach emphasizes cooperative learning, frequent assessment of student progress, and at least 90 minutes of daily reading instruction. The program also features a family support team to encourage parental support and involvement as well as to address problems at home, and a local facilitator to provide mentoring, counseling, and support to the school as needed.
www.successforall.net

Talent Development High School with Career Academics

The Talent Development High School with Career Academies (TDHS) was first implemented in 1995, informed in part by the research on dropout prevention. The core elements of TDHS include a Ninth-Grade Success Academy (teams of four to five teachers are responsible for 150–180 ninth-grade students), Career Academies for the Upper Grades, Core Curriculum in a Four-Period Day (includes English, social studies, science, and math), Catch-Up Curriculum and Extra Help (for math and English classes), and Twilight School (an alternative after-hours program for students with poor attendance, discipline problems, or who come from prison or suspension from another school). *www.csos.jhu.edu*

More details on most of these programs, including some evaluative data, can be found in An Educators' Guide to Schoolwide Reform (*www.aasa. org/issues_and_insights/district_organization/Reform/index.htm*) or from the Comprehensive School Reform Quality Center (*www.csrq.org/reports.asp*).

Notes

Introduction

1. With respect to teaching to the test, however one defines that slippery term, note that teaching to the test is pretty clearly a higher level of instruction than children in bottom-tier schools traditionally got. In Chicago, it would seem that the cheating problem is not an enormous one. One analysis estimated that fewer than 2 percent of elementary classrooms were cheating (Duffrin 2001). When it occurred, it seemed to be initiated by individual teachers rather than by principals. As a deterrent, the Chicago Board annually retests some classrooms randomly and some others where scores seemed questionable. In addition, under Paul Vallas principals got the message that low scores might cost them their jobs, but cheating could cost them their pensions. Duffrin found that when schools were put on probation, cheating went up sharply, by 75 percent compared to a year earlier, with nearly all the increase coming from the bottom third of schools and especially from those classrooms where students had scored most poorly the year before. Cheating on the math test, which did not count toward probation, did not increase. On the other hand, when the board instituted its policy of ending social promotion, there was no significant increase in cheating, suggesting that cheating is more closely tied to sanctions against schools or teachers than to sanctions against students. At the other end of the spectrum, there have been many plausible allegations of fraud in Texas—i.e., pushing weaker students to drop out so that scores look better and then lying about the dropout rate.

2. A wave of gentrification currently affecting Chicago's inner-city neighborhoods may play havoc with the mobility rate, especially in conjunction with a policy of aggressively closing schools. Chicago's sprawling housing projects are largely a thing of the past.

Chapter 1 Dimensions of Demoralization

1. The Utah teacher also suggested that women were "much more likely to ask his advice, trade ideas, and express interest in his techniques than men." It would be important to find out whether this is a general pattern. It would not be difficult to think of reasons why male teachers, especially at the elementary school level, would be more status-threatened than women.

2. Some forms of traditional African American culture sanction strict disciplining of children (e.g., Hale-Benson 1986: 123–24). Anyon (1997) suggests that in the angry climate of the contemporary inner city, some African American teachers use that tradition to legitimate behavior toward children that is in fact abusive. The point is well taken, but teachers of all races can do it: "You have to smack 'em. That's what their parents do. It's all they understand." That reductionist language—"all they understand"—should be a red flag.

3. Happy Talk culture is encouraged by other factors, including the generally low standards that some professionals in urban schools have been exposed to and their sensitivity to the negative images of themselves in most public dialogue about urban schools.

Chapter 2 "I Don't Want Your Nasty Pot of Gold"

1. I am indebted to Michelle Adler-Morrison, Chicago Comer facilitator, for the Pot of Gold story.

2. In order to protect the anonymity of schools, descriptive details have been changed.

3. The material on Westside predates Chicago school reform. See Charles Payne, *Getting What We Ask For: The Ambiguity of Success and Failure in Urban Education* (Westport, CT: Greenwood Press, 1984), esp. 58–71.

Chapter 3 Weak Skills and Bad Attitudes

1. Gouldner notes that patterns of interaction in school seemed to replicate patterns at home. Children with high rates of negative interaction with teachers also tended to have high rates of negative interaction at home. Children with low frequency of interaction in one context tended to have low frequency of interaction in the other. If these are generalizable patterns, the implications are truly frightening.

2. The current rush in many cities to open new high schools as quickly as possible may actually be exacerbating these patterns. The new schools—charters, magnets, academies, and so on—may be attracting a disproportionate share of the better teachers and students, leaving neighborhood schools with even fewer human resources. (On Chicago, see Chicago Acorn 2001.)

3. One can argue that Festinger's arguments apply better to education than to millenarian movements. For criticisms of Festinger and his colleagues, see Dein 2001.

4. There is a parallel phenomenon at the school level. In Chicago, where so many schools had fewer than 15 percent of kids performing on grade level in the early 1990s, schools with 20–30 percent performing on grade level could be very difficult to work with. Compared to their neighboring institutions, they were doing well and nobody could tell them anything. At the individual teacher level, we need to better understand how successful teachers negotiate their success. The "acting white" literature (Fordham 1996) suggests that high-achieving inner-city students may be at some pains to hide their success, or at least not flaunt it. In failing schools, relatively successful students and relatively successful teachers may have to negotiate their social status in similar ways.

5. American students have a longer school day than students in many other countries, yet less time devoted to instruction. The discrepancies are largest in middle and high schools (Smith 1998: 9). A compressed schedule like Chicago's is also dysfunctional in that it reduces the opportunities teachers have for spending informal, get-to-know-you time with students. This seems to be even more of a problem in high schools where security guards, who do have unstructured time, often seem to have the greatest store of knowledge about students' out-of-school lives. Note, too, that one used to hear from progressive educators (with their characteristic bias toward teaching style) that if students don't learn something, spending more time teaching them with the same methods can't be expected to do much good. One does not hear that comment much anymore, which is good since it's almost certainly wrong. It fails to take into account how teaching attention is actually distributed. In point of fact, a strong relationship between instructional time and learning is well established. Various studies (summarized by Smith 1998: 9) find relationships ranging from modest to substantial, with the most powerful relationships found among disadvantaged and/or lower-performing students.

6. The 6 percent figure is probably low; smart principals avoided the Sub Center and developed their own pools of substitutes, assuring themselves of higher quality.

Chapter 4 Sympathy, Knowledge, and Truth

1. I have not directly addressed culturally relevant pedagogy because of issues of the generalizability of its research base, but see Lee (2007) for a sense of how powerful that pedagogy can be. For similar reasons, I have not addressed

the issue of didactic vs. interactive pedagogy. One of the Consortium's best-known instructional studies (Smith, Lee, and Newmann 2001) concludes that while many teachers believe poor children have a particular need for didactic instruction, in fact, students do best in classrooms where the instruction is more interactive. The problem is that the study doesn't have any way to measure the quality of the teaching done under each label. It is possible that it is, in fact, comparing interactive teaching done reasonably well to didactic teaching done badly. In test-happy Chicago at the time of the study, it seems likely that interactive teaching was most likely to be done by young, energetic, recently trained teachers who were ideologically committed to student-centered pedagogies. On the other side, it's likely that many of the people doing didactic instruction aren't so much committed to it as resigned to it. In fact, I do believe, largely because of my personal experience as a teacher, that kids get more out of progressive pedagogies done well, but with Lisa Delpit, I will take structured pedagogies done well over progressive done poorly. At this juncture in the discussion, I am not sure how helpful this debate is, given my suspicion that the spirit which animates teaching is more important than the style of teaching, perhaps especially so for disadvantaged children. Nevertheless, the findings that didactic teaching is particularly dominant in African American schools and that kids get more of it as they get older are very disturbing. We can be almost certain this represents poorly executed didactic teaching.

2. Interesting in this respect is Uri Treisman's Agile Mind program for teaching mathematics, a feedback-rich instructional approach to math that seems to be making significant headway in the Chicago schools that have implemented it. For a guide to developing a school-wide assessment program, see Boudett, City, and Murnane (2005).

3. It would be interesting to think about some of the no-nonsense charter schools in this light. KIPP (Knowledge Is Power Program) comes to mind, but that is only one example. One could see how they could get the demand component down but have more trouble sending the signals that legitimated demanding behavior. The latter can call for a fairly nuanced set of signals, and even within the same program, it wouldn't be surprising if some sites got it right and some didn't.

4. Ferguson (2002) finds that teacher encouragement is more important for nonwhite students than teacher demand, but his sample is largely suburban, so a threshold level of demands may be less an issue there. Moreover, the way the questions are phrased—"My teachers encourage me to work hard" against "The teacher demands it (hard work)"—doesn't distinguish between demand-

ing behavior and supportive behavior in the way those terms are being used here. Both questions have an element of demand to them.

5. In the early years of the Algebra Project, it was uncommon to see sixth graders doing algebra, certainly in urban schools. Students understood that algebra was for smart kids, not kids like themselves. In Chicago, we used to see students arrange their books so that their Algebra Project materials were prominently displayed, their way of hurling counternarrative.

6. Among Latinos, Sciarra and Whitson (2007), trying to find predictors of academic attainment, find that locus of control is the strongest predictor of the variables examined and is substantially stronger than self-esteem. Cummings (1977) notes that the family seems to have a much larger—three times larger—impact on shaping the sense of fate control among girls than among boys. For an example of reductionist interpretation of these ideas, see Justin (1970), who decides that "fatalism" among Mexican American students is just a function of that old ancestral culture. There is no consideration of the possibility that at least some of it is a function of experiences outside of the family.

7. With younger students, Cohen et al. (2006) have demonstrated that the racial gap in achievement on an experimental task can be reduced by 40 percent by reducing the sense of stereotype threat among African American middle schoolers.

8. The work on the long-term effect of class size should be considered in light of the evidence gathered by Sawhill and Ludwig (2007) about the long-term benefits of intervening in the lives of disadvantaged children before they reach the age of ten. It is worth noting that the idea of Black and Latino children as particularly school-vulnerable appears in Coleman's data in several ways. For example, "Thus, if a white pupil from a home that is strongly and effectively supportive of education is put in a school where most pupils do not come from such homes, his achievement will be little different than if he were in a school composed of others like himself. But if a minority pupil from a home without much educational strength is put with schoolmates with strong educational backgrounds, his achievement is likely to increase (Coleman et al. 1966: 22).

9. This is not necessarily a self-concept issue in a direct way. We can accept that the group we are identified with is of little worth and yet decide that we are the exception. What that would do, of course, is complicate intra-group bonding.

10. For a critique of the static assumptions about youth identity that inform some Afrocentric schools, see Ginwright 2004.

Chapter 5 "You Can't Kill It and You Can't Teach It"

1. Hess sees superintendents as the dominant actors in their districts. This is too simple, and his own argument seems to undercut it. If they were in fact dominant, they would not feel so pressured to impress quickly. Note, too, that Hess really adduces little evidence as to the motives of superintendents. His interpretation is plausible, but there are other possibilities, some more normative (i.e., superintendents may believe that the nature of dysfunctional bureaucracy demands that a lot needs to be changed at once). Some may just believe that they are responding to the diverse needs of children.

2. Paul Hill and his collaborators contend that "When opponents feel free to come out and attack reform supporters, an initiative is dead," which seems an overstatement (Hill, Campbell, and Harvey 2000: 39). It is hard to find a reform of any consequence that does not get attacked, and conflict need not be all bad. Bryk and Schneider (2002) point out that conflict means more viewpoints are likely to be aired and examined publicly, so that if consensus does emerge, it may be more firmly based than would be the case where fewer ideas were vetted.

3. Hess (1999: 79) finds unions to be supportive of most reforms, but he also notes that "the need to win union acquiescence discourages local policymakers from emphasizing reforms that require significant change from teachers" (60), which is a problem since those seem to be the only changes that matter long-term.

4. Because of their size, many charters do not have to do NCLB reporting, but there is a larger issue of charters in various locales being able to avoid accountability in ways that make it easier for them to produce misleading results. KIPP Academies, for example, have been accused of producing glitzy numbers by pushing some kids out, retaining some kids, and so forth (see El-Amine and Glazer 2007).

Chapter 6 Missing the Inner Intent

1. The long-running, but now dying, debate over whether money matters in education was always a racist and class-biased discourse in the sense that it is really a question about poor children and children of color. Someone asking the same question about middle-class children would hardly be taken seriously. In that sense, it is part of the dominant ideological discourse justifying existing distributions of privilege. In the context of this chapter, however, the point to note is that just as inattention to context is one of the most impor-

tant factors leading to poor program implementation, discussions as wrong-headed as this one remain viable by ignoring context. In the class-size litera-ture, for example, we have people who look at cases where reduced class size makes no difference in learning and conclude class size doesn't matter. In the most literal sense, of course, this is true. Class size—like most structural changes—seldom makes a difference in and of itself. It doesn't make a differ-ence if teachers don't believe their children can learn; it doesn't make a dif-ference if teachers teach the smaller classes the same way they taught larger ones; it doesn't make a difference if staffing a greater number of smaller classes requires hiring less qualified teachers (as happened in California). The litera-ture telling us that class size doesn't matter is weak on these untidy details of context. Reframing the discussion to something like, What has to happen to make class size (or whatever resource) matter?, would have yielded a much more useful conversation.

2. Despite its track record of implementation, when philanthropist Walter An-nenberg decided to make a $500 million gift for the improvement of ur-ban education, he essentially put the Coalition in charge of it, which was widely read as another example of the disconnect between performance and influence.

3. This may be a problem in the longer term. It is not clear how programs that import so much structure—Sylvan Learning is another example—typically interact with what is already there. One could foresee a scenario in which such programs became isolated from the life of the school, raising scores but not contributing to broader cultural or organizational change. There are also some questions about how lasting the gains are from some of the early-grade reading programs. For a more critical reading of the SFA case, see Pogrow (2000).

4. If we consider the period of rapidly expanding programs in the early 1990s to be the second developmental generation for whole-school reforms, there are some reform models, notably First Things First and Talent Development, that could be considered third generation. These are very self-conscious about learning from the mistakes of their predecessors; more comprehensive than most of their predecessors in the way they conceive the issues, which includes an awareness of the importance of social capital; and more careful about providing stronger instructional and organizational scaffolding, to use Lisa Delpit's term. We know that their early implementations are running into the usual thicket of problems, but cannot say yet whether what they've learned from their predecessors will help them move through it more quick-ly (Quint and Byndloss 2003; Quint 2006; Kemple, Herlihy, and Smith 2005).

5. These tensions overlap with another common split: between different cohorts of implementers, including the founders and subsequent staff. Founders are typically most intimately involved with schools when the programs are small, trying to change only one or a few schools. As programs grow, they become administrators speaking to the outside world. For later cohorts, it may seem that the founders grow out of touch with the complexities of dealing with many more schools, typically with a program trying to do more things than was the case when the founders were in the field and typically within a changed political environment. (The founders didn't have to be bothered with NCLB and the like.) To the latter cohorts, the "fact" that founders are out of touch with day-to-day realities accounts for the willingness of founders to think it's safe to expand. At worst, cohort tensions become battles over authenticity, with each cohort thinking that their experience represents the real version of the program and all others represent co-optation or dilution.

6. In another example of the endless capacity of bureaucracy to trivialize good ideas, the federal government has built having a faculty vote of confidence into its *definition* of comprehensive school reform.

7. I would argue that Berman and McLaughlin undervalue administrative pressure and overvalue local development of program materials.

8. One of the most sensible and thoughtful overviews of what the research actually does tell us is provided by David and Cuban (2006).

9. From afar, both the America's Choice program and the Knowledge Is Power Program might be at this kind of juncture, where their track record attracts resources that could tempt them to grow beyond their capacity.

10. The numbers and categories here are not completely divorced from reality. They have been (loosely) extrapolated from several conversations with members of the Math Directors Network, math directors from nine urban areas at various stages of implementing reform-based mathematics. The network grew out of the work of the Pew Charitable Trusts. I thank particularly Jane David and Brenda Turnbull, organizers of the network, for comments on an earlier version of this discussion.

References

Achieve, Inc. (2007). *Closing the expectations gap, 2007*. Washington, DC: American Diploma Project Network. *www.achieve.org* (accessed April 21, 2007).

Allensworth, E. (2004). *Ending social promotion: Dropout rates in Chicago after implementation of the eighth-grade promotion gate*. Chicago: Consortium on Chicago School Research.

Allensworth, E., and Easton, J. Q. (2007). *What matters for staying on-track and graduating in Chicago public schools*. Chicago: Consortium on Chicago School Research.

Allensworth, E., Newmann, F. M., Smith, B., and Bryk, A. S. (2001). *School instructional program coherence: Benefits and challenges*. Chicago: Consortium on Chicago School Research.

Allport, G. W. (2001). *The nature of prejudice*. Garden City, NY: Doubleday (orig. pub. 1954).

Anderson, J. (1988). *The education of Blacks in the South, 1860–1953*. Chapel Hill, NC: University of North Carolina Press.

Anderson, V., and Lenz, L. (2001). Duncan charts a new path for Chicago public schools. *Catalyst Chicago*, September. *www.catalyst-chicago.org/news/index. php?item=142&cat=22* (accessed June 29, 2004).

Anderson, V., Lenz, L., and Ortiz, M. (2001). Solid footing for city's new school leaders. *Catalyst Chicago*, June. *www.catalyst-chicago.org/news/index. php?item=129&cat=19.*

Anyon, J. (1997). *Ghetto schooling: A political economy of urban educational reform*. New York: Teachers College Press.

———. (2005). *Radical possibilities: Public policy, urban education, and a new social movement*. New York: Routledge.

Archer, J. (2006). Beefing up personnel skills. *Education Week*, October 4.

———. (2006). Time on his side. *Education Week*, June 7.

Ayers, W., and Klonsky, M. (1994). Navigating a restless sea: The continuing struggle to achieve a decent education for African American youngsters in Chicago. *Journal of Negro Education 63*(1), 5–18.

Berends, M., Bodilly, S., and Kirby, S. (2002). Looking back over a decade of whole-school reform: The experience of new American schools. *Phi Delta Kappan 84*(2), 168–175.

Berman, P., and McLaughlin, M. (1978). *Federal programs supporting educational change, Vol. 8: Implementing and sustaining innovations.* Santa Monica, CA: Rand Corporation.

Black, P., Harrison, C., Lee, C., Marshall, B., and William, D. (2004). Working inside the black box: Assessment for learning in the classroom. *Phi Delta Kappan 86*(1), 8–21.

Black, P., and William, D. (1998). Inside the black box: Raising standards through classroom assessment. *Phi Delta Kappan 80*(2), 139–148.

Blair, J. (2004). D.C. union leader sentenced to nine-year prison term. *Education Week*, February 11.

Bloom, H., Ham, S., Melton, L., and O'Brien, J. (2001). *Evaluating the accelerated schools approach: A look at early implementation and impacts on student achievement in eight elementary schools.* New York: MDRC.

Blume, H., and Rubin, J. (2006). Brewer gets no honeymoon at L.A. Unified. *Los Angeles Times*, November 15. *www.latimes.com/news/education/la-me-lausd15 nov15,1,4645152.story?coll=la-news-learning* (accessed October 17, 2007).

Boghossian, N. (2005, December 27). Kirst urges LA to study mayoral takeover before making decisions. *Los Angeles Daily News. http://ed.stanford.edu/ suse* (accessed October 21, 2007).

Bonilla-Silva, E. (2004). *Racism without racists: Color-blind racism and the persistence of racial inequality in the United States.* Lanham, MD: Rowman & Littlefield.

Borman, G., Hewes, G. M., Overman, L. T., and Brown, S. (2002). *Comprehensive school reform and student achievement: A meta-analysis.* Baltimore, MD: Johns Hopkins University.

Boston Globe. (2005). School-wise teachers. March 30.

Boudett, K. P., City, E. A., and Murnane, R. J. (Eds.). (2005). *Data wise: A step-by-step guide to using assessment results to improve teaching and learning.* Cambridge, MA: Harvard Education Press.

Bowles, S., and Gintis, H. (1976). *Schooling in capitalist America: Educational reform and the contradictions of economic life.* New York: Basic Books.

Boyd, D., Lankford, H., Loeb, S., Rockoff, J., and Wyckoff, J. (2007). *The narrowing gap in New York City teacher qualifications and its implications for student achievement in high-poverty schools.* Washington, DC: Urban Institute. *www.urban.org/url.cfm?ID=1001103* (accessed October 6, 2007).

Bradley, A. (1995). What price success? *Education Week*, November 22.

Brehm, J. (2003). Review of *Social capital and poor communities*, by Susan Saegert, J. Phillip Thompson, and Mark R. Warren. *Contemporary Sociology 32*(3), 345–346.

Brehm, J., and Gates, S. (1994). When supervision fails to induce control. *Journal of Theoretical Politics.*

———. (2004). Social work supervisors as trust-brokers. In K. Cook (Ed.), *Trust in Organizations.* New York: Russell Sage Foundation.

Brimelow, P. (2003). *The worm in the apple: How the teacher unions are destroying American education.* New York: HarperCollins.

Bryk, A., Easton, J. Q., Kerbow, D., Rollow, S. G., and Sebring, P. B. (1993). *A view from the elementary schools: The state of reform in Chicago.* Chicago: Consortium on Chicago School Research.

Bryk, A., Thum, Y. M., Easton, J. Q., and Luppescu, S. (1997). *Assessing school productivity using student achievement: The Chicago public elementary schools.* Chicago: Consortium on Chicago School Research.

Bryk, A., Lee, V., and Holland, P. (1993). *Catholic schools and the common good.* Cambridge, MA: Harvard University Press.

Bryk, A., Nagaoka, J. K., and Newmann, F. M. (2000). *Chicago classroom demands for authentic intellectual work.* Chicago: Consortium on Chicago School Research.

Bryk, A. S., and Schneider, B. (2002). *Trust in schools: A core resource for improvement.* New York: Russell Sage Foundation.

Burney, D., and Elmore, R. (1998). Improving instruction through professional development in New York City's community district #2. Philadelphia: Consortium for Policy Research in Education. *www.cpre.org.*

Catalyst Chicago. (2000). An annotated guide to rising elementary test scores. *www.catalyst-chicago.org.*

———. (2001). Solid footing for city's new leaders. June. *www.catalyst-chicago.org.*

———. (2002). Voices of Chicago school reform. June. *www.catalyst-chicago.org.*

Cavanagh, S. (2007). Scores on urban NAEP inch up. *Education Week*, November 15.

Cecelski, D. (1994). *Along freedom road: Hyde County, North Carolina and the fate of Black schools in the South.* Chapel Hill, NC: University of North Carolina Press.

Chicago Acorn. 2001. Instructional inequality and its impact on ACORN neighborhood high schools. Unpublished paper.

Chicago Tribune. (1988). Chicago schools: Worst in America.

———. (2004). A disappointing history lesson. June 18.

————. (2007). 25,000 "superior" teachers. August 13. *www.chicagotribune. com* (accessed August 28, 2007).

Chubb, J., and Moe, T. (1990). *Politics, markets, and America's schools.* Washington, DC: Brookings Institution.

Cohen, G. L., Garcia, J., Apfel, N., and Master, A. (2006). Reducing the racial achievement gap: A social-psychological intervention. *Science 313*(5791), 1307–1310.

Coleman, J. (1988). Social capital in the creation of human capital. *American Journal of Sociology* 94, 95–120.

Coleman, J., Campbell, E., Hobson, C., McPartland, J., Mood, A., Weinfeld, F. D., and York, R. (1966). *Equality of educational opportunity.* Washington, DC: United States Department of Education.

Comer, J. (1980). *School power: Implications of an intervention project.* New York: Free Press.

————. (1997). *Waiting for a miracle: Why schools can't solve our problems—and how we can.* New York: Penguin Group.

Comer, J., Haynes, N. M., Joyner, E. T., and Ben-Avie, M. (Eds.). (1996). *Rallying the whole village: The Comer process for reforming education.* New York: Teachers College Press.

Conley, S. (1991). Review of *Research on teacher participation in school decision making.* In G. Grant (Ed.), *Review of Research in Education* 17, 225–266. Washington, DC: American Educational Research Association.

Cooper, M. (2003). City is selling symbol of its troubled schools. *New York Times,* July 9.

Cortes, R. (2006). Herman Badillo has a plan. *New York Latino Journal,* December 20.

Cosby, B. (2004). The pound cake speech. *www.blackpast.org/?q=2004-bill-cosby-pound-cake-speech.*

Council of Great City Schools. (2004). *Restoring excellence to the District of Columbia public schools.* Washington, DC: Council of Great City Schools.

Cremin, L. (1965). *The genius of American education.* New York: Vintage.

Cuban, L. (1984). *How teachers taught: Constancy and change in American classrooms, 1890–1980.* New York: Longman.

Cuban, L., and Usdan, M. (Eds.). (2003). *Powerful reforms with shallow roots: Improving America's urban schools.* New York: Teachers College Press.

Cummings, S. (1977). Family socialization and fatalism among Black adolescents. *Journal of Negro Education 46*(1), 62–75.

Datnow, A., Hubbard, L., and Mehan, H. (2002). *Extending educational reform: From one school to many.* New York: Routledge Farmer.

David, J. L., and Cuban, L. (2006). *Cutting through the hype: A taxpayer's guide to school reforms.* Mt. Morris, Illinois: Education Week Press.

David, J. L., and Shields, P. (2001). *When theory hits reality: Standards-based reform in urban districts* (Final Narrative Report). Palo Alto, CA: SRI International. *www.sri.com/policy/cep/pubs/pew/pewfinal.pdf.*

Davis, M. (2003). Student scores show progress but critics question price. *North Jersey Media Group,* June 23. *www.edlawcenter.org/ELCPublic/ELC_in_Media_030623.pdf.*

Davis, M. R. (2006). After four years, NCLB impact seen as positive and negative. *Education Week,* March 28. *www.edweek.org/ew/artilces/2006/03/28/30cep_web.h25.html* (accessed April 5, 2007).

Dein, S. (2001). What really happens when prophecy fails: The case of Lubavitch. *Sociology of Religion 62*(3), 383.

Devine, J. (1996). *Maximum security: The culture of violence in inner-city schools.* Chicago: University of Chicago Press.

Dillon, S. (2007). Democrats make Bush school act an election issue. *New York Times,* December 23.

Dingerson, L. (2007). *Unlovely: How a market-based educational experiment is failing New Orleans children.* New York: Open Society Institute. *www.tilsonfunds.com/Personal/KeepingthePromiseWhitePapers.pdf* (accessed September 1, 2007).

DiPardo, A. (1997). Of war, doom and laughter: Images of collaboration in the public-school workplace. *Teacher Education Quarterly 24*(1), 89–104.

Du Bois, W. E. B. (1935). Does the Negro need separate schools? *Journal of Negro Education 4*(3), 328–335.

———. (1961). *Souls of Black Folk.* Greenwich, CT: Fawcett.

Duffrin, E. (1998). Chicago comes up short on what it takes to improve teaching. *Catalyst Chicago. www.catalyst-chicago.org.*

———. (2000). New numbers confirm good, bad of promotion policy. *Catalyst Chicago,* April. *www.catalyst-chicago.org/arch/04-00/0400main.htm.*

———. (2001). Test cheating analysis finds little in CPS, *Catalyst Chicago,* September. *www.catalyst-chicago.org/news/index.php?item=145&cat=30* (accessed June 29, 2004).

Dunbar, P. L. (1915). *The complete poems of Paul Laurence Dunbar.* New York: Dodd, Mead.

Easton, J. (2006). Presentation to senior Chicago Public School staff and the Board of Education. Chicago. July 27.

Easton, J., Rosenkranz, T., and Bryk, A. (2001). *Annual CPS test trend review, 2000.* Chicago: Consortium on Chicago School Research.

Easton, J., and Storey, S. (1994). The development of local school councils. *Education and Urban Society 26*(3), 220–237.

Eccles, J., and Templeton, J. (2002). Extracurricular and other after-school activities for youth. In W. Secada (Ed.), *Review of Research in Education 26,* 113–180. Washington, DC: American Educational Research Association.

Editorial Projects in Education. (2007). Diplomas count, 2007. *www.edweek.org/ew/toc/2007/06/12/index.html.*

Education Alliance (2006). Through different lenses: West Virginia school staff and students react to school climate. *www.educationalliance.org* (accessed October 6, 2007).

Education Week. (2007). Graduation profiles. June 12. *www.edweek.org/ew/articles/2007/06/12/40gradprofiles.h26.html* (accessed November 1, 2007).

El-Amine, Z., and Glazer, L. (2007). *The "evolution of public education": A critical look at Washington, D.C., charter schools.* New York: Open Society Institute. *www.tilsonfunds.com/Personal/KeepingthePromiseWhitePapers.pdf* (accessed September 1, 2007).

Elmore, R. (1996). Getting to scale with good educational practice. *Harvard Educational Review 66,* 1–26.

———. (1999). *Leadership of large-scale improvement in American education.* Unpublished manuscript, Graduate School of Education, Harvard University.

Elrich, M. (1994). The stereotype within: Why students don't buy Black history month. *Washington Post,* February 13.

Enoch, R., and Zuviri, G. (2006). *What Olney teachers say about their students and school.* Philadelphia: Research for Action.

Erlichson, B. A., and Goertz, M. (2001). *Implementing whole-school reform in New Jersey, year two.* New Brunswick, NJ: Department of Public Policy and Center for Government Services.

Erlichson, B. A., and Slavin, R. (n.d.) *Achievement data presented to Supreme Court* (ELC memo). Newark, NJ: Education Law Center. *www.edlawcenter.org/ELCPublic/Alert_0403_DataSummary.htm.*

Evans, P. (2003). A principal's dilemmas: Theory and reality of school redesign. *Phi Delta Kappan 84*(6), 424–437.

Fairclough, A. (2007). *A class of their own: Black teachers in the segregated South.* Cambridge, MA: Harvard University Press.

Ferguson, F. (2002). What *doesn't* meet the eye: Understanding and addressing racial disparities in high-achieving suburban schools. *www.ncrel.org/gap/ferg* (accessed November 1, 2007).

Ferguson, R. (2003). Teachers' perception and expectations and the black–white test score gap. *Urban Education 38,* 460–507.

————. (2006). Recent research on the achievement gap: How lifestyle factors and classroom culture affect black–white differences. *Harvard Education Letter*, November/December 2006. *www.edletter.org/current/ferguson.shtml* (accessed March 3, 2007).

Fessenden, F. (2006). Abbot school district among the top spenders. *New York Times*, October 30.

Fessenden, F., and Hu, W. (2007). Data show wide differences in New Jersey school spending. *New York Times*, March 24. *www.nytimes.com/2007/03/24/nyregion/24spend.html*.

Festinger, L., Riecken, H. W., and Schachter, S. (1956). *When prophecy fails: A social and psychological study of a modern group that predicted the destruction of the world.* New York: Harper & Row.

Fine, M. (1991). *Framing dropouts: Notes on the politics of an urban public high school.* Albany, NY: SUNY Press.

Fineman, S. (1993). *Emotions in organizations.* Thousand Oaks, CA & London: Sage Publications.

Finn, C. (2000). *Charter schools in action: Renewing public education.* Princeton, NJ: Princeton University Press.

Flores-González, N. (2002). *School kids / street kids: Identity development in Latino students.* New York: Teachers College Press.

Fordham, S. (1996). *Blacked out: Dilemmas of race, identity, and success at Capital High.* Chicago: University of Chicago Press.

Fuchs, E. (1969). *Teachers talk.* New York: Anchor.

Gaines, K. K. (1996). *Uplifting the race: Black leadership, politics, and culture in the twentieth century.* Chapel Hill: University of North Carolina Press.

Gal, R., and Mangelsdorff, A. D. (Eds.). (1991). *Handbook of military psychology.* New York: Wiley.

Garet, M., Porter, A. C., Desimone, L., Birman, B. F., and Yoon, K. S. (2001). What makes professional development effective? Results from a national sample of teachers. *American Educational Research Journal 38*(4), 915–945.

Gehring, J. (2004). New Orleans board blocked from firing superintendent. *Education Week*, June 16.

Gennetian, L. A., Miller, C., and Smith, J. (2005). *Turning welfare into a work support: Six-year impacts on parents and children from the Minnesota Family Investment Program.* New York: MDRC.

Gewertz, C. (2002). Miami-Dade board OKs tougher ethics policies. *Education Week*, May 22.

————. (2003). Miami-Dade superintendent announces his departure. *Education Week*, November 12.

————. (2006). N.J. panel eyes changes in school funding. *New York Times*, November 28.

————. (2007). Miami "zone" gives schools intensive help. *Education Week*, October 16. *www.edweek.org/ew/articles/2007/10/17/08miami.h27.html* (accessed October 18, 2007).

Gibboney, R. (1994). *The stone trumpet: A story of practical school reform.* Albany, NY: SUNY Press.

Ginwright, S. (2004). *Black in school: Afrocentric reform, urban youth and the promise of hip hop culture.* New York: Teachers College Press.

Glantz, O. (1977). Locus of control and aspiration to traditionally open and traditionally closed occupations. *Journal of Negro Education 46*(3), 278–290.

Goodnough, A. (2002). Half of new teachers lack certificates, data say. *New York Times*, May 15.

Gordon, D. T. (Ed.). (2003) *A nation reformed? American education 20 years after a nation at risk.* Cambridge, MA: Harvard Education Press.

Gordon, E. (2004). Closing the gap: High achievement for students of color. *AERA Research Points 2*(3). *www.aera.net.*

Gouldner, H. (1978). *Teachers' pets, troublemakers and nobodies.* Westport, CT: Greenwood Press.

Grogger, J., and Neal, D. (2000). Further evidence on the effects of Catholic secondary schooling. *Brookings-Wharton Papers on Urban Affairs.* The Brookings Institution.

Guarino, C., Santibañez, L., and Daley, G. (2006). Teacher recruitment and retention: A review of the recent empirical literature. *Review of Educational Research 76*(2), 173–208.

Hale-Benson, J. (1986). *Black children: Their roots, culture and learning styles.* Baltimore, MD: Johns Hopkins University Press.

Hansberry, L. (1968). The Black revolution and the white backlash. In J. Grant (Ed.), *Black Protest.* New York: Fawcett.

Hargreaves, A. (1991). Contrived collegiality: The micropolitics of teacher collaborations. In J. Blasé (Ed.), *The politics of life in schools: Power, conflict and cooperation.* Thousand Oaks, CA: Corwin Press.

Hartocollis, A. (2000). Tough task: Uniting teachers in learning. *New York Times*, November 22.

Haynes, D., and Keating, D. (2007). Can D.C. schools be fixed? *Washington Post*, June 10, A01. *www.washingtonpost.com/wp-dyn/content/article/2007/06/09/AR2007060901415.html* (accessed October 18, 2007).

Haynes, N. and Comer, J. (1993). The Yale school development program: Process, outcomes and policy implications. *Urban Education 28*(2), 166–199.

Hendrie, C. (2001). N.J.'s "whole school" approach found hard for districts. *Education Week*, February 21. *www.edweek.org/ew/ew_printstory.cfm?slug=23nj.h20*.

Herald Sun. (2004). Local schools must make do with less. August 11.

Hess, F. (1998). The urban reform paradox. *The American School Board Journal 185*(2), 24–27.

———. (1999). *Spinning wheels: The politics of urban school reform*. Washington, DC: Brookings Institution Press.

Hess, G. A. (2001). *Reconstitution: Three years later—monitoring the effect of sanctions on Chicago high schools*. Evanston, IL: Center for Urban School Policy, Northwestern University.

Hill, P. T. (2007). Waiting for the "tipping point." *Education Week*, September 4. *www.edweek.org/ew/articles/2007/09/05/02hill.h27.html?qs=paul_hil*.

Hill, P. T., Campbell, C., and Harvey, J. (2000). *It takes a city: Getting serious about urban school reform*. Washington, DC: Brookings Institution Press.

Hill, P. T., Pierce, L., and Guthrie, J. (1997). *Reinventing public education: How contracting can transform America's schools*. Berkeley, CA: University of California Press.

Hinton, W. (1966). *Fanshen: A documentary of revolution in a Chinese village*. New York: Vintage.

Hoff, D. J., and Kennedy Manzo, K. (2007). Bush claims about NCLB questioned: Data on gains in achievement remain limited, preliminary. *Education Week*, March 9. *www.edweek.org/ew/articles/2007/03/09/27evidence.h26.html* (accessed April 5, 2007).

Holloway, L. (1998). The principal as Gulliver: Rule-bound school leaders rely on clever diplomacy. *New York Times*, November 4.

———. (2000). Union thwarts effort to replace teachers in school for deaf. *New York Times,* July 2.

Hu, W. (2006). In New Jersey, system to help poorest schools faces criticism. *New York Times*. *www.nytimes.com/2006/10/30/education/30abbot.html* (accessed October 20, 2007).

Irvine, R., and Irvine, J. (1983). The impact of the desegregation process on the education of Black students: Key variables. *Journal of Negro Education 52*(4), 410–422.

Jackall, R. (1980). Structural invitations to deceit: Some reflections on bureaucracy and morality. Paper presented at the Little Three Colloquium on Lying and Deceit, Amherst College, January 18.

———. (1983). Moral mazes: Bureaucracy and managerial work. *Harvard Business Review*, September 1.

James, C. L. R. (1963). *The Black Jacobins*. New York: Random House.

Jeffrey, M. (1993). School reform, Chicago style. *Urban Education 28*, 116–149.

Johnson, D. (1970). *The social psychology of education*. New York: Holt, Rinehart and Winston.

Johnston, R. C. (2001). "Failing" Detroit faces job cuts, privatization. *Education Week*, April 18.

Jones-Wilson, F. C. (1981). *A traditional model of educational excellence: Dunbar High School of Little Rock, Arkansas*. Washington, DC: Howard University Press.

Justin, N. (1970). Culture conflict and Mexican American achievement. *School and Society 98*(2322), 27–28.

Kane, P. R. (1992). *The first year of teaching: Real world stories from America's teachers*. New York: Penguin.

Katz, M., Fine, M., and Simon, E. (1997). Poking around: Outsiders view Chicago school reform. *Teachers College Record 99*(1), 117–158.

Keating, D., and Haynes, D. (2007, June 10). Can D.C. Schools Be Fixed? *Washington Post*, A01. *www.washingtonpost.com/wp-dyn/content/article/2007/06/09* (accessed October 18, 2007).

Kelleher, M. (2001). "Team player" Duncan named CEO. *Catalyst Chicago*, June. *www.catalyst-chicago.org/news/index.php?item=134&cat=30* (accessed June 29, 2004).

———. (2004a). CPS a leader in AP growth. *Catalyst Chicago*, June. *www.catalyst-chicago.org/news/index.php?item=1277&cat=23*.

———. (2004b). Suspension up in CPS. *Catalyst Chicago*, December. *www.catalyst-chicago.org/arch/12-04/1204main.htm*.

Kemple, J., and Herlihy, C. (2004). *The talent development middle school model*. New York: MDRC.

Kemple, J. J., Herlihy, C. M., and Smith, T. J. (2005). *Making progress toward graduation: Evidence from the talent development high school model*. New York: MDRC.

Kerckhoff, A., and Campbell, R. (1977). Race and social status differences in the explanation of educational ambition. *Social Forces 55*(3), 701–714.

King, L. (2006). Gap in teacher quality falls on income lines. *USA Today*, April 26. *www.usatoday.com/news/education/2006-04-26-teachers-poor_x.htm* (accessed April 16, 2007).

King, M. B., and Newman, F. (2000). Will teacher learning advance school goals? *Phi Delta Kappan 81*(8), 576–580.

Kingon, J. (2001). A view from the trenches. *New York Times*, April 8.

Kohl, H. (1967). *Thirty-six children*. New York: New American Library.

Kohn, A. (2000). *The case against standardized tests: Raising the scores, ruining the schools*. Portsmouth, NH: Heinemann.

Kozol, J. (1967). *Death at an early age.* Boston: Houghton-Mifflin.

Krueger, A., and Whitmore, D. (2002). Would smaller classes help close the black–white achievement gap? In J. Chubb and T. Loveless (Eds.), *Bridging the achievement gap.* Washington, DC: Brookings Institution Press.

Kruse, S. D., and Seashore, K. (1997). Teacher teaming in middle schools: Dilemmas for a schoolwide community. *Educational Administration Quarterly 33*, 261–289.

Kruse, S., Seashore-Louis, K., and Bryk, A. (1995). Teachers build professional communities. *Wisconsin Center for Education Research Highlights 7*(1), 6–8.

Leacock, E. (1969). *Teaching and learning in city schools.* New York: Basic Books.

Lee, C. D. (2007). *Culture, literacy, and learning: Taking bloom in the midst of the whirlwind.* New York: Teachers College Press.

Lee, C. D. (2008). Profile of an independent Black institution: African-centered education at work. In C. Payne and C. Strickland (Eds.), *Teach freedom: Education for liberation in the African American tradition.* New York: Teachers College Press.

Lee, V. (1998). Comments on Charles Payne's "So much reform, so little change." Paper presented at the Chicago Assembly's Education Reform for the 21st Century, Chicago.

Lee, V. E., and Burkam, D. (2002). *Inequality at the starting gate: Social background differences in achievement as children begin school.* Washington, DC: Economic Policy Institute.

Lee, V. E., Smith, J. B., Perry, T. E., and Smylie, M. A. (1999). *Social support, academic press, and student achievement: A view from the middle grades in Chicago.* Chicago: Consortium on Chicago School Research.

Lenz, L. (2004). NAEP test shines light on racial gap. *Catalyst Chicago*, February. *www.catalyst-chicago.org/news.*

Leonard, L., and Leonard, P. (2003). The continuing trouble with collaboration: Teachers talk. *Current Issues in Education 6*(15). *http://cie.ed.asu.edu/volume6/number15* (accessed August 14, 2004).

Levin, J., Mulhern, J., and Schunck, J. (2005). *Unintended consequences: The case for reforming the staffing rules in urban teachers union contracts.* New York: The New Teacher Project. *www.tntp.org/newreport/TNTP%20Unintended%20Consequences.pdf* (accessed October 18, 2007).

Lewis, A. E. (2003). *Race in the schoolyard: Negotiating the color line in classrooms and communities.* New Brunswick, NJ: Rutgers University Press.

Lieberman, A., and Millers, L. (Eds.). (1979). *Staff development: New demands, new realities, new perspectives.* New York: Teachers College Press.

Lipman, P. (1998). *Race, class and power in school restructuring*. Albany, NY: State University of New York Press.

Ludwig, J., and Sawhill, I. V. (2007). *Success by ten: Intervening early, often, and effectively in the education of young children*. Washington, DC: Brookings Institution. *www.brookings.edu/papers/2007/02education_ludwig.aspx* (accessed October 31, 2007).

Lytle, J. (2002). Whole school reform from the inside. *Phi Delta Kappan 84*(2), 164–167.

MacDonald, Christine. (2004). Detroit schools chief asked to resign. *Detroit News*, July 8.

Madden N., Slavin, R. E., Karweit, N. L., Dolan, L. J., and Wasik, B. A. (1993). Success for all: Longitudinal effects of a restructuring program for inner-city elementary schools. *American Educational Research Journal 30*(1), 123–148.

Mahoney, J., Larson, R., and Eccles, J. (Eds.). (2005). *Organized activities as contexts of development*. Mahwah, NJ: Lawrence Erlbaum.

Malen, B., Ogawa, R., and Kranz, J. (1990). What do we know about school-based management? A case study of the literature—A call for research. In W. Clune and J. Witte (Eds.), *The practice of choice, decentralization and school restructuring*. Vol. 2 of *Choice and control in American education*. New York: Falmer.

Manning, F. J. (1991). Morale, cohesion and esprit de corps. In R. Gal and A. D. Mangelsdorf (Eds.), *Handbook of military psychology*. Chichester, NY: John Wiley & Sons.

Marshall, K. (2003). A principal looks back: Standards matter. *Phi Delta Kappan 85*, 104–113.

Martinez, M. (2001). City teachers rate training as ineffective. *Chicago Tribune*, February 7.

Maxwell, L. A. (2006). L.A. building program faces possible $2.5 billion shortfall. *Education Week*, October 30. *www.edweek.org/ew/articles /2006/11/01/10 facilside.h26.html?qs=L.A.+Building+Program+Faces+Possible+2.5+Billion+ Shortfall* (accessed October 17, 2007).

———. (2007). As school year looms, Detroit predicts enrollment drop. *Education Week*, August 29.

McDiarmid, G. (1999). *Still missing after all these years: Understanding the paucity of subject matter professional development in Kentucky*. Lexington, KY: Partnership for Kentucky Schools.

Medina, J. (2007). Team forms to analyze city schools. *New York Times*, October 3. *www.nytimes.com/2007/10/03/education/03research.html* (accessed October 5, 2007).

Meier, D. (1991). The little schools that could. *The Nation*, September 23.

————. (2002). *The power of their ideas: Lessons for America from a small school in Harlem.* Boston: Beacon Press.

Merton, R. K. (1948). The self-fulfilling prophecy. *Antioch Review 8*(1), 193.

Miller, E. (1995). The old model of staff development survives in a world where everything else has changed. *Harvard Education Letter 11*(1), 1–3.

————. (1996). Hard-won lessons from the school reform battle: A conversation with Ted Sizer. *Harvard Education Letter 12(*4), 3–6.

Miller, J. (2001). The super. *Washington Monthly,* June.

Mirel, J. (1993). School reform, Chicago style: Educational innovation in a changing urban context, 1976–1991. *Urban Education 28*(2), 116–149.

Mooney, J. (2003). Rise in test scores leads to a debate. *Star-Ledger,* June 16.

Moore, W. (1999). *William of Cape May: The autobiography of William J. Moore.* Cape May, NJ: William J. Moore Scholarship Fund.

Muncey, D., and McQuillen, P. (1996). *Reform and resistance in schools and classrooms: An ethnographic view of the coalition for essential schools.* New Haven, CT: Yale University Press.

Nagourney, A. (1997). As Messinger turns cool on Dr. Crew, the mayor tries warm. *New York Times,* July 20.

National Center for Education Information. (2005). *Profile of teachers in the U.S. 2005.* Washington, DC.

Neal, D., and Schanzenbach, D. W. (2007). Left behind by design: Proficiency counts and test-based accountability. *http://home.uchicago.edu/~n9na/web_ver_final.pdf.*

Newmann, F., Bryk, A., and Nagaoka, J. (2001). *Authentic intellectual work and standardized tests: Conflict or coexistence?* Chicago: Consortium on Chicago School Research.

Newmann, F., Lopez, G., and Bryk, A. (1998). *The quality of intellectual work in Chicago schools: A baseline report.* Chicago: Consortium on Chicago School Research.

Newmann, F., Smith, B., Allensworth, E., and Bryk, A. S. (2001). *School instructional program coherence: Benefits and challenges.* Chicago: Consortium on Chicago School Research.

New York City Department of Education. (2007). *Mayor Bloomberg announces that high school graduation rate reaches historic high of 60%.* May 21. *www.nyc. gov* (accessed October 5, 2007).

Noguera, P. (2003). *City schools and the American dream: Reclaiming the promise of public education.* New York: Teachers College Press.

————. (2005). The racial achievement gap: How can we assure an equity of outcomes? In L. Johnson, M. Finn, and R. Lewis (Eds.), *Urban education with an attitude.* Albany: SUNY Press.

Olson, L. (1997). Pushing the envelope of what makes a public school. *Education Week*, September 10.

Olszewski, L. (2004). Holding kids back fails too, study says: U. of C. report finds repeating grade no help. *Chicago Tribune*, April 7.

Ortiz, M. (2002a). Candidate recruitment off to typically slow start. *Catalyst Chicago*, March.

———. (2002b). Growing up: Local leaders say it's now or never for LSC's. *Catalyst Chicago*, March.

Parish, R., and Aquila, F. (1996). Cultural ways of working and believing in school. *Phi Delta Kappan 78*(4), 298–308.

Patterson, J. (2001). *Brown v. Board of Education: A civil rights milestone and its troubled legacy*. New York: Oxford University Press.

Payne, C. (1984). *Getting what we ask for: The ambiguity of success and failure in urban education*. Westport, CT: Greenwood Press.

———. (Forthcoming). Making it past the little box: An interview with the Baltimore Algebra Project. In T. Perry (Ed.), *Quality education as a civil right*. Boston: Beacon Press.

Pederson, S., and Seidman, E. (2005). Contexts and correlates of out-of-school activity participation among low-income urban adolescents. In J. Mahoney, R. Larson, and J. Eccles (Eds.), *Organized activities as contexts of development*. Mahwah, NJ: Lawrence Erlbaum.

Perry, T., Steele, C., and Hilliard, A. (2003). *Young, gifted, and Black: Promoting high achievement among African-American students*. Boston: Beacon Press.

Peske, H., and Haycock, K. (2006). *Teaching inequality: How poor and minority students are shortchanged on teacher quality*. Washington, DC: Education Trust.

Peters, W. (1971). *A class divided*. Garden City, NY: Doubleday.

Peyser, J. (2007). The schools that Katrina built? How New Orleans could end up saving public education in America. *Boston Globe*, October 14. *www.lexisnexis.com* (accessed October 17, 2007).

Pogrow, S. (1998). What is an exemplary program, and why should anyone care? A reaction to Slavin and Klein. *Educational Researcher 27*(7), 22–28.

———. (2000). Success for all does not produce success for students. *Phi Delta Kappan 82*(1), 67–80.

———. (2000). The unsubstantiated "success" of Success for All. *Phi Delta Kappan 9*(4), 596–600.

Pollock, M. (2004). *Colormute: Race talk dilemmas in an American school*. Princeton, NJ: Princeton University Press.

Portner, H. (2005). Success for new teachers. *American School Board Journal 192*(10), 30–33.

Presley, J., White, B., and Gong, Y. (2005). *Examining the distribution and impact of teacher quality in Illinois.* Edwardsville, IL: Illinois Education Research Council. *http://ierc.siue.edu.*

Putnam, R. (2000). *Bowling alone: The collapse and revival of American community.* New York: Simon & Schuster.

Quint, J. (2006). *Meeting five critical challenges of high school reform: Lessons from research on three reform models.* New York: MDRC. *www.mdrc.org /publications/428/full.pdf.*

Quint, J., and Byndloss, C. (2003). *Scaling up First Things First: Findings from the first implementation year.* New York: MDRC.

Rasheed, A., and Thevenot, B. (2004). Move may be afoot to fire Amato: Hasty meeting today to review performance. *New Orleans Times-Picayune*, June 4.

Rathbone, C. (1998). *On the outside looking in: A year at an inner-city high school.* New York: Atlantic Monthly Press.

Reid, K. (2003). New Orleans schools focus of fraud probe. *Education Week*, October 22.

———. (2004). District of Columbia schools facing leadership dilemma. *Education Week*, March 31.

Resnick, L. (Ed.). (2005). Teaching teachers: Professional development to improve student achievement. *AERA Research Points*, *3*(1). *www.aera.net.*

Resnick, L., and Zurawsky, C. (2006). Do the math: Cognitive demand makes a difference. *AERA Research Points 4*(2). *www.aera.net.*

Reville, P. (2007). *A decade of urban school reform: Persistence and progress in the Boston Public Schools.* Cambridge, MA: Harvard Education Press.

Rimer, S. (2002). Philadelphia school's woes defeat veteran principal. *New York Times*, December 15.

Roderick, M., Nagaoka, J., and Allensworth, E. (2006). *From high school to the future: A first look at Chicago public school graduates' college enrollment, college preparation, and graduation from four-year colleges.* Chicago: Consortium on Chicago School Research.

Rogers, D. (1969). *110 Livingston Street: Politics and bureaucracy in the New York City school system.* New York: Vintage.

Rosenfeld, G. (1971). *"Shut those thick lips!": A study of slum school failure.* New York: Holt, Rinehart and Winston.

Rosenthal, R., and Jacobson, L. (1968). *Pygmalion in the classroom: Teacher expectation and pupils' intellectual development.* New York: Holt, Rinehart and Winston.

Rowan, B. (2004). Teachers matter: Evidence from value-added assessments. AERA Research Points 2(2). *www.aera.net.*

Russo, A. (2004). *School reform in Chicago: Lessons in policy and practice.* Cambridge, MA: Harvard Education Press.

————. (2004). *Chicago school reform.* Cambridge, MA: Harvard Education Press.

Ryan, S., Bryk, A. S., Lopez, G., Williams, K. P., Hall, K., and Luppescu, S. (1997). *Charting reform: LSCs-local leadership at work.* Chicago: Consortium on Chicago School Research.

Samuels, A. (2007). Oprah goes to school. *Newsweek*, January 8.

Sanchez, R. (1997). Mixed returns on gifts to education. *Washington Post*, October 13.

Sanders, W., and Rivers, J. (1996). *Cumulative and residual effects of teachers on future student academic achievement.* Knoxville, TN: University of Tennessee Value-Added Research and Assessment Center.

Sarason, S. (1996). *Revisiting "the culture of the school and the problem of change."* New York: Teachers College Press.

————. (1998). *Political leadership and educational failure.* San Francisco, CA: Jossey-Bass.

Sawhill, I. V., and Ludwig, J. (2007). *Success by ten: Intervening early, often, and effectively in the education of young children.* The Brookings Institution. *www. brookings.edu/papers/2007/02education_ludwig.aspx.*

Schemo, D. J. (2007). Failing schools see a solution in longer day. *New York Times*, March 27. *www.nytimes.com/2007/03/26/us/26schoolday.html* (accessed March 29, 2007).

Schneider, B. (2001). The ubiquitous emerging conception of social capital. In D. Levinson, P. Cookson, and A. Sadovnik (Eds.), *Education and sociology: An encyclopedia.* New York: Garland.

Sciarra, D., and Whitson, M. (2007). Predictive factors in postsecondary educational attainment among Latinos. *Professional School Counseling 10*(3), 307–316.

Sconzert, K., Smylie, M., and Wenzel, S. (2004). *Working for school improvement: Reflections of Chicago Annenberg external partners.* Chicago: Consortium on Chicago School Research.

Sebring, P. B., Allensworth, E., Bryk, A. S., Easton, J. Q., and Luppescu, S. (2006). *The essential supports for school reform.* Chicago: Consortium on Chicago School Research.

Sebring, P. B., Bryk, A. S., and Easton, J. (1995). *Charting reform: Chicago teachers take stock.* Chicago: Consortium on Chicago School Research.

Sebring, P. B., Bryk, A. S, Roderick, M., Camburn, E., Luppescu, S., Thum, Y. M., Smith, B., and Kahne, J. E. (1996). *Charting reform in Chicago: The students speak. A report.* Chicago: Consortium on Chicago School Research.

————. (2006). *The essential supports for school improvement*. Chicago: Consortium on Chicago School Research.

Sennett, R., and Cobb, J. (1972). *The hidden injuries of class*. New York: Alfred A. Knopf.

Shibutani, T. (1978). *The derelicts of Company K: A sociological study of demoralizations*. Berkeley, CA: University of California Press.

Siddle Walker, V. (1996). *Their highest potential: An African American school community in the segregated South*. Chapel Hill, NC: University of North Carolina Press.

Simon, D. (2001). What really happens when prophecy fails? The case of Lubavitch. *Sociology of Religion 62*(3), 383.

Slavin, R., and Madden, N. A. (1996). Success for all: A summary of research. *Journal of Education for Students Placed at Risk 1*(1), 41–76.

Smith, B. (1998). *It's about time: Opportunities to learn in Chicago's elementary schools*. Chicago: Consortium on Chicago School Research.

Smith, J., Lee, V., and Newmann, F. (2001). *Instruction and achievement in Chicago elementary schools*. Chicago: Consortium on Chicago School Research.

Smith, J., Smith, B., and Bryk, A. (1998). *Setting the pace: Opportunities to learn in Chicago's elementary schools*. Chicago: Consortium on Chicago School Research.

Smylie, M., Bilcer, D. K., Kochanek, J., Sconzert, K., Shipps, D., and Swyers, H. (1998). *Getting started: A first look at Chicago Annenberg schools and networks*. Chicago: Consortium on Chicago School Research.

Snipes, J., Doolittle, F., and Herlihy, C. (2002). Foundations for success: Case studies of how urban school systems improve student achievement. New York: MDRC.

Snipes, J., Williams, A., Horwitz, A., Soga, K., and Casserly, M. (2007). *Beating the odds: A city-by-city analysis of student performance and achievement gaps on state assessments. Results from the 2005–2006 school year*. Washington, DC: Council of the Great City Schools. *www.cgcs.org/pdfs/BTO7_Analysis.pdf* (accessed October 1, 2007).

————. (2007). *Beating the odds: An analysis of student performance and achievement gaps on state assessments*. Washington, DC: Council of the Great City Schools. *www.cgcs.org/pdfs/BTO7_Analysis.pdf* (accessed April 22, 2007).

Snyder, S. (2007a). An inside call to fire six school managers. *Philadelphia Inquirer*, May 20. *www.philly.com/inquirer/home_region/20070520_An_inside_call_to_fire_6_school_managers.html* (accessed September 1, 2007).

————. (2007b). Philadelphia school district's state test scores improve. *Philadelphia Inquirer*, August 8.

Sommerfeld, M. (1994). Grant to implement Comer model in Detroit school. *Education Week*, July 13.

Sowell, T. (1974). Black excellence: The case of Dunbar high school. *Public Interest 35*, 3–21.

———. (1976). Patterns of Black excellence. *Public Interest 43*, 26–58.

Stevens, W. D. (2006). *Professional communities and instructional improvement practices: A study of small high schools in Chicago.* Chicago: Consortium on Chicago School Research.

Success for All: A summary of research. (1996). *Journal of Education for Students Placed at Risk 1*(1), 41–76.

Supovitz, J., May, H., and Perda, D. (2004). *A longitudinal study of the impact of America's choice on student performance in Rochester, New York, 1998–2003.* Philadelphia, PA: Consortium for Policy Research in Education.

Sykes, G. (1990). Organizing policy into practice: Reactions to the cases. *Educational evaluation and policy analysis 12*(3), 243–247.

Taylor, P. (2007). *American and social trust: Who, where and why.* Washington, DC: Pew Research Center. *http://pewresearch.org/assets/social/pdf/SocialTrust. pdf* (accessed March 1, 2007).

Taylor, P., Funk, C., and Clark, A. (2007). *Social trends: Americans and social trust—who, where and why.* Washington, DC: Pew Research Center. *www. pewtrusts.org/our_work_ektid21060.aspx* (accessed March 1, 2007).

TheNewOrleansChannel.com. (2004). Court hears testimony in school board-Amato fight. June 8. *www.wdsu.com/education/3389764/detail.html* (accessed October 28, 2007).

———. (2005). Nagin: School in "state of emergency." April 13. *www.wdsu. com/news/4375682/detail.html* (accessed October 28, 2007).

Thernstrom, A., and Thernstrom, S. (2003). Left behind. *Boston Globe*, October 26.

Thevenot, B. (2004). Seeds of discord planted in January. *New Orleans Times Picayune*, June 5.

Thomas, W. I., and William, T. (1928). *The child in America: Behavior problems and programs.* New York: Alfred A. Knopf.

Thompson, C., and Quinn, S. (2001). *Eliminating the black-white achievement gap: A summary of research.* Special report. Chapel Hill, NC: North Carolina Education Research Council. *http://erc.northcarolina.edu/docs/publications/ gapspecialreport.pdf.*

Thompson, C., and Zeuli, J. (1999). The frame and the tapestry: Standards-based reform and professional development. In G. Sykes (Ed.), *The heart of the matter: Teaching as a learning profession.* San Francisco, CA: Jossey-Bass.

Timmer, D. (2001). *Leave no school behind: Instructional inequality and its impact on ACORN neighborhood high schools.* Chicago: ACORN.

Trotter, A. (2007). Glitches in Los Angeles payroll system spark furor. *Education Week*, June 15. *www.edweek.org/ew/articles/2007/06/20/42lapay.h26.html?qs=roy+romer* (accessed October 17, 2007).

Tyack, D., and Cuban, L. (1995). *Tinkering toward utopia: A century of public school reform.* Cambridge, MA: Harvard University Press.

Useem, E., Offenberg, R., and Farley, E. (2007). *Closing the teacher quality gap in Philadelphia: New hope and old hurdles.* Philadelphia: Research for Action.

Vander Weele, M. (1994). *Reclaiming our schools: The struggle for Chicago school reform.* Chicago: Loyola University Press.

Viadero, D. (1994). Success with coalition reforms seen limited in some schools. *Education Week*, April 13.

———. (2001a). Memphis scraps redesign models in all its schools. *Education Week*, July 11. *www.edweek.org/ew/articles/2001/07/11/42memphis.h20.html?qs=Memphis+scraps+redesign+models+in+all+its+schools+viadero.*

———. (2001b). Whole-school projects show mixed results. *Education Week*, November 7. *www.edweek.org/ew/articles/2001/11/07/10memphis.h21.html?qs=Memphis+scraps+redesign+models+in+all+its+schools+viadero.*

———. (2001c). RAND finds mixed results for school reform models. *Education Week*, April 18. *www.edweek.org/ew/articles/2001/04/18/31rand.h20.html?qs=RAND+finds+mixed+viadero.*

———. (2007). In whole-school reform, staying true to model matters: Study shows models' practices also spread to other schools. *Education Week*, May 16.

Viteritti, Joseph. (2002). Abolish the board of education. *New York Times*, January 6.

Walberg, H., and Niemiec, R. (1994). Is Chicago school reform working? *Phi Delta Kappan 75*(9), 713–715.

Walsh, K. (2003). *After the test: How schools are using data to close the achievement gap.* San Francisco: Bay Area Research Collaborative. *www.springboardschools.org/research/studies/GAPstudy-ES.pdf* (accessed October 10, 2006).

Wasley, P. (1991). Stirring the chalkdust: Three teachers in the midst of change. *Teachers College Record 93*(1), 28–58.

Webb, A. L. (2004). Lesson plans. *City Paper*, August 2004. *www.citypaper.net/articles/2004-08-26/cover.shtml.*

Wellman, D. (1977). *Portraits of white racism.* New York: Cambridge University Press.

Whyte, W. F., et al. (1955). *Money and motivation: An analysis of incentives in industry*. New York: Harper (orig. pub. 1914).

Williams, D. (2003). Shock absorbers. *Catalyst Chicago*, November. *www.catalystchicago.org/news/index.php?item=1186&cat=23*.

Winerip, M. (2005). New York's revolving door of good teachers driven out. *New York Times*, June 1.

Witt, A. (2007). Worn down by waves of change: Bureaucracy, politics beat back succession of superintendents and plans. *Washington Post*, June 11.

Witt, H. (2007). School discipline tougher on African Americans. *Chicago Tribune*, September 25.

Wohlstetter, P., and Mohrman, S. (1994). *School-based management: Promise and process*. New Brunswick, NJ: Consortium for Policy Research in Education.

Wolk, R. (1998). Introduction: Strategies for fixing failing public schools. *Education Week*, November 18.

Woodall, M. (2004). Test results for teachers are not public, the state says. *Philadelphia Inquirer*, April 13.

Woolley, M., and Bowen, G. (2007). In the context of risk: Supportive adults and the school engagement of middle school students. *Family Relations 56*(1), 92–104.

Woolley, M., and Grogan-Kaylor, A. (2006). Protective family factors in the context of neighborhood: Promoting positive school outcomes. *Family Relations 55*(1), 93–104.

York, D. (1996). The academic achievement of African American students in Catholic schools: A review of the literature. In J. J. Irvine and M. Foster (Eds.), *Growing up African American in Catholic schools*. New York: Teachers College Press.

About the Author

Charles M. Payne is the Frank P. Hixon Professor in the School of Social Service Administration at the University of Chicago. He is author of *Getting What We Ask For: The Ambiguity of Success and Failure in Urban Education* (1984) and *I've Got the Light of Freedom: The Organizing Tradition in the Mississippi Civil Rights Movement* (1995); the latter book won awards from the Southern Regional Council, *Choice*, the Simon Wiesenthal Center, and the Gustavus Myers Center for the Study of Human Rights in North America. He is coauthor of *Debating the Civil Rights Movement* (1999), coeditor of *Time Longer Than Rope: A Century of African American Activism, 1850–1950* (2003), and coeditor of *Teach Freedom: Education for Liberation in the African American Tradition* (2008).

Payne has served on the board of the Chicago Algebra Project, the Steering Committee for the Consortium on Chicago School Research, the Research Advisory Committee for the Chicago Annenberg Project, and the editorial boards of *Catalyst*, *Sociology of Education*, and *Educational Researcher*. He is cofounder of the Duke Curriculum Project, which involves university faculty in the professional development of public school teachers, and cofounder of the John Hope Franklin Scholars, which prepares high school youngsters for college. He is among the founders of the Education for Liberation Network, which encourages the development of educational initiatives to help young people to think critically about social issues and to understand their own capacity for addressing them. He was also the founding director of the Urban Education Project in Orange, New Jersey, a nonprofit community center that broadens educational experiences for urban youngsters.

Payne has taught at Southern University, Williams College, Northwestern University, and Duke University. He has won several teaching awards; he held Northwestern's Charles Deering McCormick Chair for Teaching Excellence and Duke's Sally Dalton Robinson Chair for excellence in teaching and research.

Index

Note: Page numbers followed by *f* or *t* indicate figures and tables, respectively.

Abbott districts, 161–164, 175, 194
Abbott v. Burke, 161
Academic press, 100–101, 104. *See also* Teacher expectations
Accelerated Schools Program, 155, 161, 165, 175, 213
Accountability, 3, 169–170
Achievement. *See* Student achievement
Ackerman, Arlene, 144
Acting white, 23
Adler, Mortimer, 217
Administrator-administrator relationships, 51–53
African Americans. *See also* Race
    and African-American leadership, 132–133
    attitudes of, 109–116
    criticism of, by same-race individuals, 192
    discipline and, 112
    and fate control, 110, 116
    in inner-city schools, 67–68
    intellectual competence of, 103–104, 109–111
    internalization of prejudices by, 115–116
    math instruction and, 78
    middle-class, 109, 111–113
    socially supportive instruction for, 95–96, 99–103, 116, 120, 211–212

student achievement of, 103–104, 110–111
teaching, 93–120, 207–212, 224n1
and trust, 109–112
Algebra Project, 2, 171, 175–176, 213, 225n5. *See also* Baltimore Algebra Project
Alienation, 69
Allport, Gordon, 108
Alvarado, Anthony, 128, 197
Amato, Tony, 141–142
American Institutes of Research, 164–165
America's Choice School Design, 161, 165, 213, 228n9
Annenberg, Walter, 227n2
Annenberg Foundation, 3, 7
Anyon, Jean, 23, 24, 73, 222n2(ch.1)
Assignments, classroom, 84–87
Assistant principals, 42
ATLAS Learning Communities, 159, 165, 214
Attendance. *See* Student attendance
Audrey Cohen College, 214
Authoritative-supportive teaching, 99–103, 99*f*, 108, 118–119, 211–212

Badillo, Herman, 192
Bailin, Michael A., 179
Baldwin, James, 191
Baltimore Algebra Project, 104–108
Bay Area School Reform Collaborative, 95
BBN Corporation, 215
Belief, processes of, 75–76

Bennett, William, 10
Berman, P., 179, 180
Best Practices, 63
Bethune, Mary McLeod, 118
Betty Shabazz International Charter
    School, Chicago, 119
Black, Paul, 95
Bloomberg, Michael R., 145
Boards of education
    corruption in, 143
    politics and, 134
    role of, 122
Borman, G., 164, 176
Boston, 133, 197
Boston Globe (newspaper), 147
Bosworth, Mahogony, 105
Bottom-tier schools. *See also* High-poverty
    schools; Urban schools
    characteristics of, 23–24, 45,
        153–154, 177
    demoralization in, 23–24
    follow-through lacking in, 58–59,
        177–178
    politics of, 39–47
    reform in, 174, 178
    resources of, 24–25, 30–31
    social relationships in, 24–27,
        31–39, 44–45
    standards-based reform and, 170
    study of, 6
    teachers in, 71–82
    Westside High School, 57–61
    Woodbine School, 50–57
    working conditions in, 17–20
Bowen, G., 102
Brooks, Bill, 140
Brown, Charlotte Hawkins, 118
Bryk, Anthony, 36, 86–87, 117
Building repairs, 150
Bullock, Barbara, 142–143
Bureaucracy, 121–152. *See also*
    Institutionalization of failure
    authoritarian type of, 124, 125*t*
    change in, 126
    characteristics of, 123, 151
    Chicago school reform and,
        130–131
    corruption in, 142–144, 152
    cronyism in, 124
    decisionmaking in, 151
    in Detroit, 140–141
    disconnection of, from school
        realities, 131–132, 151
    insularity of, 124
    internal conflicts of, 130
    leadership in, 131–132
    of Los Angeles, 134–136
    models of, 125*t*
    morality and, 150–152
    in New Orleans, 141–142,
        147–149
    in New York City, 144–145
    pathologies of, 18, 122–134, 146,
        150
    professional type of, 125*t*
    school reform principles in
        opposition to, 126–128,
        130–131
    self-serving nature of, 124, 126
    teachers' unions and, 136–140
    in Washington, D. C., 142–143,
        149–150
Burkham, D., 70
Burnley, Kenneth, 140–141
Bush, George H. W., 158
Business community, 10, 11, 194
Byrd, Manfred, 131–132

Campbell, R., 110
Casserly, Michael, 143, 144
Casswell County Teaching School, North
    Carolina, 97
Catalyst (journal), 2, 9–10, 12–13
Catholic schools, 99, 117–118
Cecelski, David, 98*f*
Central Park East, New York City, 63
Change
    in bureaucracy, 126
    conservative view of, 192–193, 195
    liberal view of, 77, 192–193,
        195–199
    pressure for, 197–198

urgency of, 198–199
voluntary, 77, 193–198
Charlotte, North Carolina, 128
Charter schools
    as change agent, 62
    economics of, 194
    effectiveness of, 149, 226n4
    in New Orleans, 148–149
    in Ohio, 149
    personnel of, 118, 189
    in Washington, D. C., 149
Chavous, Kevin, 143–144
Chesterton, G. K., 17
Chicago. *See also* Chicago school reform
    teacher retention in, 72
    teachers' unions in, 136–139
    urban schools in, 82–90
Chicago Annenberg Challenge, 2, 37,
    172, 174, 214
Chicagoans United for the Reform of
    Education, 2
Chicago Consortium. *See* Consortium on
    Chicago School Research
Chicago school reform
    bureaucratic failure and, 130–131
    civic infrastructure and, 10
    difficulties of, 2
    educational journalism and, 9–10
    effectiveness of, 11–14
    history of, 10–15
    importance of, 9–10
    origins of, 1, 130
Chicago Tribune (newspaper), 10–11, 83,
    130–132, 134, 139
China, 205
Christmas tree schools, 173
Citywide Coalition for School Reform, 2
Civic culture, 146–149
Clark, Septima, 93
Class. *See* Social class
Class Divided, A (video), 119
Classroom assignments, 84–87
Classroom climate, 69
Class size, 114, 227n1
Coaches. *See* Instructional coaches
Coalition of Essential Schools, 182, 214

Annenberg and, 227n2
"doing less but better" philosophy
    of, 89
implementation of, 166–167
and maintenance of reform,
    177–178
overview of, 215
as progressive, 171
and scaling up, 174
Coleman, James, 110, 225n8
Color blindness, 27–30
Comer, James, 1, 2, 26, 28, 155, 167,
    173–174, 178, 180–181, 214, 218
Comer Process. *See* School Development
    Program
Common school model, 117–118
Communication
    bureaucratic, 123–124
    demoralization and, 31–32
Community activists, 127
Community for Learning/Adaptive
    Learning Environment Model, 161
Community organizations, 10
Competitive Admission of Failure, 75
Comprehensive school reform. *See*
    Whole-school reform
Comprehensive School Reform
    Demonstration Program, 156, 165
Co-nect Schools, 159, 161, 215
Conservatives
    change theory of, 192–193, 195
    Chicago school reform and, 10
    and the poor, 203–204
    principles of, 194–195
    and resource use, 31, 39, 194
    and school choice, 62
    standards-based reform and, 171
Consortium for Policy Research in
    Education, 165
Consortium on Chicago School Research,
    2, 9, 11, 35, 46, 81–82, 90, 101
Context, school reform dependent on,
    46–47, 63, 77, 154, 163–164, 181,
    226n1(ch.6)
Core Knowledge, 156, 215–216
Corridor Principle, 59

Corruption, 142–144, 152
Cortines, Ramon, 128, 135
Cosby, Bill, 192, 199
Council of the Great City Schools, 142
Covert, Charnell, 105
Cremin, Lawrence, 180
Crew, Rudy, 128
Cronyism, 124
Cross City Campaign for Urban School
    Reform, 7
Cuban, Larry, 180, 181
Culture of failure, 74–75
Cummings, S., 225n6
Curriculum
    adherence to, 33–34
    coherence and coordination in,
      88–90, 178
    Woodbine School, 53–55

Data-gathering, 187–188
David, Jane, 170–171
Decentralization
    Chicago school reform and, 12,
      130–131
    problems with, 43
Decisionmaking
    bureaucratic, 151
    decentralization of, 43
    shared, 43, 51–53
Delpit, Lisa, 224n1, 227n4
Demoralization, 17–47
    in bottom-tier schools, 23–24
    change and, 196–197
    collegial relationships and, 20–23,
      27, 32–38, 73
    communication and, 31–32
    factions and, 26–27, 30
    negative interpretations and, 25
    politics of, 39–47
    professional culture and, 23, 73
    resources unused because of, 30–31
    school organization and, 49–50
    social relationships and, 24–27,
      31–39, 44–45

teacher, 60–63, 176
teacher-administrator relationships
    and, 17–20
trust and, 35–38
working conditions and, 17–20
Desegregation, 96
Detroit, 140–141
Didactic instruction, 224n1
Direct Instruction, 216
Discipline
    procedures for, 19–20
    race and, 30, 112, 222n2(ch.1)
    teaching quality and, 103
    at Westside High School, 57–59
    at Woodbine School, 55–56
Distar, 193
District Two, New York City, 197
Donorschoose, 92
Dropouts, 69–70
Du Bois, W. E. B., 93, 96, 104
Dunbar, Paul Laurence, 97
Duncan, Arne, 13, 177, 184

Early childhood education, sorting in,
    68–71
Edmonds, Ron, 33
Edna McConnell Clark Foundation, 179
Educational journalism, 9–10
Educational Technologies Group, 215
Education Development Center, 214
Educators, contempt for, 146–147,
    182–185, 194
Eighth-grade students, 70
Eisenhower, Dwight David, 198
Elmore, Richard, 73, 181–182
Elrich, Marc, 115
"Encouraged" (Dunbar), 97
Engelmann, Siegfried, 216
Equality of Educational Opportunity
    (Coleman), 110
Essential Schools, 166
Ethnicity. *See also* Latinos; Race
    educational opportunity and,
      113–114

expectations and, 77–78, 112
   politics and, 132–133
   social relationships and, 27
Evans, Paula, 181
Expectations. *See* Teacher expectations
Expeditionary Learning, 155, 159, 171, 216
External partners, 28–29
Extracurricular activities, 97, 116

Facilitators. *See* Program facilitators
Factions, 26–27, 30
Failure. *See also* Bottom-tier schools; Institutionalization of failure
   causes of, 5, 45–47, 180
   culture of, 74–75
   environment created by, 45
   necessity of studying, 5
   as norm, 21–22, 74–76
   social factors in, 6
   teacher/administrator investment in, 21–22, 76–77, 196
Fairclough, Adam, 93, 96, 98*f*
Fanshen (Hinton), 205
Farkas, George, 217
Fate control, 110, 116, 225n6
Feinberg, Mike, 216
Fenty, Adrian, 144
Ferguson, Ron, 77, 102, 110, 112, 201
Fernandez, Joseph A., 145
Festinger, Leon, 75–76
First Things First, 227n4
Five Fundamentals for school improvement, 46
Flores-Gonzalez, Nilda, 69–70
Franklin, John Hope, 113
Free speech, 44

Gaines, Kevin, 211
Gandhi, Mohandas, 204
Gangs, 57, 70
Gardner, Howard, 214
Gates Foundation, 128
Gender, teacher relationships and, 221n1(ch.1)

Gibboney, R., 166
Giuliani, Rudolph, 128, 145
Glantz, O., 110
GOSPELL Academy, New Jersey, 1
Gouldner, Helen, 67–69, 77, 102, 114
Gradualism, 198
Grogan-Kaylor, A., 102
Grogger, J., 117

Hansberry, Lorraine, 111
Happy Talk, 30, 222n3(ch.1)
Health code violations, 150
Hess, Frederick M., 129–130
High-poverty schools. *See also* Bottom-tier schools; Urban schools
   extracurricular activities in, 116
   instructional pacing in, 87–88
   size of, 88
   teacher quality in, 71–72
High schools
   achievement in, 13
   instructional time in, 84
   new, 222n2(ch.3)
   problems in, 57
   reform of, 47
Hill, Paul, 17
Hilliard, Asa, 7, 93
Hinton, William, 205
Hirsch, E. D., Jr., 215–216
Holidays, 83–84
Home-school relationship, 222n1(ch.3)
House, Gerry, 157
Howard, Cordelia, 211
Howard, Weaver, 211
Hudson Institute, 217
Hurston, Zora Neale, 109

Identities, school, 69–70
Ideology. *See* Conservatives; Liberals
"If" (Kipling), 207
Illinois, 71–72
Implementation of reform
   Comer process and, 167
   customization of models and, 163
   effective, 160

failure to analyze, 158
intensity of, 179
leadership and, 159
New American Schools and,
   159–160
in New Jersey, 161–162
personnel as factor in, 176–178
problems in, 154, 172*f*, 181–182,
   189–190
reformers versus educators and,
   182–185
research on, 166
scale issues in, 95, 117, 160,
   173–175
standards of, 185–189
Success for All and, 167–168
teacher buy-in and, 175–176
time allotted for, 172–173
Inadequate Personnel Paradigm, 32
Inner-city schools. *See* Bottom-tier
   schools; High-poverty schools; Urban
   schools
Institutionalization of failure. *See also*
   Bureaucracy; Failure
absence of teacher support, 23
administrative control, 57–59
bottom-tier schools, 23–24, 91
failure to learn from experience,
   31–32
irrational organization, 61–65
reinforcement of failure, 45
sorting of students, 68–70
teacher expectations, 74–79
Institutional learning, 31–32, 183–184
Instruction. *See* Teaching
Instructional coaches, 41–42, 127, 187
Intent of reform efforts, 154, 189–190
Interactive instruction, 224n1

Jackall, Robert, 150–151
Jacobson, L., 74
James, C. L. R., 15
Janey, Clifford, 144
Johns Hopkins University, 47, 156, 218
Johnson, Cornelius, 211

Jones-Wilson, Faustine, 98*f*
Journalism, educational, 9–10
Justin, N., 225n6

Kennedy, James, 207
Kentucky, 3
Kerckhoff, A., 110
King, Martin Luther, Jr., 119, 204, 218
Kingon, Joyce, 17–20
Kipling, Rudyard, 207
Kirst, Michael, 136
Kluger, Richard, 96
Knowledge Is Power Program (KIPP),
   216, 226n4, 228n9

Labeling. *See* Sorting, of students
Lam, Diana, 128
Latinos. *See also* Ethnicity
criticism of, by same-race
   individuals, 192
discipline and, 112
and fate control, 225n6
math instruction and, 78
student achievement of, 225n6
Lawyers, 144
Leadership
African-American, 132–133
authoritative, 197–198
bureaucratic, 131–132
democratic, 197
effectiveness of, 5–6
implementation role of, 159
legitimacy of, 40–41
liberal view of, 194, 197
teacher-administrator relationships
   and, 39–40
Lee, Valerie, 117–118
Lee, V. E., 70
Lenz, Linda, 14
Leonard, L., 32
Leonard, P., 32
Levin, Dave, 216
Levin, Henry, 213
Liberals
change theory of, 77, 193, 195–199

Chicago school reform and, 10
pedagogy fetishized by, 119, 193
and the poor, 193, 199, 204
principles of, 193–194
and rationality, 62–63
reform practices of, 133
Limbaugh, Rush, 200
Lipman, P., 27
Los Angeles, 134–136
Low-group students, 68–70, 74
Ludwig, J., 225n8
Lynch, Deborah, 138–139
Lytle, James, 163–164, 168, 172–173, 183

MacArthur Foundation, 184
Madden, Nancy, 218
Marcy School, Newark, New Jersey, 24
Marshall, Kim, 33–35
Marx, Karl, 204
Marxism, 69
Math Directors Network, 228n10
Mathematics instruction. See also Algebra
Project
race/ethnicity and, 77–78, 104–108
standards for, 185–188
Mather School, Boston, 33–35
Mayoral control, 11, 136, 144
Mays, Benjamin, 118
McLaughlin, M., 179, 180
McQuillen, P., 166, 182
Memphis, 157–158
Merton, Robert, 7, 59, 109
Miami, Florida, 128, 143
Miami Herald (newspaper), 143
Middle-class Black students, 109, 111–113
Miller, Matthew, 121
Minnesota Family Investment program, 200–201
Mobility rate. See Student mobility rate
Model developers, 163–164, 182–183.
See also Program facilitators
Modern Red SchoolHouse, 159, 173, 217
Money, conservatives' view of, 194

Moore, Mildred Payne, 210–211
Moore, William J., 208–211
Moral community, 104, 118
Moral responsibility, 150–152
Moses, Robert P. (Bob), 176, 213
Muncey, D., 166, 182
Murphy, John, 128

Nagin, Ray, 141–142
National Alliance for Restructuring
Education, 159
National Assessment of Educational
Progress (NAEP), 14
National Board for Professional Teaching
Standards, 22
National Council of Teachers of
Mathematics, 185–186
National Executive Service Corps, 24
National Science Foundation, 3, 173, 185–186
Neal, D., 117
Neighborhoods, social capital in, 38–39
New American Schools, 157–160, 176
New Concept Development Center,
Chicago, 119
New Jersey, 157, 161–164, 175, 194
Newmann, F., 89–90, 178
New Orleans, 20–21, 141–142, 147–149, 189
New York City, 4, 71, 72, 128, 138, 197
New York City Board of Education, 122, 126, 130, 144–145
New York Times (newspaper), 145
No Child Left Behind (2002)
accountabililty and, 3
charter schools and, 149, 226n4
conservative principles of, 193
drawbacks of, 169
effectiveness of, 4
urgency of, 198–199
Noguera, Pedro, 103
North Carolina, 3, 71, 79

Ohio, 149
110 Livingston Street (Rogers), 122

Order, in school organization, 60–61
Organizational culture, 44, 59, 61. *See also* School organization
Outside agencies. *See* External partners
Outsiders, disregard for, 25
Outward Bound. *See* Expeditionary Learning

Paideia, 217
Parents. *See also* Teacher-parent relationships
    pressure on school reform from, 174–175
    responsibility of, 199–200
    as school volunteers, 202–203
    student support from, 100, 203–204
    trust between teachers and, 35–36, 38
Parker, Channell, 105
Payzant, Thomas, 133
Peers, 100
Performance pay for teachers, 62
Perry, Theresa, 97, 103, 115
Personality issues, 32, 80
Pew Charitable Trusts, 169
Philadelphia, 4, 71, 75, 136
Policy churn, 129–130, 157
Politics
    of demoralization, 39–47
    of Los Angeles educational system, 134–136
    of New York educational system, 145
    program facilitators and, 42–43
    race/ethnicity and, 132–133
    resources and, 24–25
    school reform and, 40, 174
    superintendents and, 128–129, 134–135
    teachers' unions and, 140
    of Washington, D.C. educational system, 143
Pot of Gold story, 49, 64
Poverty and the poor. *See also* High-

poverty schools; Urban schools
    causes of, 201–202
    change strategies for, 201–202
    childrearing and, 203
    conservatives' view of, 203–204
    liberal view of, 193, 199, 204
    resources and, 200–201
    and responsibility, 192, 199–205
    of students, 13–14, 116
Principals. *See also* Administrator-administrator relationships; Teacher-administrator relationships
    authorities overseeing, 41, 45, 52
    implementation role of, 159
    ineffective, 19–20
    and instructional supervision, 73
    obstacles faced by, 41, 45, 52–53
    replacement of, 197
    trust between teachers and, 36–37
    unions versus, 137–138
Principle of Negative Interpretation, 25
Professional development, 127
Program facilitators. *See also* Model developers
    in Comer process, 167
    hands-off versus hands-on, 166–168
    race and, 28–29
    school politics and, 42–43
Progressive pedagogy, 80, 171, 193, 224n1
Progressives. *See* Liberals
Project Zero, 214
Purpose-Centered Education, 159, 214
Pygmalion in the Classroom (Rosenthal and Jacobson), 74

Quantification, evaluative criteria dependent on, 194
Quantitative research, 35

Race. *See also* African Americans; Ethnicity
    color blindness and, 27–30
    discipline and, 30, 112

educational opportunity and,
113–114
expectations and, 77–79, 112
gradualism and, 198
politics and, 132–133
resources and, 112–113
salience of, 109, 113, 120
school climate and, 112
school programs and, 28
school vulnerability and, 225n8
social construction and
reproduction of, 108–120
social relationships and, 27–29
RAND Corporation, 158
Rate-busters, 22, 76
Rathbone, Cristina, 96, 114–115
Reading One-to-One, 167, 217
Reading Recovery, 167, 217
Reagon, Bernice Johnson, 96
Relational trust, 36–38
Religion, 38
Research, of school reform history and
practices, 181–182, 185
Resources
conservatives' view of, 31, 39, 194
failure to use, 24–25, 30–31, 91
instructional goals and, 90
morale as factor in use of, 30–31
political factors and, 24–25
of the poor, 200–201
race and, 112–113
South's use of, 96
teacher expectations and, 75
Rice, Jane, 119–120
Rindge and Latin High School,
Cambridge, Massachusetts, 181, 191
Rochester, New York, 165
Rodney, Walter, 191
Rogers, David, 121–126, 130, 132, 133,
139, 151, 180
Rolling, Ken, 172
Romer, Roy, 134–136
Roots and Wings, 159, 173
Rosenfeld, Gerry, 74–76
Rosenthal, R., 74

Ross, Diana, 7
Russo, Alexander, 10

Saint-Exupéry, Antoine de, 153
San Antonio, Texas, 128
Sanders, William, 72
San Diego, California, 129
Sarason, Seymour, 166, 180, 182
Sawhill, I. V., 225n8
Scarsdale, New York, 72
Schneider, Barbara, 36
School-based management, 130–131
School choice, 62
School climate, 112
School council, 52
School Development Program (Comer
Process), 171, 214
administrative problems in, 42
in Chicago, 1, 2, 173–174,
202–203
implementation of, 167
in New Jersey, 161
overview of, 218
parent participation in, 202–203
and personnel issues, 177–178
principles of, 155–156
race as factor in, 28
schools using, 156
and social relationships, 26
School for the Deaf, New York City, 138
School identities, 69–70
School organization
demoralization and, 49–50
irrational, 50, 61–65, 77
order and disorder in, 60–61
at Westside High School, 57–61
at Woodbine School, 50–57
School programs. See also Program
facilitators
frequent changing of, 18–19, 31,
173
multiple, attempted
implementation of, 173
partisanship concerning, 156
replicability of, 167

teacher reception of, 79–81
teacher support in, 166–167
School reform. *See also* Change; Chicago
  school reform; Implementation of
  reform; School programs
  bureaucratic characteristics in
    opposition to, 126–128,
    130–131
  coercion in, 77
  conduct principles for, 153
  context-specificity of, 46–47,
    63–64, 77, 154, 163–164, 181,
    226n1(ch.6)
  debate over, 226n2
  difficulties of, 180–182
  effectiveness of, 4, 7, 35
  factors in, 7
  failure of, 180
  Five Fundamentals for, 46
  founders versus followers in, 228n5
  honest assessments necessary for,
    5–6, 44, 61–62, 64, 153
  inner intent of, 154, 189–190
  institutional learning in, 183–184
  insularity of proponents of,
    163–164, 182–185
  micropolitical barriers to, 40
  national movement for, 2–3
  novelty in, 64, 145
  pattern of, 29–30, 184–185
  policy churn in, 129–130, 157
  politics and, 40, 174
  and reversion to former practices,
    180
  scale issues in, 95, 117, 160,
    173–175
  simplistic nature of, 45–47
  skepticism about, 64, 79–80, 162,
    195 (*see also* teacher buy-in and)
  social barriers to, 26*f*
  standards-based movement,
    169–171
  study of, 4–5, 180–182, 185
  systemic, 169, 173
  teacher buy-in and, 175–176 (*see*

    also skepticism about)
  teacher role in, 179
  teacher training and, 179
  whole-school reform, 155–169
School size, 88. *See also* Small schools
Sciarra, D., 225n6
Self-fulfilling prophecies, 59. *See also*
  Teacher expectations
Shibutani, T., 44, 59
Shields, Patrick, 170–171
Shropshire, Michele, 105
Shut Those Thick Lips (Rosenfeld), 74
Simmons, Warren, 7, 189
Sizer, Theodore (Ted), 166, 180–181,
  214, 215
Slavin, Robert, 218
Small schools, 5–6, 127–128, 146–147,
  175
Smith, B., 86–87
Smith, BetsAnn, 82–84
Smith, J., 86–87
Smith, Jerome, 189
Social capital
  of African-American parents, 201
  low/negative, 6, 47, 147, 183
  in neighborhoods, 38–39, 47
  school engagement and, 102
  significance of, 146
  in urban schools, 37, 174
Social class, expectations and, 77, 79
Social factors
  significance of, 6
  in sorting of students, 68, 77
Social relationships
  in bottom-tier schools, 24–27,
    31–39, 44–45
  in neighborhoods, 38–39
  at Woodbine School, 50–57
Social support
  from parents, 100
  from peers, 100
  from teachers, 99–102, 116, 120
Solkov, Janice I., 136
Solomon, Rochelle Nicholls, 199
Sorting, of students, 68–70, 74, 118

South Bronx, New York, 17–20
Sowell, Thomas, 98*f*
Standards-based reform, 169–171
Steele, Claude, 110–111
Stereotype threat, 110–111, 225n8
Stewart, Marilyn, 139
Stierheim, Merrett R., 143
St. Petersburg Times (newspaper), 121
Street kids, 70
Student achievement
    African-American, 103–104,
        110–111
    authoritative-supportive teaching
        and, 100–101
    diagnostic teaching and, 95
    fate control and, 110
    high-quality assignments and, 86
    instructional coherence and, 90,
        178
    Latino, 225n6
    proficiency levels, 3–4, 13–14
    stereotype threat and, 110–111,
        225n7
    teacher expectations and, 74–76
    teacher quality and, 71–72
    whole-school reform and, 164–165
Student attendance, 60, 101–102
Student mobility rate, 14, 88, 221n2
Student Nonviolent Coordinating
    Committee, 205
Students. *See also* Student achievement
    attitudes of, toward teachers,
        102–103
    home environment of, 222n1(ch.3)
    incoming high school, 70
    opportunities for, 87, 91, 113–114
    school identities of, 69–70
    social support from parents for, 100
    social support from peers of, 100
    social support from teachers for,
        99–103, 116
    sorting of, 68–70, 74, 118
Study halls, 84
Substitute teachers, 83
Success for All, 18–19, 159, 161

effectiveness of, 165
implementation of, 167–168
overview of, 218
performance review in, 163
schools using, 156
time required by, 173
Superintendents of schools
    administrative offices versus, 130
    politics and, 128–129, 134
    power of, 226n1(ch.5)
    reforms proposed by, 129
    role of, 122
    tenures of, 128
Sykes, Gary, 154
Sylvan Learning, 227n3
Systemic reforms, 169, 173

Talent Development High School, 47,
    156, 218–219, 227n4
Teacher-administrator relationships
    dysfunctional, 17–20, 34
    instructional supervision and, 73
    leadership and, 39–40
    trust and, 36–37
    at Woodbine School, 50–52
Teacher expectations. *See also* Academic
press
    class and, 77, 79
    factors contributing to low, 76
    race/ethnicity and, 77–79, 112
    resources needed for support of,
        74–75
    rigidity of, 75–76
    social factors in, 77
    in urban schools, 104
Teacher-parent relationships
    negative, 26–27, 203
    parental involvement and, 26–27
    trust in, 35–36, 38, 101
Teacher persistence, 77
Teacher Quality Index (Illinois), 71–72
Teachers. *See also* Teacher-administrator
    relationships; Teacher-parent
    relationships; Teacher-teacher
    relationships; Teaching

absences by, 83, 137
attitudes of, 72–81
in bottom-tier schools, 71–82
and buy-in to school reform,
175–176 (*see also* skepticism of,
about school reform)
in Catholic schools, 118
coaches for, 41–42, 127
demoralized, 60–63, 176
didactic versus interactive, 224n1
dismissal of, 137–138
disrespect for, in school reform
movements, 45, 91, 182–185,
194
minority, 78–79
performance pay for, 62
policy involvement of, 43
popular contempt for, 146–147
quality of, 71–82, 95
resistance of, 79–80, 195
retention of, 72
reversion of, to accustomed
practices, 177–178, 180
role of, 118
self-improvement of, 22–23
seniority of, 135, 137–138
skepticism of, about school reform,
64, 79–80, 162, 195 (*see also*
and buy-in to school reform)
student attitudes toward, 102–103
training of, 179
Teachers' unions
in Chicago, 10–11, 136–139
corruption in, 142–143
goals of, 139
in Los Angeles, 134–135
member relations in, 22
in Philadelphia, 136
politics and, 140
power of, 139–140
principals versus, 137–138
protectiveness of, 60
seniority rules of, 135, 137–138
strikes by, 10–11
Teacher Support Network, 2

Teacher-teacher relationships
in bottom-tier schools, 73
collaboration and, 32–33
factions in, 27
gender and, 221n1(ch.1)
race and, 30
resentment in, 20–23, 76
trust and, 35–38
at Woodbine School, 53–56
work performance and, 30
Teach for America, 20–21
Teaching, 81–92
African Americans, 93–120,
207–212, 224n1
authoritative-supportive, 99–103,
99*f*, 108, 118–119, 211–212
coherence in, schoolwide, 88–90,
178
conception of, 95, 101
diagnostic, 95
focus on, 33
high-impact, characteristics of, 94*f*
impediments to, 81*f*
quality of, 84–88, 94–95, 103, 119
reversion to accustomed, 177–178,
180
social support function of, 95–96,
99–103, 116, 120
time devoted to, 82–84, 94, 223n5
traditional Black, 96–97, 98*f*, 99
Teaching to the test, 221n1(introduction)
Tennessee, 72, 114
Test scores
liberal view of, 194
school cheating and,
221n1(introduction)
value of, 6–7, 221n1(introduction)
Texas, 3
Thomas, W. I., 109
Thompson, Charles, 170–171
Time
instructional, 82–84, 94, 223n5
for program implementation,
172–173
Title I, 155

Tracking. *See* Sorting, of students
Train the Trainer model, 23
Trenton, New Jersey, 163
Trust
 race and, 109–112
 relational, 36–38
 teacher-parent, 35–36, 38, 101
 teacher-principal, 36–37
 teacher-teacher, 35–38

Uniforms, 177
Union. *See* Teachers' union
Urban schools. *See also* Bottom-tier
 schools; High-poverty schools
 high-impact instructional programs
  for, 94*f*
 instructional capacity in, 81*f*
 instructional coherence in, 88–90
 instructional quality in, 84–88
 instructional time in, 82–84
 problems in, 90–91
 reform in, 179–180
 teacher expectations in, 104
 traditional Black teaching model
  for, 99–100
U.S. Congress, 156

Vallas, Paul, 11–13, 132–133, 198,
 221n1(introduction)
Vance, Paul, 142
Veteran teachers, resistance and
 skepticism of, 21, 42, 49, 80, 179, 195
Victim-blaming, 203
Voucher plans, 62, 194

Walker, Vanessa Siddle, 97, 98*f*
Washington, Booker T., 84
Washington, D. C., 142–144, 149–150
Watson, Johnnie, 157
Weaver, Reg, 39
Weber, Max, 61, 151
West Cape May, New Jersey, 207–211
Westside High School, Chicago, 57–61,
 102

West Side High School, New York City,
 114–115
Whitla, Janet, 214
Whitson, M., 225n6
Whole-school reform, 155–169
 America's Choice model of, 165
 assessment of, 168–169
 benefits of, 164
 Coalition of Essential Schools
  model of, 166–167
 Comer process model of, 167
 effectiveness of, 164–166
 field staff versus national staff in,
  175
 in Memphis, 157–158
 models of, 155–156
 New American Schools model of,
  158–160
 in New Jersey, 161–164
 origins of, 155
 progressive background of, 171
Wilcox, Brian, 21
Williams, Anthony, 144
Winfrey, Oprah, 192
Wisconsin Center for Educational
 Research, 61–62
Woodbine School, Chicago
 administrative style in, 50–53
 curriculum reform in, 53–55
 staff relations in, 50–57
Woolley, M., 102
World Lab, 173
Wright, Richard, 10

York, D., 118

Zeuli, John, 170–171